THE
EVERYTHING.
PARENT'S GUIDE TO COMMON CORE ELA:
GRADES 6–8

Dear Reader,

As an eighth grade teacher, I've seen firsthand some of the challenges that parents face with the new Common Core State Standards. Change can be challenging, and although some school districts are able to provide parents with workshops to help them understand new requirements, not all have the resources to do so. Faced with revised annual assessments, parents may feel like they've been left out of an important part of their children's lives.

I hope that, to some degree, this book can help you feel like you're in the loop as you gain a good understanding of what your child is learning and how she is learning it. I explain the standards in plain language and provide examples so that you can support your child as she navigates these new, more rigorous learning requirements.

I suggest that you read through all three grade levels covered in the book, focusing closely on the grade your child is currently in. To understand the expectations for each grade, it is important to understand what your child has already accomplished or will be expected to accomplish.

Your child's teacher may take a different approach to some skills than what I note in this book. That certainly doesn't mean that he or she is wrong. The best sources of information about what your child is learning are, of course, your child and her teacher. Furthermore, the ELA (English language arts) standards can be taught using a wide range of texts. You may be able to ask for a copy of the grade-level curriculum to learn more about the texts and topics that are used to meet the standards. If that option is available, I encourage you to do so.

I hope you find this book helpful and that you and your child enjoy a productive school year.

Jill Mountain

Welcome to the EVERYTHING® Series!

These handy, accessible books give you all you need to tackle a difficult project, gain a new hobby, comprehend a fascinating topic, prepare for an exam, or even brush up on something you learned back in school but have since forgotten.

You can choose to read an Everything® book from cover to cover or just pick out the information you want from our four useful boxes: e-questions, e-facts, e-alerts, and e-ssentials.

We give you everything you need to know on the subject, but throw in a lot of fun stuff along the way, too.

We now have more than 400 Everything® books in print, spanning such wide-ranging categories as weddings, pregnancy, cooking, music instruction, foreign language, crafts, pets, New Age, and so much more. When you're done reading them all, you can finally say you know Everything®!

QUESTION

Answers to common questions

FACT

Important snippets of information

ALERT

Urgent warnings

ESSENTIAL

Quick handy tips

PUBLISHER Karen Cooper

MANAGING EDITOR, EVERYTHING® SERIES Lisa Laing

COPY CHIEF Casey Ebert

ASSISTANT PRODUCTION EDITOR Alex Guarco

ACQUISITIONS EDITOR Hillary Thompson

ASSOCIATE DEVELOPMENT EDITOR Eileen Mullan

EVERYTHING® SERIES COVER DESIGNER Erin Alexander

Visit the entire Everything® series at *www.everything.com*

THE
EVERYTHING®
PARENT'S GUIDE TO
Common Core ELA: GRADES 6-8

**Understand the new English standards
to help your child learn and succeed**

Jill Mountain, MA

Aadamsmedia
Avon, Massachusetts

An Everything® Series Book.
Everything® and everything.com® are registered trademarks of F+W Media, Inc.

Published by
Adams Media, a division of F+W Media, Inc.
57 Littlefield Street, Avon, MA 02322. U.S.A.
www.adamsmedia.com

ISBN 10: 1-4405-9059-1
ISBN 13: 978-1-4405-9059-7
eISBN 10: 1-4405-9060-5
eISBN 13: 978-1-4405-9060-3

Printed in the United States of America.

10 9 8 7 6 5 4 3 2 1

Many of the designations used by manufacturers and sellers to distinguish their products
are claimed as trademarks. Where those designations appear in this book and F+W Media,
Inc. was aware of a trademark claim, the designations have been printed with initial capital
letters.

Interior illustrations copyright © 2015 by Adams Media.

This book is available at quantity discounts for bulk purchases.
For information, please call 1-800-289-0963.

Contents

Acknowledgments

With thanks to my husband, Lewis, and children, William and Michael, who supported me in my decision to change careers ten years ago to become a teacher. Thanks also to Susan Haske, the principal of JWY Middle School, who gave me the opportunity to teach and has since become a mentor and a friend.

Introduction

THE PROCESS OF DEVELOPING the Common Core State Standards began in 2009. Governors and state education leaders from all over the United States met to review the standards already in place in all fifty states and look for a way to develop a common approach to K–12 education. This approach did not prescribe curriculum, but instead determined what skills students should achieve in each grade level.

The standards were based, in part, on standards already in place in states that demonstrated a high degree of success in K–12 education in outcomes like graduation rates, state testing, and competitive international testing. Using a wide range of inputs, the developers of the Common Core determined the key skills in math and English language arts that seemed to most consistently lead to student success in post–high school careers or in college.

Several criteria were established for the ideal standards. They should be rigorous, and success should be based on mastery of complex concepts by grade level. They should be clear, so that different interpretations would not interfere with learning. And they should be measurable, so that student achievement could be evaluated—a student in Alaska could be compared to a student in Florida, for example, and the analysis would generate meaningful results.

After several years of testing, reviewing, revising, and soliciting feedback, the developers released the standards to the states in 2011 for consideration. Forty-three states chose to adopt the standards and began the process of implementing them in schools. Teachers and administrators were provided training and support as existing curricula were revised and new curricula added. Finally, state by state standardized testing was revised to reflect the new learning standards.

The one significant hurdle in the rollout was that the standards were implemented for grades K–12, even though each grade relied on instruction that had included the standards in the preceding grades. For example, a student in the eighth grade was expected to have mastered all of the skills in grades K–7, even though she had not been taught using the standards in those grades. Teachers were required to "spiral" the skills for the first few years, moving up and down the grade levels to ensure students had access to all of the information necessary for success in their current grade. After a few years of spiraling, students were deemed on track for grade-level success.

Recently, in some states there has been backlash regarding testing related to the Common Core standards. It is important to avoid conflating the standards and the testing. Many testing opponents support the standards, but feel the testing is inappropriate. Regardless of how mastery is assessed in individual states, the standards, as they stand, provide a consistent and rigorous framework for classroom instruction.

This book offers an overview of the English language arts standards for grades six through eight. These standards cover reading, writing, speaking, listening, and language skills. Mastery of these skills prepares your child for success in high school, college, and the workplace.

CHAPTER 1

The Key Shifts in Common Core Standards for ELA

The Common Core standards have introduced three key shifts in how ELA (English language arts) instruction is structured. The goal of these shifts is to better prepare students for life beyond grades K–12, giving them the literacy skills they will need as college students and when they enter the workforce. This isn't necessarily a shift in what students learn. Indeed, the Common Core standards do not ignore what many people consider a cornerstone of ELA instruction—the conventions of language, including points of grammar, punctuation, spelling, and types of figurative language or literary elements. Instead, the Common Core shifts how students learn, and how much time and focus occurs in different learning areas. Common Core standards encourage students to build knowledge independently, through reading, and share that knowledge with classmates. The goal of the National Governors Association and the Council of Chief State School Officers, two organizations that were instrumental in developing the standards, was to create fewer standards that focused more clearly on higher-order skills.

Regular Practice with Complex Texts

Research indicates that there is a significant gap between what students read independently in grades K–12 and what they are expected to read independently in college. College students are expected to read and learn from textbooks and other resource materials with little one-on-one support for surmising the meaning of those texts. In fact, most college lectures are supplemental to the text, and most professors lecture with the assumption that their students have completed the reading assignments and therefore have the necessary background knowledge. What happens, then, if college students cannot independently learn from a text? In many cases, for such students lectures are less valuable and a true understanding of the subject is never achieved. Professors may respond by slowing down the pace of the course or devoting more time to explaining the text. While these strategies seem supportive, both result in students actually learning less. To succeed in college, and to have access to the educational experiences they need, students must enter college able to read and understand complex texts.

FACT

ELA stands for English Language Arts. ELA instruction combines the study of literature, grammar, and academic forms of writing.

What Is a Complex Text?

Complex texts are information-dense. They present complicated ideas using longer sentences, longer paragraphs, and specialized vocabulary. A complex text doesn't review or remind the reader of points that have already been covered. Instead, the text builds ideas one upon the next to link together several main points or themes.

Have you ever watched a television program that reviews everything it has covered after every commercial break? Someone who wasn't paying attention to the first segment gets an overview of the main idea before the second segment continues. Have you ever been annoyed by these frequent reviews? Often, the program has to sacrifice a certain amount of new content in order to review content that already has been covered. A complex text does not offer these types of reviews. It is up to the reader to delve into the information and figure out the meaning independently.

ESSENTIAL

Prior to the implementation of Common Core standards nationwide, most states had their own learning standards for all subjects. Educational standards set out specific learning goals that students are expected to master by the completion of a grade. Standards are important as they ensure that students are receiving the same educational experience regardless of who their teacher is or where they live. Common Core standards are intended to provide a framework that will ensure a consistent, high-quality classroom experience for every child in every school.

The Standards use a two-part model to determine the complexity of a text and its most appropriate grade level:

Quantitative Measures: Quantitative measures use readability formulas to assign a number score to a text. This measure is known as a Lexile. The Common Core standards most often refer to a text's Lexile. The Lexile and other readability measurements analyze concrete aspects of a text such as the number of words in a sentence, the number of syllables in words, and how frequently words are repeated. The result is a number that can be correlated to suggested readability, or Lexile score, of a text by grade level.

Qualitative Measures: A readability score, like a Lexile, is a good place to start when considering a text. More information is needed to determine if a student at a certain grade level should be able to understand a given text. Your child's teacher considers many other factors before determining if a given text is appropriate for her students. Some of these include:

- **Layout:** How long are passages that require sustained reading? How much analysis is required to understand graphics or images that accompany the text?
- **Purpose:** Does the author explicitly state the main point or purpose of the text? Or does the reader have to process different concepts to determine the meaning and purpose independently?

- **Structure:** How do events or ideas work together? If, for example, the text is a biography, do events unfold chronologically in a way a student-reader could plot on a timeline, or are key events presented in other ways so that student-readers must reconstruct a timeline?
- **Language:** Is the language simple, using words common to a typical student's vocabulary, or does it include specialized vocabulary unique to the topic that the student must learn as she reads? Are ideas communicated with concrete specific details, or does the author use figurative and abstract language?
- **Knowledge demands:** Does the reader need extensive background knowledge to read and understand the text? If a reader does not have the necessary background knowledge, or cannot understand what knowledge is required to fully understand a text, he will not get the most from that text.

Teachers provide direct instruction that shows students how to read a text closely and build support systems to help students take on increasingly difficult texts. Your child's teacher will use strategies such as multiple readings, guided reading out loud, and chunking larger texts into smaller passages for close study. With the Common Core instruction and support is provided *while* students read the text, which is a shift from merely preparing students to read a text.

Using Text Evidence to Support Analysis

Prior to the implementation of Common Core standards, many ELA teachers used a balanced literacy teaching model that focused on the personal connections students made with what they read. This model was, in part, inspired by reader-response theory, a type of literary criticism that is based on how individuals find meaning based on their own knowledge and experiences. The Common Core approach inverted that model. The focus of reading now is on what is often called "author's craft," or the intent of the author.

Under the Common Core, when your child reads and analyzes a text she will be required to support her ideas with evidence from the text. That doesn't mean she can't use her own ideas or opinions; it only means that she must find evidence to support those ideas or opinions.

The use of text evidence extends into writing as well. Your child will be required to support her ideas with details and evidence. Sometimes this evidence will come from personal experiences, such as in a personal narrative that includes extensive details. In other cases, your child will have the opportunity to use research materials to find evidence to support a point of view.

Your child's teacher will often pose text-based questions about a reading. These questions will require your child to draw a conclusion or perform some sort of analysis that is supported with evidence from the text.

Building Knowledge with Informational Texts

This shift in focus brought on by new Common Core standards has the potential to change how classroom instruction happens. Because it is so important that your child and all students learn to *independently* gather knowledge, teachers are learning to provide more and more opportunities for this to happen in a supported learning environment.

This standard is emphasized throughout students' academic careers by means of a continually shifting balance of literary and informational texts. Elementary students begin their reading instruction with accessible literary texts, such as narratives or stories with predictable organization and outcome. An example would be a chronologically organized story about a day at the beach. By the 5th grade, half of all the texts a student reads will be informational. By the time a student reaches high school, 70 percent of texts will be informational. Year by year, more and more informational texts are introduced, and are often paired with literature.

The selection of informational texts is not random. Rather, the chosen texts cover subjects that are relevant to all disciplines of study, including science, math, and social studies.

Although the purpose of this shift to informational text is to help students learn independently, rest assured that your child's teacher will not simply assign complex texts and expect your child to have perfect and full comprehension. Classroom teachers often use a technique called scaffolding to help students work with complex texts. An example of scaffolding is when a teacher reads aloud in the classroom a work that is far above a grade level as a way to model comprehension skills.

What is scaffolding?
Scaffolding is a teaching technique that supports students learning by gradually allowing them to become more independent learners.

Because the Common Core standards are intended to be applied across disciplines, you will likely notice that teachers in other subjects, including science, social studies, and math, will assign independent reading to your child more frequently as well.

Here is a list of comprehension strategies that are crucial to independent learning:

- **Investigating unfamiliar vocabulary:** Gone are the days when a student-reader might skip an unfamiliar word. Instead, students are taught to read slower and more deliberately, and are instructed to use context clues, reference books, or other strategies to confirm understanding of unfamiliar words.
- **Paraphrasing an author's ideas:** When a reader understands a text, he can restate the author's ideas in his own words. Your child will learn to paraphrase as he reads as a way to capture important concepts.
- **Reading with purpose:** If a student intends to build knowledge using informational text, he should begin reading the text with a learning goal. Your child will learn to determine a purpose for reading before beginning any text, and make connections between his purpose for reading and the information in the text as he reads.

A deliberate approach to reading is crucial to knowledge building. In addition, the amount of time spent reading is also important. To support the use of text for learning, encourage your child to take her time with reading assignments. If a text is challenging, encourage her to apply strategies and chunk the text into manageable passages. Foster and encourage independence by reminding and supporting your child as she reads on her own.

An Overview of the Anchor Standards

The overarching focus for the Common Core ELA standards is found in the anchor standards. Anchor standards indicate the expectations for students who are college and career ready. These standards, formally called the College and Career Readiness anchor standards, span all content areas from kindergarten through grade 12. An anchor standard is a skill that a student should master by the time he graduates from high school. This mastery is the ultimate goal of a student's ELA education from grades K–12 and is built over the course of many years. The standards are intended to be general so that different teachers can approach them in different ways, and so that different students can master them via different learning paths. They are rigorous and consistent from year to year. Anchor standards have been established for reading, writing, speaking, listening, and language use.

Each of the anchor standards is covered in more detail in the following chapters. The grade-specific chapters demonstrate how the anchor standards are interpreted for each grade level to help students work toward mastery that, in turn, will prepare them for college and the workplace.

CHAPTER 2

The Anchor Standards for Reading

The ten anchor standards for reading fall into four different groups. The anchor standards address several key skills that are crucial for students' future success in college and in their careers. By mastering grade level skills year after year, students will learn to use reading skills to acquire knowledge, contemplate ideas critically, and consider different ideas that relate to one another. The four groups of reading anchor standards are: Key ideas and details, craft and structure, integration of knowledge and ideas, and range of reading and level of text complexity.

The Ten Anchors for Reading

The following is a list of the ten anchors for reading:

- Students will read a text carefully to understand stated and unstated ideas and be able to use evidence from the text to support their conclusions about the text.
- Students will be able to determine the main idea of a text.
- Students will be able to explain how different ideas, events, or individuals interact and develop in the text.
- Students will be able to use context clues and text evidence to determine the meaning of unfamiliar words and phrases.
- Students will be able to identify and explain the different structural parts of a text, such as paragraphs, sentences, stanzas, etc.
- Students will understand point of view and how it shapes a text.
- Students will be able to evaluate information presented in many different ways—in text, film, on the Internet, etc.
- Students will be able to identify an argumentative claim and explain how the author supports it.
- Students will be able to evaluate two texts on similar topics or themes and compare the authors' approaches.
- Students will read complex texts independently.

Read Closely

The first anchor standard says: Read closely to determine what the text says explicitly and to make logical inferences from it; cite specific textual evidence when writing or speaking to support conclusions drawn from the text. (CCSS.ELA-LITERACY.CCRA.R.1)

This anchor standard requires three specific skills. First, students must learn to read closely. Your child will likely spend more time on shorter texts in an effort to learn to read attentively and to thoughtfully interact with the text. Those interactions are usually in the form of *annotations*. Your child will learn to make marginal notes in what he reads, noting important ideas, complex arguments, relevant evidence, and even personal reactions. Ideally, by using these close reading and annotating skills, all students will gain the skills and confidence to tackle texts once thought far beyond their comprehension.

The second part of this anchor standard focuses on determining what the *text* says explicitly, and the ability of students to make inferences based on what is explicitly stated in the text. For example, a student can read *The Adventures of Huckleberry Finn* to follow the story and identify explicit important plot points, characterizations, and even the author's biases. Inferences from the text, however, also reveal cultural bias, racism, and commentary on family relationships that are not explicitly stated. A skilled close reader can make any assertion about the text that can be supported *with* the text.

For example, review the following excerpt from *The Adventures of Huckleberry Finn* by Mark Twain:

> Now the way that the book winds up, is this: Tom and me found the money that the robbers hid in the cave, and it made us rich. We got six thousand dollars apiece—all gold. It was an awful sight of money when it was piled up. Well, Judge Thatcher he took it and put it out at interest, and it fetched us a dollar a day apiece all the year round—more than a body could tell what to do with. The Widow Douglas she took me for her son, and allowed she would sivilize me; but it was rough living in the house all the time, considering how dismal regular and decent the widow was in all her ways; and so when I couldn't stand it no longer I lit out. I got into my old rags and my sugar-hogshead again, and was free and satisfied. But Tom Sawyer he hunted me up and said he was going to start a band of robbers, and I might join if I would go back to the widow and be respectable. So I went back.

Now, consider the following questions:

1. What evidence from the text supports the claim that the narrator felt confined at the Widow Douglas's house?
   a. The narrator describes himself as being "free and satisfied" after running away from the Widow.
2. What can the reader infer about the narrator's life before he and Tom found the money?

    a. He was very poor and perhaps an orphan. He was uncivilized, and may have been involved in illegal activities or minor crimes.

This text provides information about the narrator's background, without explicitly stating it. The reader can make inferences about the narrator, the widow, and even the narrator's friend, Tom, who tricks him into returning.

Your child will also learn the importance of using text evidence to support a conclusion. Too often the loudest opinions get the most attention, even if there is no supporting evidence. While that might be satisfying for those who are the loudest, or even those who agree with them, unsupported assertions have the potential to undermine the quality of information available to everyone. Students will learn the value of their own analysis and conclusions, but also the importance of supporting those ideas with evidence, both when reading and writing.

Central Ideas and Themes

The second anchor standard says: Determine central ideas or themes of a text and analyze their development; summarize the key supporting details and ideas. (CCSS.ELA-LITERACY.CCRA.R.2)

Main ideas and themes are potentially abstract concepts that have to be constructed by the reader. The second anchor standard addresses this by requiring students to build information based on the content of a text. This anchor standard is handled differently depending on whether a text is literary or informational. Informational texts often directly state the main idea or theme. There is often a thesis statement or controlling idea that tells a reader what the point of the text is. That thesis is often found within the first paragraph or introduction.

Determining a central theme or main point of a literary text can also be challenging. Sometimes the reader has to think about the point of view of the narrator, and the details he or she chooses to share. Sometimes the characters reveal the theme through their own development. The theme or main point of a literary text may not be apparent until the end of the text, and it may be dependent on how and when the narration reveals important details. Annotating a literary text helps students find clues to the theme or main point.

In a longer, more complex text, a reader will likely identify more than one theme. The theme is a lesson, or observation about life, that is revealed through the characters' experiences. As your child advances from grade to grade, he will learn that a story can have more than one theme, and that every detail and every interaction in a well-written story relates to and supports one of these themes. While your child is annotating a text, he might consider several strategies to help identify themes:

1. Notice words, ideas, or challenges that are repeated.
2. Consider where the text focuses its attention. For example, is there a long passage describing the way the sun plays through the leaves on a tree? Consider that the text focuses on certain details for a reason, and tease out those reasons.
3. How does the title of the work focus the reader's attention? Is the title cryptic? Is it straightforward?
4. What common life experience is examined? Is it perhaps done in a unique way to come to a conclusion about that experience?

In an informational text the author's purpose is to explain, describe, provide an argument, or in some way offer information. Finding the main point of an informational text, even when it is not explicitly stated, is relatively easy. Focusing on the examples the author provides, the statistics used, and the facts elaborated on will reveal what the author considers important.

Analyze How Ideas Develop

The third anchor standard says: Analyze how and why individuals, events, or ideas develop and interact over the course of a text. (CCSS.ELA-LITERACY.CCRA.R.3)

QUESTION

What is the difference between a concrete detail and an abstract detail?
Concrete details are directly stated in the text. Concrete questions include those asking for dates, names, locations, etc. Abstract details have to be inferred. Abstract questions often ask about motivation, feelings, or for predictions.

The third anchor standard focuses on concrete details such as the setting, the characters, and the points in the plot. In grades 6–8 your child, having mastered the ability to identify the concrete components of a text, will begin to evaluate how they interact and to advance a purpose. Take, for example, the classic middle school text *The Outsiders*. The protagonist, or main character, Ponyboy, has a worldview formed by the details of his life: His parents have died, and he lives with his two older brothers. The brothers are poor, and they may be separated if any of them gets into trouble. They live in a community that vilifies them and their friends as "hoods" or "gangsters," and celebrates the wealthy teenagers in the same community. When Ponyboy has the opportunity to get to know a girl who is part of the wealthy clique, he realizes that wealth does not necessarily diminish the struggles teenagers face. Although, at the beginning of the novel, he believes that the only solution is violence between the poor and rich teenagers, by the end he realizes that violence leads to the deaths of his friends and does nothing to change his status.

At the beginning of the novel the reader is sympathetic to Ponyboy, who seems to be a victim caught up in a conflict he has no choice but to participate in. But, as the narrative progresses, the reader understands that opportunities exist for him to change his personal outcome by adjusting his worldview.

FACT

A coming-of-age novel, or bildungsroman, is a specific genre of literature. Both *The Outsiders* and *The Adventures of Huckleberry Finn* fit within this genre. These novels often have a first-person narrator who is experiencing a change in understanding as a result of growing up. There is often internal dialog, as the narrator explains his feelings and thoughts.

Because informational texts don't have plots or characters, the third anchor standard focuses on how the text elaborates on a topic, and on which details act as the focus of an explanation or argument. This anchor standard asks readers to consider why details are ordered in a specific way. This standard also encourages analysis of examples and anecdotes, and how different examples of a single concept work together to explain an idea.

Interpret Words and Phrases

The fourth anchor standard says: Interpret words and phrases as they are used in a text, including different technical, connotative, and figurative meanings, and analyze how specific word choices shape meaning or tone. (CCSS.ELA-LITERACY.CCRA.R.4)

Complex texts contain complicated ideas that are explained with specialized vocabulary and figurative language. The meaning of the text is constructed through comparisons, precise terms, and the use of carefully chosen words. This anchor standard focuses on the idea that plain language, or concrete ideas expressed in simple sentences, limits a writer's ability to communicate a complex idea.

Your child will learn how to decipher technical language and understand how familiar terms may have different meanings. For example, the word *windows* will likely mean something different in a text about using a computer than it does in a text about building a house. Likewise, the term *drive* can mean a ride in a car, or a disk on which data is stored in a computer. While these are simple examples, they serve to illustrate how common words become technical terms in some contexts.

In reading literary texts, your child will encounter many different types of figurative language. While she is likely familiar with figurative language such as similes, metaphors, or personification, in simple texts she will be required to understand more complicated comparisons and how figurative language is used to transfer very precise information from the text to the reader.

Analyze the Structure of Texts

The fifth anchor standard says: Analyze the structure of texts, including how specific sentences, paragraphs, and larger portions of the text (e.g., a section, chapter, scene, or stanza) relate to each other and the whole. (CCSS. ELA-LITERACY.CCRA.R.5)

Texts are composed of parts. Each section of a text functions to fulfill an overall purpose. In earlier grades your child learned about the parts of a text, from sentences to chapters and stanzas. Now she'll consider what links these parts and ask critical questions such as, "What is the unifying idea of this chapter?" or "How did the author transition from one paragraph to the next?" Understanding how the parts of a text are used to build meaning requires close reading, and, of course, annotation.

Your child will likely learn how to write a "gist statement" or statement of a main idea, theme, or concept that is developed in a part of a text. Then, she'll learn to analyze those gist statements to understand how multiple parts contribute to a whole.

While reading literary texts, your child might identify chapters that make up parts of the plot, from the exposition that establishes the characters and setting, to the climax that offers a turning point in the story, and finally to the resolution that ties together all of the plot threads to create a satisfying ending.

In a literary text your child will analyze how an author organizes information to present it logically. For example, a text intended to describe a location might use spatial organization and break information into paragraphs that offer descriptions of unique parts of the whole setting. In an argumentative text, the writer might begin with the most compelling evidence, and then offer decreasingly important evidence in subsequent paragraphs.

Within each part of a text, such as each paragraph or stanza, your child will focus on individual sentences and consider the role each plays in developing an idea. For example, a topic sentence expresses the main point of an informational paragraph. Like the other anchor standards, standard five encourages close, critical reading that regards all parts of a text as being equally valuable.

Assess Point of View

The sixth anchor standard says: Assess how point of view or purpose shapes the content and style of a text. (CCSS.ELA-LITERACY.CCRA.R.6)

Both literary and informational texts are written from a particular point of view. In an informational text, the author's purpose (to inform, persuade, or entertain) is determined by the point of view. In the 6th grade your child will be asked to determine the point of view and explain how it is revealed in the text. For example, a reader might identify what an author's argument is in a persuasive text, what an author thinks is important about a subject in an informational text, or what the author considers to be amusing in a text intended to entertain. Your sixth grader will use text evidence to support an analysis of the point of view.

In the 7th grade your child will begin to look for ways in which an author distinguishes her point of view from those of others on the same subject. For example, the author of an informational text on transportation might focus on the development of public transportation solutions, such as trains and buses, and explain that she supports public transportation instead of other strategies such as increasing the number of bicycle lanes on public roads.

By the 8th grade your child will analyze the author's point of view, how it differs from other points of view, and how the author acknowledges and responds to opposing points of view. For example, in the same text about public transportation, your child would identify the author's position (in favor of trains and buses), a position the author does not support (the bicycle lanes), and how the author responds to the argument that bicycle lanes are a better approach. Furthermore, in the 8th grade your child might read two different texts, one that advocates trains and buses and another that advocates bicycle lanes, and explain how each author supports her position. Finally, your child will develop a point of view on an issue based on analysis of multiple texts that offer different points of view on the same issue.

Integrate and Evaluate Content

The seventh anchor standard says: Integrate and evaluate content presented in diverse media and formats, including visually and quantitatively, as well as in words. (CCSS.ELA-LITERACY.CCRA.R.7)

Texts often include images. Part of being a strong reader is to have the ability to decode diverse media that is intended to bring meaning to a text. This anchor standard addresses how information can be provided in different ways. For example, your child may be asked to evaluate photographs or art included in a literary text, or read a graphic novel that relies on images to tell a story. He may also read informational texts that include diagrams and graphs that support the specific ideas within the text. Your child's teacher will frequently present information using presentation software, short videos, and images from websites. Finally, your child will be given the opportunity to compare a literary text and a filmed or audio performance of that text to identify similarities, differences, and production choices that can influence meaning.

FACT

Graphic novels are an excellent reading choice for reluctant readers. While many focus on fantasy or adventure, there are several graphic novels that cover history, retell classic literature, or focus on contemporary, realistic characters. Some recent titles of interest include *Anne Frank: The Anne Frank House Authorized Graphic Biography* by Sid Jaboson and Ernie Colón (2010) and *The Demon of River Heights*, by Stefan Petrucha (2005), which is a reimagining of the classic Nancy Drew girl detective.

Evaluate the Argument

The eighth anchor standard says: Delineate and evaluate the argument and specific claims in a text, including the validity of the reasoning as well as the relevance and sufficiency of the evidence. (CCSS.ELA-LITERACY.CCRA.R.8)

To delineate an argument is to identify the central claim or the main point the author intends to prove. Additionally, the reader must identify the evidence the author uses to support that claim. Your child will be asked to trace an argument; that is, he will be asked to point out where in a text the argument is stated, and then trace the evidence that supports that argument.

The next step is to evaluate the argument. Evaluation requires critical thought and analysis of the evidence. Readers are expected to consider how an author builds an argument and whether the information is typical, relevant, and sufficient.

Typical evidence is evidence that is supported by multiple sources. For example, if an author has constructed an argument on how to slow global warming and supports that argument with evidence from an outlying or extremist source, the argument is weakened. Typical evidence is confirmed in multiple credible resources.

Relevant evidence is evidence that is directly related to the argument. One might argue, for example, that global warming is caused by burning fossil fuels, but support that claim with irrelevant evidence, such as the fact that hybrid cars burn less fuel than traditional cars. The evidence may be accurate and typical, but it isn't relevant and may only be present as a way to support the author's personal bias.

Sufficiency refers to the amount and quality of evidence presented. An argument that is not supported with specific evidence is weak. There must be enough evidence to convince the reader to agree with the author.

Finally, when evaluating an argument your child will be asked to consider the logic of the argument. She will study different types of logical fallacies that can mislead a reader. The ability to delineate and evaluate an argument is a crucial life skill. The media bombard people with ideas, claims, and conspiracies that critical consumers of information must be prepared to evaluate and understand in order to make informed decisions.

How Texts Are Similar

The ninth anchor standard says: Analyze how two or more texts address similar themes or topics in order to build knowledge or to compare the approaches authors take. (CCSS.ELA-LITERACY.CCRA.R.9)

By analyzing multiple texts on the same topic, readers can develop a more thorough and accurate understanding of a topic. Competent readers learn to synthesize information from multiple sources to create a broad understanding of a subject.

This anchor standard can be approached in many different ways. For example, students will likely read informational texts to accompany literary texts. Students reading *Little Women* might also read nonfiction texts about the Civil War or other topics that are related to the narrative.

Students may also read multiple literary texts on the same subject. For example, students might read several historical fiction literary texts set during the Civil War and compare the points of view of the authors and the experiences of the characters in the story.

Additionally, students may read informational texts to provide background for literary texts such as dramas, short stories, novels, and poetry. For example, before reading the poetry of Wilfred Owen, a WWI poet, students could read from a history text about specific battle lines or wartime experiences in order to better understand Owen's point of view.

Reading multiple texts on the same general subject can lead to insightful analysis and the building of a more complete understanding of a topic. Under this standard, students are asked to compare information within complementary texts and notice how different authors and different forms of literature address similar topics.

Read and Comprehend

The tenth anchor standard says: Read and comprehend complex literary and informational texts independently and proficiently. (CCSS.ELA-LITERACY .CCRA.R.10)

This standard focuses on each student's growth as a reader. For each grade level there is a range of appropriate text-complexities. By the end of a grade level, students should be able to independently read and understand works near the high (or more complex) end of that range.

As students move from kindergarten toward graduation they should read increasingly complex texts that provide more and more nuanced information. These ten anchor standards develop a staircase of complexity that provides scaffolding or support to help struggling readers rise to grade level proficiency year after year.

In each grade students will be presented with texts that are more complex than those read in the preceding grade. For each grade there is a range of text complexity. This range offers support texts for those students who struggle with reading and enrichment texts for students who excel in reading.

Not only do texts become more complex year by year, they also become increasingly focused on information, rather than literary topics. Because the majority of texts one encounters in college and in a career are informational, developing skills necessary to read and understand informational texts is crucial for success.

CHAPTER 3

The Anchor Standards for Writing, Speaking, and Listening

Writing has ten anchor standards, and speaking and listening has six anchor standards. There is some overlap in these anchors, as both the writing standards and the speaking and listening standards establish pathways for students to use evidence and research to support their own points of view. Both sets of standards also emphasize content and how to most effectively communicate ideas to different audiences.

The Sixteen Anchor Standards

The writing, speaking, and listening standards may be rooted in classroom tasks, but they are intended to help students gain valuable life skills. As your child progresses through the standards, help him understand the long-term benefits of mastering these skills. Doing so will help the work seem even more relevant to your child, and make the learning more authentic. The ten anchor standards for writing are:

- Write arguments to support claims.
- Write informative/explanatory texts to examine and convey complex ideas.
- Write narratives to develop real or imagined experiences.
- Produce clear and coherent writing that considers task, purpose, and audience.
- Develop writing by planning, revising, editing, rewriting, or trying a new approach.
- Use technology, including the Internet, to produce and publish writing and to interact and collaborate.
- Conduct short and more sustained research projects.
- Gather relevant information from multiple sources.
- Draw evidence from literary or informational texts to support analysis.
- Write routinely over extended and shorter time frames for a range of tasks, purposes, and audiences.

The six anchor standards for speaking and listening are:

- Prepare for and participate in a range of conversations and collaborations with diverse partners.
- Integrate and evaluate information presented in diverse media and formats.
- Evaluate a speaker's point of view, reasoning, and use of evidence.
- Present information, findings, and supporting evidence such that listeners can follow a line of reasoning.
- Make strategic use of digital media and visual displays of data to express information.
- Adapt speech to a variety of contexts and communicative tasks.

Mastering these standards can help students communicate their ideas effectively. Writing, speaking, and listening are career and college skills. Of course, these skills are developed over time, with each grade bringing more independence and higher expectations.

Writing Arguments

The first anchor for writing says: Write arguments to support claims in an analysis of substantive topics or texts using valid reasoning and relevant and sufficient evidence. (CCSS.ELA-LITERACY.CCRA.W.1)

When writing argumentative texts, the goal is to establish a subjective point of view and support it with evidence. In grades 6–8 your child will develop argumentative writing skills, beginning with learning how to develop a precise claim or argument. An argument or claim takes a stance on a topic or issue that has more than one reasonable point of view. For example, a writer might argue that California is the best state in the United States. That argument could be supported with information about climate, standards of living, opportunities for recreation, and so forth. While the argument in favor of California could be well-supported and convincing, an equally effective argument might be made for another state, such as Florida.

An argument might be based on a reading. For example, your child might be asked to explain which character is most responsible for an important event in the text. When the argument is text based, so too is the evidence. Students will learn to pull key details from a text to support a claim about what the text says.

ESSENTIAL

Your child's teacher will support him as he learns how to generate a thesis statement. The thesis statement is often one of the most challenging aspects of argumentative writing. Students often state facts or statistics, rather than argumentative points. It takes time, practice, and a lot of confidence to make an independent claim. The best way to support the development of this skill is to give students time to work through different arguments as they learn which can be supported and which cannot.

It can also be challenging for students to find supporting evidence. The sooner your child understands that she'll be asked to use evidence when arguing about a text, the better. Gathering evidence while reading is a much easier task, and leads to much more effective arguments, as compared to going back through a text after reading to search out important evidence.

In 7th and 8th grade your child will also be called upon to review a counterargument made within an essay. A counterargument is a logical argument that presents an opposing point of view. Strong writers can present and rebut a counterargument with strong evidence. Throughout grades 6–8 your child will also learn how much evidence is "sufficient" to support a claim, and about the structure of an effective argumentative paper. The standards for each of these three grades elaborate on the structure and requirements that are needed to make formal connections between ideas.

Writing Information/Explanatory Texts

The second anchor standard says: Writing informative/explanatory texts to examine and convey complex ideas and information clearly and accurately through the effective selection, organization, and analysis of content. (CCSS. ELA-LITERACY.CCRA.W.2)

The goal of informative/explanatory writing is to share factual information with the reader. Examples your child might be familiar with include textbooks, newspaper and magazine articles, and encyclopedia entries. Teachers will likely assign some sort of how-to topic as a first step in helping students develop grade-level explanatory writing skills. Writing a how-to essay is an excellent way to practice organizing material in a logical, step-by-step manner. Other writing tasks might include explaining a quote from a text or explaining a concept from a different area of study like science or social studies.

QUESTION

I've also heard the term *expository essay*. What does that mean?
An expository essay combines argument and explanatory. Writers research or investigate a topic and develop an argument related to the topic.

Once a topic is established, your child will need content, or what could be reasonably called evidence, in order to develop the topic. Evidence can be information from a text, research such as facts and statistics, or what the writer already knows about the topic. Once the topic is established and the evidence in place, the final step is to organize the text. Some types of informational texts are best organized chronologically. For example, the events in a biography are often presented in the order they occurred in time, or chronologically. Other types of informational texts call for different organizational structures. A text that explains a location might use spatial organization, or describe elements in terms of their relationship to others.

Finally, your child will learn the importance of writing objectively when creating an explanatory text. The explanatory text is unique in that the writer's opinion or bias should not be evident. The information should be presented clearly in a way that the reader cannot determine the writer's opinion on the topic.

Writing Narratives

The third anchor standard says: Write narratives to develop real or imagined experiences or events using effective techniques, well-chosen details, and well-structured event sequences. (CCSS.ELA-LITERACY.CCRA.W.3)

A narrative is basically a story. The story can be something imagined by the writer or a retelling of events that actually occurred. Storytelling is different from informative or argumentative writing in several ways.

A narrative includes characters and setting. Characters are developed with details that make them seem realistic. One of the biggest challenges of writing a narrative is developing realistic characters who are different from one another. Your child will likely study characterization in literary texts and learn to model these aspects of character in his own writing.

A narrative is further developed using several techniques:

Dialogue: Dialogue is the words characters speak to one another. Dialogue moves the plot, or series of events in a story, and establishes who the characters are, what they want, need, or think, and how they are different from one another.

Pacing: In a narrative, details are revealed in a way that builds suspense or interest. If the reader knows the ending of a narrative from the first paragraph he or she might not be interested in reading the entire story. Pacing refers to how information is developed to move the story from one event to the next.

Description: Descriptive language provides information that makes a story lively and interesting. The goal of effective description is for the writer to communicate, as precisely as possible, what she imagines a setting, character, or event to be.

Reflection: After a writer finishes writing her narrative, she reflects on and shares the point of her story. A narrative is intended to make an observation that is specifically meaningful. The reflection, which usually occurs near the end of the story, establishes what that point is, and why it matters.

Storytelling: Finally, a narrative has a purpose: It tells a specific story. Many young writers are challenged to write a story that has a clear beginning, middle, and end. It is likely that your child will struggle at first to get beyond simply describing events in an effort to create an actual story plot.

Clear and Coherent Writing

The fourth anchor standard says: Produce clear and coherent writing in which the development, organization, and style are appropriate to the task, purpose, and audience. (CCSS.ELA-LITERACY.CCRA.W.4)

Once your child understands the three forms of writing (argumentative, informative/explanatory, and narrative), she will be prepared to develop writing for specific situations. This fourth anchor standard focuses on several key ideas that can be applied to all writing:

- The task determines the type of writing your child will use. Is the assignment to write an e-mail, a script, a short story, or an essay? Knowing the task is a necessary aspect of effective writing.
- The purpose of why the task is being completed. For example, a writer might write an e-mail to argue in favor of a change in policy, or she might write a script for a humorous play in order to entertain an audience. The same tasks can be written for different purposes. For example, an essay can be written to persuade, to entertain, or to explain.
- The audience for whom the writing is intended. Writers learn that writing for an academic audience (other students studying a similar topic) is different than writing for an audience that is unfamiliar with the topic,

or even skeptical of it. Making this distinction is essential for creating an explanatory piece of writing or an argumentative essay.

- Development includes everything that goes into the piece of writing before the writer creates a draft. Development includes brainstorming, prewriting, outlining, and all the other activities that help a writer get ideas on paper and become ready to create a finished written product.
- The organization of writing is both its structure and how its ideas relate to one another. In a narrative the organization might include all the components of the plot. In an argument, the organization determines what evidence is used to support distinct components of the argument. Finally, in explanatory writing, organization helps the reader understand the relationship between details so as to understand a complex idea.
- The style is how the writing sounds, including the level of formality. Your child will learn the difference between formal and informal writing, and the best times to use each style.

Develop and Strengthen

The fifth anchor standard says: Develop and strengthen writing as needed by planning, revising, editing, rewriting, or trying a new approach. (CCSS. ELA-LITERACY.CCRA.W.5)

Writing is a process and this anchor standard focuses on that process. Any project, including writing, begins with planning. This is also covered in the development stage, noted in the fourth anchor standard for writing. Planning can include brainstorming, outlining, or creating any number of planning maps that begin the writing process. From planning, writers move on to drafting, or creating a rough, first-pass at a text. The draft usually includes all of the writer's key ideas and much of the research, but little attention is paid to organization, connecting ideas, or developing a strong introduction or conclusion.

ALERT

Student writers are often reluctant to plan or pre-write. Very often, students write one draft and turn it in. While that may be sufficient for younger writers to earn middling marks, skipping these steps in the writing process can lead to lower scores on more complex essays. Encourage your child to plan ahead to utilize every step in the writing process.

After planning, a writer revises his work. Revising focuses on ideas, not mechanics. In the revising stage the writer considers how ideas are related, how to make connections between concepts, and how to hold the essay or story together with an effective introduction and conclusion.

Once revising is complete, the writer edits her work. Editing focuses on the mechanics of a text, including spelling and grammar. It is always a good idea to save editing for near the end of the process, as revising often leads to changes and may require multiple edits.

Good writers are able to recognize when a text just isn't working. There are times when a writer realizes that the evidence or details he has presented are not sufficient and that the paper does not serve the purpose it was intended to serve. Good writers are able to recognize these moments and take advantage of opportunities to try a new approach to the same task or engage in rewriting.

Your child is not unique if she is not thrilled with the writing process. Being a good writer takes patience and perseverance. Good writers also need encouragement to understand that needing to try a new approach to a writing task is not the same as failing at that task. In fact, taking a new approach may be the best path to a successful writing assignment.

Collaborate with Others

The sixth anchor standard says: Use technology, including the Internet, to produce and publish writing and to interact and collaborate with others. (CCSS.ELA-LITERACY.CCRA.W.6)

Writing is meaningful when it is shared with an authentic audience. While there will be times when your child's only audience is his teacher, there will also be several opportunities each year for your child to reach a wider audience with his work. That audience might be an authentic recipient, such as the editor of a newspaper or the customer service center of a company. The audience might also consist of other students who are invited to comment and interact with your child's writing.

Most people are familiar with different ways people can publish writing using the Internet, such as blog posts, product reviews, or posts to social media. While these might be informal publishing settings, they all rely on knowledge of the audience and adherence to a specific style.

One of the benefits of publishing writing on the Internet is the opportunity for comment and collaboration. Your child's teacher will likely set up peer review/peer comment opportunities using a class LMS (learning management system) such as Edmodo or Noodle tools, or with a collaborative writing platform such as Google Docs. No matter the venue, learning to share and respond to the writing of others is part of the writing experience in middle school.

Conduct Research Projects

The seventh anchor standard says: Conduct short as well as more sustained research projects based on focused questions, demonstrating understanding of the subject under investigation. (CCSS.ELA.LITERACY.CCRA.W.7)

Research begins with a question. Your child will have the opportunity to use his own curiosity to develop research projects that address a wide range of topics. A focused research question is complex. It isn't something that can be answered with a quick Internet search or by looking something up in a textbook. The keyword in this standard is *investigation*, and like a detective, your child will use clues from multiple sources to craft thoughtful writing pieces based on what he learns during the investigation.

Sometimes your child's teacher will provide a research question, which could be something broad, such as, "Should students attend school year-round?" In other situations, especially in the higher grades, your child's teacher will guide him to develop his own research question based on a subject that is provided. For example, the teacher might offer the general subject of education, and then support students as they develop a wide range of topics. Research questions don't have a single correct answer. Rather, they are a starting point that leads to exploration and greater understanding of a topic.

The point of research is to better understand a topic. The point of writing the research paper is to demonstrate that understanding. The research question provides direction so that your child's work will be focused and valuable.

Gather Information

The eighth anchor standard says: Gather relevant information from multiple print and digital sources, assess the credibility and accuracy of each source, and integrate the information while avoiding plagiarism. (CCSS.ELA-LITERACY .CCRA.W.8)

To conduct research, your child will need to choose and use sources. Sources can include the same sorts of resources you used when you were in grades 6–8: the trusty encyclopedia, reference books, biographies, textbooks, and so on. Twenty-first century sources also include digital media. Your child's school library most likely subscribes to many academic databases. Academic databases offer research conducted by university professors and scholars, and are, with few exceptions, credible. Of course, there is also the Internet. Google or other search engines will pull up thousands, if not millions, of websites on just about any topic. In grades 6–8 your child will learn to determine which of those websites offers information that is credible, accurate, and appropriate for his academic paper. Being a critical consumer of the Internet is a skill that will carry on beyond a single research project, as this skill is something even adults struggle with.

Your child will also learn more about the importance of writing in his own words and giving appropriate credit to those he quotes. The Internet offers seemingly endless resources and there is always the temptation to simply copy and paste information that seems relevant. However, doing so violates academic integrity, and, especially in later grades and in college, can lead to serious consequences. Your child will learn to summarize and paraphrase information from his research, and will become familiar with the basics of citing sources to indicate where information originated. Most teachers have access to some sort of originality-checking resource, such as Turnitin (*http://turnitin.com*), which, in the middle years, will likely be used as a teaching tool to help your child see where he or she may have inadvertently plagiarized.

ESSENTIAL

There are several free plagiarism/grammar checkers available on the Internet. You may want to check out *www.grammarly.com* or *www .plagtracker.com* to see how these tools work and to familiarize your child with the importance of academic integrity.

Learning to use programs that assess originality and generate citations will likely be part of your child's middle school writing instruction.

Reflect on Research

The ninth anchor standard says: Draw evidence from literary or informational texts to support analysis, reflection, and research. (CCSS.ELA-LITERACY. CCRA.W.9)

Learning to use outside sources isn't necessary for only research projects. Your child will be asked to support her ideas, analyses, and answers to questions with evidence from texts. Learning to find relevant evidence starts with learning close reading strategies. Your child will be instructed how to identify keywords and concepts, make inferences based on reading, and use that information to support independent analyses and conclusions. Throughout middle school your child's teachers will focus on close-reading strategies and how to successfully respond to text-based questions. Even in class discussion, teachers will require evidence to support ideas.

Write Routinely

The tenth anchor standard says: Write routinely over extended time frames (time for research, reflection, and revision) and shorter time frames (a single sitting or a day or two) for a range of tasks, purposes, and audiences. (CCSS. ELA-LITERACY.CCRA.W.10)

This anchor standard pulls together all of the others, and, basically, expresses the idea that writing assignments don't occur in a vacuum and are not special events. Your child will have frequent opportunities to write for many different reasons. All writing assignments will be constructed in a way that is intended to support ongoing mastery of all of the writing standards. To prepare for longer essays, it is likely your child will undertake many short writing assignments, including tasks such as writing paragraphs, e-mails, and responses to short-answer questions. He will practice the same skills over and over again, and be consistently held to the same writing standards regardless of the assignment.

Speaking and Listening Standards

The anchor standards for speaking and listening will help your child learn to express himself and absorb information as best as he can. Each of the six standards builds on the previous one in an effort to impart a well-rounded instruction.

Prepare and Participate

The first anchor standard says: Prepare for and participate effectively in a range of conversations and collaborations with diverse partners, building on others' ideas and expressing their own clearly and persuasively. (CCSS. ELA-LITERACY.SL.1)

To be career and college ready all students must be able to communicate and exchange ideas effectively. That happens through discussion. Your child will learn the basics of presenting and sharing information, and her teacher may introduce this standard through traditional question and answer sessions about a text or concept. Your child will learn to express her ideas, support them with evidence, and compare them to ideas others have offered. Slowly, your child will learn to respond not only to a teacher's questions but also to what her peers have to say.

Students will also learn to collaborate in achieving a single learning goal. Collaboration might consist of a group project, or maybe something shorter and more immediate, like working together on a set of text-based questions. In collaborative assignments students learn to present their own ideas clearly, and to respectfully discuss the ideas of others in order to combine information. With support your child will learn to work within a group to assign roles and divide tasks in order to achieve a common goal.

Evaluate Information

The second anchor standard says: Integrate and evaluate information presented in diverse media and formats, including visually, quantitatively, and orally. (CCSS.ELA-LITERACY.CCRA.SL.2)

This anchor standard addresses another "real world" skill—the ability to decipher all different kinds of information. Visual information can include things like maps, charts, photos, diagrams, drawings, and graphs. Quantitative data includes numbers, such as statistics. Oral data includes spoken information such as speeches, podcasts, and lectures.

Learning how to process different kinds of information will not only help your child become better at gathering information for writing assignments, but it will also support independence in learning. Of course, being able to decipher different media starts with instruction and practice. Your child's teacher will offer frequent opportunities to work with different types of information, answer questions on that information, and share and develop strategies for doing so.

Evaluate the Speaker

The third anchor standard says: Evaluate a speaker's point of view, reasoning, and use of evidence and rhetoric. (CCSS.ELA-LITERACY.CCRA.SL.3)

This standard addresses the strategies your child will use to assess the credibility and believability of a speaker. Speakers often have agendas—they have a point they want to prove. It takes skill and experience for listeners to identify that agenda and learn how to separate objective statements from subjective opinion. To be able to identify a speaker's point of view is another "real world" skill that your child will need to effectively engage in the workplace. These skills are also critical for consuming media and conducting daily commercial interactions. Rhetoric consists of different persuasive techniques used in an argument. Rhetorical techniques are ways a speaker works to convince her audience that her ideas are relevant and credible. Different rhetorical appeals call on the audience to relate to the subject on an emotional level, because of the accuracy and logic of facts presented, or because of the credibility of the speaker. For example, if a doctor were to present statistics expressing the number of people who die from lung cancer each year as a way to persuade an audience to quit smoking, she would be using rhetoric to convince the audience because she is an expert, and because her facts are convincing.

As your child learns more about evaluating speakers and rhetoric, he will begin to learn about strategies for identifying flaws in logic and for discerning persuasion techniques. Logical fallacies attempt to build connections, like cause and effect, without the evidence to support them. Untrained speakers might use fallacies unintentionally, although deceptive speakers use fallacies to create seemingly logical arguments that are actually not well supported.

Presenting Information

The fourth anchor standard says: Present information, findings, and supporting evidence such that listeners can follow the line of reasoning and the organization, development, and style are appropriate to a task. (CCSS.ELA-LITERACY.CCRA.SL.4)

This anchor standard is similar to a standard in the writing area, and it applies the same skills to speaking. By the time your child graduates from high school he should be able to understand the difference between effective and ineffective speakers, and know what he must do to communicate his ideas to others. The first step in developing a presentation for a group is to understand both the audience and the information needs of that audience. For example, someone speaking to a group of seventh graders about education would not spend a lot of time explaining how the typical seventh grader spends her school day. Instead, the speaker would assume the audience has that information, and build his presentation from that base of knowledge.

To be an effective speaker, your child will also learn how to use research and evidence to support a point. He will evaluate sources, as he did as a writer, and choose precise information that proves the points he is trying to make. He will connect those points with logical connections and help the audience see how the ideas are related. Finally, he will use visuals where necessary to make sure points are made clearly.

Make Visual Displays

The fifth anchor standard says: Make strategic use of digital media and visual displays of data to express information and enhance understanding of presentations. (CCSS.ELA-LITERACY.CCRA.SL.5)

Students have access to an almost endless supply of digital media. YouTube alone offers more video than any person could watch in a lifetime. The current culture is an increasingly visual one. As more and more people become accustomed to visual media being a part of any information gathering, students must develop the skills necessary to sort and curate visual data in order to support their own presentations. Your child's teacher will provide opportunities for him to learn how to use visual presentation software programs, and how to best include visuals so that they enhance, rather than overwhelm, his speaking.

Adapt Speech

The sixth anchor standard says: Adapt speech to a variety of contexts and communicative tasks, demonstrating command of formal English when indicated or appropriate. (CCSS.ELA-LITERACY.CCRA.SL.6)

If your child spends time texting or interacting on social media, you may have already noticed that a different type of language emerges when she's engaged with her friends in these tasks, and you might be worried that she'll continue to use this sort of shorthand, informal speech when she goes out someday to look for a job or write a college essay. Obviously the use of informal English is an appropriate way for friends to communicate in informal situations, but it is not appropriate in more formal settings like a professional workplace.

This anchor standard is focused on helping your child to understand the difference between formal and informal situations, and how to adjust her speech and vocabulary for different situations. Because your child will eventually grow into an adult who needs to find a job, communicate with colleagues, and navigate in the world, it's important she understands that chatting during an interview requires a more formal way of speaking than does arguing with a little brother. This standard will offer her many opportunities to explore and experiment with different ways of communicating ideas.

CHAPTER 4

The Anchor Standards for Language

These standards cover what you might remember most from your own middle school ELA courses: grammar and vocabulary. In every grade, language instruction in the Common Core focuses on specific aspects of grammar and specific strategies for acquiring vocabulary. All standards in the Common Core are cumulative, and assume mastery of the prior year's material. The language standards are especially demanding in this regard. Once a point of grammar has been covered, it is then assumed to be part of a student's background knowledge.

The Six Anchor Standards

The language anchor standards, like all of the other anchor standards, provide the basic framework for grade-level standards, which in turn are more detailed and focus on very specific skills. Teachers and parents can use the anchor standards as a touchstone for understanding grade-level instruction and assignments within the context of the overall goals of a standards-based education. The anchor standards for language require students to:

- Demonstrate command of the conventions of Standard English grammar and usage.
- Demonstrate command of the conventions of Standard English capitalization, punctuation, and spelling when writing.
- Understand how language functions in different contexts, and make effective choices for meaning and style.
- Determine or clarify the meaning of unknown and multiple-meaning words and phrases.
- Demonstrate an understanding of figurative language, relationships among words, and nuances of word meaning.
- Acquire and use accurately a range of general academic and domain-specific words and phrases.

Grammar

The first anchor standard says: Demonstrate command of the conventions of standard English grammar and usage when writing or speaking. (CCSS.ELA-LITERACY.CCRA.L.1)

Grammar and writing conventions are important. For better or for worse, people often judge others based on their use of language conventions and grammar. A subject/verb agreement error like, "He don't know the current valuation of that investment portfolio," can overwhelm the message. Even if someone is competent in his field, as this hypothetical investor might be, to many people that single verb error screams ignorance.

Obviously, it is important that your child has the instruction and practice necessary to avoid these types of errors. In each grade, this anchor standard leads to a specific focus on a point of grammar and mechanics. In the 6th grade, the focus of the grammar conventions standard is pronouns: pronoun case, pronoun agreement, avoiding vague pronouns, and avoiding pronoun shifts. In the 7th grade, the focus is on sentence structure, and how phrases and clauses make up compound and complex sentences. Finally, in the 8th grade, the grammar conventions standard takes students through the use of verbs and verbal phrases.

Your child's teacher will work to make the language study interesting and authentic, tying it to texts and sample documents, but, at some point, there will be grammar rules that your child must learn and practice. Despite the fact that this element of instruction can be dull, this area of study remains crucial to helping your child become an effective communicator.

Punctuation and Spelling

The second anchor standard says: Demonstrate command of the conventions of standard English capitalization, punctuation, and spelling when writing. (CCSS.ELA-LITERACY.CCRA.L.2)

Word processing programs are amazing and offer a lot of help in the form of grammar and spell checking tools. These programs will identify almost every error in a document. To repeat: *almost* every error. There will be times when your child, either as a student or as an adult, may have to write without the benefit of software-assisted spelling and grammar checking. Knowing the rules and application of those rules still matters. Each grade-level standard includes the simple directive: spell correctly. Your child will have opportunities to practice spelling throughout elementary school, and will be required to learn the spelling of common words, and how to confirm the spelling of uncommon words. By grades 6–8, it is unlikely she will receive ongoing spelling instruction.

QUESTION

What if my child still struggles with spelling?
There are many online games and resources you can use with your child to improve her spelling. You may want to visit Merriam-Webster Dictionary online at *www.m-w.com*. Click on games for a list of spelling and word games.

By 6th grade, all of the capitalization standards have been covered as well, meaning that your child's teacher will expect her to correctly capitalize proper nouns, titles, words at the beginning of sentences, and so on.

Punctuation standards continue to develop through grades 6–8. In the 6th grade, students learn to use commas, parentheses, and dashes to set off information that is relevant but not crucial to a sentence. In the 7th grade, your child will learn to apply a comma to separate adjectives in a sentence. In the 8th grade, he will learn to apply commas, ellipses, and dashes to indicate a pause in information, or where information has been omitted.

Applying Knowledge

The third anchor standard says: Apply knowledge of language to understand how language functions in different contexts, to make effective choices for meaning or style, and to comprehend more fully when reading or listening. (CCSS.ELA-LITERACY.CCRA.L.3)

This is a very general anchor standard. It acts as a sort of a catchall of writing and speaking mechanics. At different grade levels this standard includes different skills, though most instruction focuses on syntax. Syntax is the construction of sentences—how words, phrases, and clauses work together to make sentences, how to differentiate between an actual sentence and a sentence fragment, and how to write effective, detailed sentences.

In the 6th grade your child will learn strategies to vary sentence patterns in order to make her speech or writing more interesting. Communication that consists only of simple subject/verb sentences, such as "the dog ran," are dull and don't hold a reader's interest. To help your child become a more effective communicator, instruction will be provided on different sentence forms and how they work together to create compelling, interesting texts or speech.

In the 7th grade your child will learn to improve her varied sentences with more precise language. Your child's teacher will help her find the best word to express her ideas. As Mark Twain once said, "The difference between the right word and the almost right word is the difference between lightning and lightning bug." In other words, meaning is dependent on precision in language. Finally, in the 8th grade, your child will learn the difference between active and passive voice in sentence construction and how each affects meaning and tone.

Determining the Meaning of Unknown Words

The fourth anchor standard says: Determine or clarify the meaning of unknown and multiple-meaning words and phrases by using context clues, analyzing meaningful word parts, and consulting general and specialized reference materials as appropriate. (CCSS.ELA-LITERACY.CCRA.L.4)

All students have a working vocabulary that is made up of words they use and encounter frequently in their daily lives. Some of those words are domain specific, that is, words that have particular meaning in a particular context. An example would be words like *goal, run*, and *touchdown* when used to describe aspects of football. Through their own experiences, children gather more and more words, and those words are often related to particular contexts. For example, middle school students are more likely to describe a locker as a storage space for their personal belongings rather than as a person who locks. That definition is based on the students' experience in a specific domain.

FACT

In 2000, *Time* magazine reported that the average Fourteen-year-old in 1950 had a vocabulary of 25,000 words. By 1999 it was just 10,000 words. Research has shown that a larger vocabulary aids in a better understanding of complex ideas.

Even though vocabulary acquisition is an almost constant part of your child's learning experience, he will at times encounter words that he doesn't know. This standard reviews methods and strategies students can use to figure out unknown words.

Your child will learn to use context clues to better understand unfamiliar words, and to determine the meaning of words that can have multiple meanings. For example, the word *box* can mean a container or it can refer to a sport. The context of a sentence provides the information necessary to understand which would apply. Your child's teacher will help her understand a wide range of strategies that will help her make an educated guess or a well-informed conclusion about the meaning of an unfamiliar word.

Students will also learn how to discover the meaning of an unknown word by using word parts. For example, once your child learns that *cent* means 100, then words like *century* and *centennial* become more meaningful.

FACT

According to the *Oxford English Dictionary*, the word *set* has the most individual definitions, with a total of 464 meanings. The word *run* has 396 definitions, and *go* has 368. While some of these meaning may be obsolete, or apply only to special situations, there are still a lot of meanings to sort through, which is why learning to use context clues is crucial.

Your child will also learn to consult reference materials to determine the meanings of words. When other strategies aren't helpful, the best thing a student can do is to look up the meaning of a word. While the dictionary is a standard resource, other resources are available, such as text-specific glossaries, technical manuals, textbooks, and, of course, the Internet. All can offer information about the meaning of an unknown word. Your child will learn how to choose the best reference source, and how to choose the best definition of a word when different definitions are offered.

Understanding Word Meaning

The fifth anchor standard says: Demonstrate understanding of figurative language, word relationships, and nuances in word meanings. (CCSS.ELA-LITERACY.CCRA.L.5)

Your child will learn about figurative language in his reading study and how to derive meaning from it during his language study. In the language standards, figurative language often refers to the use of idioms—particular meanings that have evolved from popular culture or standard readings. Common figures of speech will be covered, as well as the relationship between words and ideas, such as cause/effect or problem/solution. In the 7th and 8th grades your child will explore allusions to biblical and mythical texts to understand how figurative language is used. For example, the "garden of Eden" is a biblical reference, but when applied to a contemporary context refers to a situation that is perfect in every way. In addition to allusions, language study will review concepts such as irony, especially verbal irony in which the words are intended to convey an idea opposite to what they literally say. Some attention will likely also be paid to puns, or other wordplay that takes advantage of words' multiple meanings to make jokes or suggest multiple meanings to a single sentence.

Using Language

The sixth anchor standard says: Acquire and use accurately a range of general academic and domain-specific words and phrases sufficient for reading, writing, speaking, and listening at the college and career readiness level; demonstrate independence in gathering vocabulary knowledge when encountering an unknown term important to comprehension or expression. (CCSS.ELA-LITERACY.CCRA.L.6)

This standard looks to the future. Your child will be prepared through direct instruction and independent practice to leave high school with a working vocabulary that will help him understand most texts in the adult world. This knowledge will help him participate in typical conversations in whatever his next situation might be, whether it is a college course, a rank in the armed forces, or his first job.

He will also be prepared to investigate unknown words and understand that it is important to do so. That is, he will see the necessity and value of continuing vocabulary acquisition outside of the classroom in order to continue to develop as an adult. Your child will be able to recognize circumstances when understanding a concept is dependent upon understanding the associated vocabulary, and have several strategies for gathering the knowledge necessary to be independent and informed.

It isn't difficult to think of situations in which adults, even those who have long completed their formal educations, must learn new words in order to continue to function in their careers and lives. For example, the advent of smartphones made it necessary for anyone interested in having such a phone to learn about apps, data plans, SIM cards, and the like, in order to make informed purchases and understand differences in products and services. Having the tools necessary to move into new domains is a relevant skill that is effectively developed throughout your child's K–12 education by way of the Common Core.

CHAPTER 5

Grade 6—Reading

By the 6th grade, your child is approaching mastery of reading essentials, including decoding words, sentences, and paragraphs. Up until this point, she has read a $^{50}/_{50}$ mix of literary and informational texts. Stories have included familiar settings and closely relatable subjects. In the 6th grade, reading becomes less child-centered. That is not to say that teachers will ignore what most interests children. Rather, now there will be more focus on learning through reading, or on using texts as a way to independently acquire knowledge. As well, in the 6th grade about 70 percent of the texts your child reads will be informational.

What Your Sixth Grader Will Learn

There are two sets of reading standards for grades K–12. The Reading Literature (RL) standards provide guidance for reading literature. The Reading Informational Text (RI) standards provide guidance for reading informational texts. There is some overlap in the standards.

It is important to note that the standards assume that the foundational skills of reading have already been established. There are no 6th grade standards that cover reading fluency. Rather, in the 6th grade and on, your child will begin to read more critically than ever before, honing her critical thinking skills by making comparisons, identifying central ideas, and learning to read between the lines to draw inferences and understand connotative meanings, or the ideas within the ideas. These skills are developed through close reading, which is a key concept within the standards. Your child will likely be taught to annotate texts, and to use text evidence to support her own analysis or to support or challenge analysis presented to her.

ESSENTIAL

Support your child as she learns to annotate a text effectively. Annotations are a sort of conversation with a text. Your child should mark or highlight important ideas. Encourage your child to write short questions, notes, or observations on sticky notes or in the margins of a text. You can model this by thinking out loud as you read with her. Circle ideas that are interesting and think of questions to ask about what you read. These annotations help a reader summarize and evaluate a narrative or informational text.

In the 6th grade, reading becomes less about what your child is reading and more about how he or she is reading it. In some classrooms, each child will read a book he or she has chosen independently. Your child may not be reading the same book as everyone else in the class. However, everyone in the class will be working on the same skills, albeit with different texts.

Reading Literature

In the 6th grade, your child will read examples of literature from many different genres, including realistic fiction, historical fiction, science fiction, fables, myths, tall tales, fantasy, folklore, and mysteries. He will also read poetry, including contemporary and classic poems. An important focus will be on making inferences, identifying themes, and getting to the bottom of what the author means literally and figuratively. The topics covered in the Reading Literature (RL) standard include:

- Using text evidence to make and support inferences
- Determining the theme or central idea of a text
- Writing an objective summary of a text
- Analyzing plot and how different episodes or events in a plot work together
- Figurative language, meaning, and tone
- Analyzing point of view
- Comparing and contrasting different genres or forms of literature

Using Text Evidence to Make and Support Inferences

An inference is a conclusion drawn from clues within a text. Inferred ideas are not explicitly stated in the text, but must be deduced. An inference is a sort of equation: The text + the reader's own knowledge = inference. Your child will learn how to be a reading detective who can use clues to support inferences and make inferences independently. Clues from the text are combined with information that the reader already knows.

Take a look at the following excerpt:

Tom picked up the bat and looked at the pitcher. He swung and missed as the ball flew by, once, twice, three times. Tom tossed the bat aside and trudged back to the bench.

What inference can a reader make from the information about Tom?

1. Tom was hit by a ball playing baseball.
2. Tom struck out.

3. Tom quit the team.

The reader brings her background knowledge to the text and recognizes relatively quickly that this text describes a boy who is up at bat during a baseball game. The text provides the information that Tom missed hitting three balls. The reader knows that missing three balls is three strikes in baseball and infers that Tom has struck out. The text supports that inference by telling us that Tom "trudged" back to the bench, since "trudged" means to walk slowly as if exhausted or defeated.

When your child encounters longer texts, it will be important for her to annotate texts and make notes as she reads to identify connections and ideas. A reader might annotate the text as follows:

Tom picked up the bat and looked at the ——— *Baseball!*

pitcher. He swung and missed as the balls

flew by, once, twice, three times. Tom tossed

three strikes ——— the bat aside and trudged back to the bench. ——— *He struck out.*

Assessment questions on making inferences can be formed in several different ways. Your child might encounter a question such as this:

WHICH STATEMENT BEST SUPPORTS THE CONCLUSION THAT TOM IS PLAYING BASEBALL?
1. He trudged back to the bench.
2. Three balls flew by.
3. Tom picked up the bat.

This question is really asking the student to think about his thinking. It is important to read the question carefully. Students often skim a question or assume they know what is being asked without thinking through the requirements. The requirement here is to show that Tom is playing baseball. Only one answer directly supports that inference: Tom picked up the bat.

The bench and the balls mentioned in the other two answer choices also can be directly associated with situations other than baseball.

Determining the Theme or Central Idea of a Text

Students find the concept of theme difficult to grasp. It is a somewhat abstract idea that can be elusive to a child who is more comfortable with concrete ideas. There are several ways to define theme. Two of the most accessible are:

- What the author wants to say about the subject of the text.
- An observation, lesson, or moral that can be taken from the text and applied to life in general.

The theme is not locked to a specific text; more than one text can have the same theme. Often, teachers will ask students to consider different texts that share a theme. That doesn't mean those texts have to be about the same topic. One of the easiest ways to introduce the concept of theme is by reading some of Aesop's Fables.

Once upon a time a tiny ant was making her way to a river to get a drink. She slipped on a wet stone and plunged into the cold water. A dove flying above saw the ant's dilemma and swooped down to the water and rescued her. "Someday," said the ant, "I shall repay you." The dove laughed, "But you're just a little ant. Please don't worry about it." Just a few days later the ant was walking through the field when she noticed a hunter pulling back his bow and aiming an arrow at her dear friend, the dove. The ant rushed to the hunter, sped up his leg and onto his hand and stung him sharply. The hunter cried out, scaring the dove, who flew away unharmed.

The subject of this story is a meeting between an ant and a dove, but the point of the story is not to describe how ants and doves typically interact. Rather, the author, Aesop, has used this story to make an observation about life, or share a moral: that one should never underestimate the value of friendship. Any number of stories could make this same observation.

Sometimes the theme can be expressed in a few words. In the case of this fable, a shorter theme might be "the value of friendship." Sometimes the author will include the theme within the story, perhaps in a concluding sentence or paragraph that explains what the narrator or other characters have learned from the plot. Other times, such as with this fable, the reader has to make an inference. To infer the theme, your child should try to use the following post-reading strategies:

1. Read the story and try to come up with a single word that captures the story.
2. Build a sentence around that single word that expresses a complete idea.

In the case of the fable discussed previously, the word might be *friendship*. The sentence that expresses a complete idea *about* friendship might be, "Never underestimate the value of friendship."

Consider the tale of the three little pigs. This story is about three pigs that each builds a home. The first and second pigs take the "easy" path and build their homes from straw and sticks. The wolf blows down the houses and eats the pigs. The third pig builds his house of bricks; the wolf cannot blow the house down, and the pig survives.

To discover a theme, begin by boiling the meaning of the story down to a couple of words: hard work. What does this story tell you about hard work? Create a longer sentence built around those words, and complete the thought. That is the theme of the story.

Writing an Objective Summary of a Text

Writing an objective summary can be challenging. It is likely that your child has spent many years engaged in reading instruction that required him to make personal connections to stories using phrases like "I think" or "I feel." Now he will have to separate himself from the text and think about how to express the main points of a story without personalizing it.

An objective summary recounts the main idea and most important details of a narrative, using only the information provided in the text. A summary is much shorter than the original text and may omit many details. There are several strategies to help students learn how to summarize a narrative text. A helpful mnemonic is C-PETE.

C—Character
P—has a Problem
E—which Escalates
T—until a Turning point
E—when it Ends

In the story of the three little pigs, the characters are the pigs. The problem is that the wolf wants to blow down their houses and eat the pigs. The problem escalates, as the wolf blows down the house of straw and the house of sticks. The turning point comes when the wolf tries to blow down the house made of brick. The problem ends when the wolf realizes it is futile to continue blowing at the brick house. The wolf leaves and the last pig survives.

Once these details are in place, the summary might be:

Three pigs try to survive a wolf attack. The wolf destroys two of the pigs' homes, which are made of straw and sticks, and eats the pigs. The wolf cannot destroy the third pig's brick house, so the third pig survives.

Notice that a central point in the classic fairy tale, the huffing and puffing of the wolf, is not part of the summary, nor is there any commentary about which pigs are lazy or hardworking. The summary does not share a moral, theme, or message and is not based on inference. It recounts "just the facts," as succinctly as possible.

Analyzing Plot

Every narrative has a plot that follows a predictable structure. Your child will learn to connect the different parts of the plot and understand and relate how they work together. The parts of the plot are as follows:

Exposition: The exposition establishes the characters and setting of the story. The central conflict is often introduced in the exposition.

Rising Action: The rising action brings in complications, or additional problems, and challenges that the main character faces.

Climax: The climax is the turning point in the story. The conflict reaches a point where something must happen to bring about change. It is the point at which the conflict must be addressed.

Falling Action: After the turning point of the story, the falling action explores the results of the climax.

Resolution: The resolution is the ending of the story. The main conflict is resolved, and the "loose ends" are tied up.

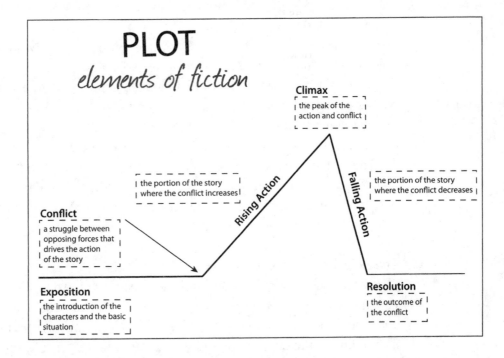

The components of the plot work together. The climax, for example, is less meaningful unless there is the buildup of the rising action. The climax doesn't complete the story, and requires falling action to move the story toward a resolution.

Aspects of Plot

Your child will learn to analyze narrative texts and identify the different aspects of the plot. The following is a short fairy tale by the Brothers Grimm:

There was once a very old man, whose eyes had become dim, his ears dull of hearing, his knees trembled, and when he sat at table he could hardly hold the spoon, and spilt the broth upon the table-cloth or let it run out of his mouth. His son and his son's wife were disgusted at this, so the old grandfather at last had to sit in the corner behind the stove, and they gave him his food in an earthenware bowl, and not even enough of it. And he used to look towards the table with his eyes full of tears. Once, too, his trembling hands could not hold the bowl, and it fell to the ground and broke. The young wife scolded him, but he said nothing and only sighed. Then they brought him a wooden bowl for a few half-pence, out of which he had to eat.

They were once sitting thus when the little grandson of four years old began to gather together some bits of wood upon the ground. "What are you doing there?" asked the father. "I am making a little trough," answered the child, "for father and mother to eat out of when I am big."

The man and his wife looked at each other for a while, and presently began to cry. Then they took the old grandfather to the table, and henceforth always let him eat with them, and likewise said nothing if he did spill a little of anything.

The **exposition** of this story is the first sentence:

"There was once a very old man, whose eyes had become dim, his ears dull of hearing, his knees trembled, and when he sat at table he could hardly hold the spoon, and spilt the broth upon the table-cloth or let it run out of his mouth."

The main character is the old man. The problem he faces is that he is hard of hearing and has trouble seeing. In addition, he trembles so much when he eats that he spills his food.

Next, there is **rising action**. The old man's son and daughter-in-law are disgusted by his eating habits and force him to eat in the corner. The old man is sad.

A new complication is introduced in the rising action. The old man drops his earthenware bowl and it is replaced with an inexpensive wooden bowl.

The **climax** is the turning point of the story or the point to which all of the conflict builds. The climax is that the grandson tries to build a trough for his own parents to eat from when they get old.

The **falling action** is the result of the climax. Once the story reaches a turning point, the falling action is where the story goes. In the Brothers

Grimm story, the falling action is the reaction of the old man's son and daughter-in-law to their son's explanation of why he's making a trough.

The **resolution** brings all the parts of the story together. Because their child has pointed out how cruel they had been, the son and daughter-in-law allow the old man to eat at the table with them and are more understanding when he spills things.

To practice identifying the components of plot, consider initiating conversations with your child about television programs, movies, and, of course, novels. In a fictional narrative, the plot is relatively predictable. More complex books may introduce additional complications in the falling action that are resolved by the end of the book. Help your child identify when the falling action occurs, and especially how a last conflict is different from the climax.

Asking Questions

For many students, understanding the plot can be a difficult task. They may have difficulty in being able to pinpoint when the climax occurs. The climax can also be called a "turning point," which is a helpful way of framing it, as it stresses what happens to the characters as a result of the climax.

Questions on this standard may require your child to make inferences. For example, in the test item that follows, the reader must make an inference to show his understanding of the relationship between elements in the plot. The question refers to the climax, or turning point of the story, and relates to the falling action of that turning point.

WHY DO THE OLD MAN'S SON AND DAUGHTER-IN-LAW DECIDE TO LET THE OLD MAN RETURN TO THE TABLE FOR MEALS?
1. They realize how sad the old man is.
2. They realize they have taught their son how old people should be treated.
3. They see that the little boy wants to eat from the same type of bowl as the old man.

The answer to the question is B. To arrive at the correct answer, readers must consider two sentences. The first is the little boy's explanation (climax), "'I am making a little trough,' answered the child, 'for father and mother to eat out of when I am big.'" From this line the reader can infer that the parents have inadvertently taught the child to treat older relatives like a barnyard animal. From the next sentence (falling action), "The man and his wife looked at each other for a while, and presently began to cry" readers can infer that the parents have realized their mistake.

Figurative Language, Meaning, and Tone

The language standard in grade 6 includes using the context of a sentence to determine the meaning of an unfamiliar word. In addition to context clues, students learn to decode figurative language to determine how it adds meaning to a text. The following kinds of figurative language should be familiar to your sixth grader:

- **Personification:** When human characteristics are assigned to nonhuman things: *The flowers* **danced** *in the wind.*
- **Simile (SIM-a-lee):** A comparison that uses *like* or *as* to show a similarity: *He ran* **like** *a cheetah.*
- **Metaphor:** A comparison between two dissimilar things, which does not use *like* or *as*: *He was a cheetah racing across the field.*
- **Hyperbole (hy-PER-bowl-ee):** An extreme exaggeration: *I've told you a million times to stop kicking the door.*
- **Onomatopoeia:** A word that mimics the sound it describes: *The bees buzzed around their hive.*
- **Alliteration:** The repetition of consonant sounds at the beginning of words: *Susan sulked in the sauna.*

In the 6th grade your child will begin to explore the nuances of a text beyond concrete ideas. Understanding figurative language is crucial to that development and is especially important in reading and understanding poetry. Sixth graders consider figurative language as part of the "big picture" of an author's intent. For example, students discuss and analyze why an author or poet makes specific comparisons or chooses to highlight certain ideas, and how those choices impact the meaning of the text. Consider the following text.

Stephen strode purposefully to the plate, confident that it was his moment to shine. His eyes met the pitcher's glance and he adjusted his stance, knees bent, arms crooked. The pitcher was a stone statue until suddenly, like a spring, he exploded into motion. The first ball whooshed by Stephen's head. He swung, but it was too late. "Strike one!" the umpire exclaimed.

Stephen took a deep breath and brushed the dirt from his shoes. He stared intently at the ground, collecting his thoughts. He looked up to the pitcher, and, once again, took his stance. The pitcher wound up and released another ball. Stephen swung, and missed again. "Strike two!" yelled the umpire.

Stephen thought to himself, "You've done this a million times. C'mon!" He looked to the stands behind him and saw his parents waving madly. He nodded to them. He looked up at the sky, saw the sun playing hide and seek with the puffy clouds. He took his stance again. The pitcher released the ball again. Stephen swung and was rewarded with the satisfying "crack" of his bat connecting with the ball. He watched it fly, for a moment, like a cannon ball toward the outfield, and set out on his trek around the bases.

HOW DOES THE AUTHOR USE METAPHOR TO SHOW THE PITCHER'S CONCENTRATION?

1. By comparing the pitcher to a spring, exploding into action.
2. By comparing the pitcher to a stone statue, silent and motionless.
3. By highlighting the sound of the ball as it flies by Stephen.
4. By contrasting the exclamation of the umpire to the quiet players.

Answer: The author compares the pitcher to a stone statue, using a metaphor to demonstrate his concentration. The pitcher is so still, so focused, that he appears to be made of stone. This metaphor is used to contrast the pitcher's apparent collected concentration to Stephen's growing anxiety.

HOW DOES STEPHEN USE HYPERBOLE TO HELP HIMSELF SUCCEED?

1. Stephen uses hyperbole to remind himself that he can hit the ball.
2. Stephen uses hyperbole to focus on the pitcher.
3. Stephen uses hyperbole to focus on his parents and their expectations.
4. Stephen uses hyperbole to distract himself from his feelings of anxiety.

Answer: Stephen uses hyperbole when he says, "You've done this a million times." In his internal dialogue, he is reminding himself that he has hit the ball in the past and can do so again.

This question did not provide any clues to the definition of hyperbole. This presents a challenge to a student who is not familiar with the names of different types of figurative language. For this reason, along with understanding how figurative language works in a story, it is important that your child know the names of different types of figurative language.

Each type of figurative language is used in the passage. In the text that follows, each type is underlined and annotated. Support your child as he learns to identify and annotate figurative language in his reading.

Alliteration
The "s" sound is repeated.

Metaphor
The pitcher is compared to a statue and something explosive.

Onomatopeia
The word "whooshed" mimics the sound the ball makes as it moves rapidly through the air.

Personification
The sun and clouds are given human attributes.

Simile
The pitcher is compared to a spring using "like."

Hyperbole
Stephen exaggerates the number of times he's been at bat.

Stephen strode purposefully to the plate, confident that it was his moment to shine. His eyes met the pitcher's glance and he adjusted his stance, knees bent, arms crooked. The pitcher was a stone statue until suddenly, like a spring, he exploded into motion. The first ball whooshed by Stephen's head. He swung, but it was too late. "Strike one!" the umpire exclaimed.

Stephen took a deep breath and brushed the dirt from his shoes. He stared intently at the ground, collecting his thoughts. He looked up to the pitcher, and, once again, took his stance. The pitcher wound up and released another ball. Stephen swung, and missed again. "Strike two!" yelled the umpire.

Stephen thought to himself, "You've done this a million times. C'mon!" He looked to the stands behind him and saw his parents, waving madly. He nodded to them. He looked up at the sky, and saw the sun playing hide and seek with the puffy clouds. He took his stance again. The pitcher released the ball again. Stephen swung and was rewarded with the satisfying "crack" of his bat connecting with the ball. He watched it fly like a cannonball toward the outfield, and set out on his trek around the bases.

Simile
The ball is compared to a cannonball.

Onomatopeia
The sound of the bat hitting the ball is similar to this sound.

Figurative language is found in literature and poetry, but it is also common in advertising and journalism. Using figurative language can change the meaning and/or tone of a text. Read the following sentence:

A flood of protests indicated the public's displeasure with the new regulations.

In this example, a comparison is made between protests and rushing water, even though the sentence doesn't explicitly say, "The protests were a flood . . ." The metaphor is effective in communicating that there are many protests simultaneously. Compare that example to this following sentence:

A trickle of protests indicated the public's displeasure with the new regulations.

Changing just one word in effect changes the meaning of the entire sentence. Now there are a few protests occurring infrequently.

The tone of a text is the author's attitude about the subject. The best way to determine the tone of a text is to consider the word choice. Keep in mind that English is an expansive language, and there is more than one way to express almost any concept. It makes sense to assume that writers are deliberate in their choices, and that those choices are based on attitude or bias. Read the following sentences:

Because he wasn't tied down to a full-time job, Martin had the freedom to spend hours hiking local trails, visiting art galleries, and taking in the latest films at the cinema.

Martin was unemployed and tried to fill his days by walking around local hiking trails, hanging around in art galleries, and spending hours in the movie theater, seeing every new release.

In the first example, Martin is taking advantage of his freedom, it seems, and using his time in a way that is almost enviable. He "hikes," "visits," and "takes in." In the second sentence, he's engaging the same activities, but now he's "walking," "hanging around," and "spending." The change in these verbs demonstrates a change in tone. In the second sentence, Martin seems to be killing time, rather than taking advantage of free time; it seems that the author pities Martin, or thinks him unproductive.

To identify the tone of a passage, consider the verbs and the adjectives used. These descriptive and active words tell you what the author was thinking when he wrote the sentence.

Analyzing Point of View

Every text, whether it is literary or informational, has a point of view. The points of view your child will encounter are:

- First person
- Second person
- Third person limited
- Third person omniscient

First Person

The first person point of view uses first-person pronouns such as *I*, *we*, and *us*, and is told by a narrator who is within the story.

John and I watched as the sun set slowly behind the mountains; I was eager to see what tomorrow would bring.

Second Person

This point of view is seldom used in literature. It can be found in instructions or directions, as the point is to explain what the reader should do. Second person point of view uses the pronoun *you*.

You and John watched the sun set slowly behind the mountains, and you were eager to see what tomorrow would bring.

Third Person Limited

This point of view narrates from outside of the story and knows the thoughts and feelings of one character. Some third person pronouns are *he*, *she*, *they*, and *them*.

Janet and John watched the sun set slowly behind the mountains; she was eager to see what tomorrow would bring.

Third Person Omniscient

Like third person limited, this point of view uses third person pronouns, *he*, *she*, *they*, and *them*. The narrator is outside of the story and knows the thoughts and feelings of all or most of the characters.

Janet and John watched the sun set slowly behind the mountains; they were eager to see what tomorrow would bring.

Comparing and Contrasting Different Genres

In the 6th grade your child will read literature from several different genres. He will be asked to identify the characteristics of different genres, and consider how the same story might be told in different ways. For example, he might encounter a mystery that is set during Paul Revere's ride and a work of historical fiction set in the same time period that centers on the ride of Paul Revere.

GENRES OF LITERATURE		
Genre	**Description**	**Example**
Mystery	Fiction that tells the story of a crime or secret that must be resolved	*The Adventures of Sherlock Holmes*
Science fiction	Fiction that deals with technology or science; it does not have to be set in the future or on a different planet	*Star Wars*
Historical fiction	Fiction that is set during a realistic time in the past; the historical events or descriptions should be accurate and factual, but the characters can be fictional	*Number the Stars*
Biography	The story of a person's life, written by another person	*Temple Grandin*

Autobiography	The story of a person's life, written by that person	*Long Walk to Freedom: The Autobiography of Nelson Mandela*
Memoir	A personal, autobiographical account of an important event or period in a person's life	*Anne Frank: The Diary of a Young Girl*
Realistic fiction	Fiction that is set during modern times and deals with realistic situations that people could face in the real world	*The Fault in Our Stars*
Fantasy	Fiction that happens in an invented setting and often includes magical creatures, magic, and situations that could not ever occur in real life	*Harry Potter and the Sorcerer's Stone*
Dystopian fiction	A more recent genre of fiction that is set in a fictional time when the society oppresses individuals and there are many harsh rules	*The Hunger Games*

In addition to these genres, your sixth grader will also read shorter, traditional stories in these genres:

GENRES OF TRADITIONAL STORIES		
Genre	**Description**	**Example**
Myth	A sacred story of how a natural phenomenon was created	Greek myths about Zeus, Hercules, and the other gods
Folklore	A tale unique to a region that has been passed down from one generation to another	Stories of Davy Crockett
Fable	A story that teaches a moral or lesson, often using animals as the main characters	Aesop's Fables
Tall tale	A kind of folklore that uses exaggeration (hyperbole) and is intended to be humorous	Paul Bunyan

In addition to genres of literature and traditional story, there are also forms of literature. The following chart highlights the forms of literature your sixth grader will study.

FORMS OF LITERATURE		
Form	**Description**	**Example**
Poetry	Literature written in verse, using stanzas that may or may not use rhyme or meter	"The Tyger" by William Blake
Songs	Verses intended to be set to music and sung	"You Are My Sunshine"
Drama	A drama is the script or text of a play; it includes the lines the actors will speak as well as stage directions and instructions for the setting	*Romeo and Juliet* by William Shakespeare
Prose	A text that is not poetry, drama, or a song; it does not feature special formatting, rhyme, or meter	Any novel

Reading Informational Texts

In the 6th grade your child will read many different kinds of informational texts, including nonfiction narratives, arguments, journalism examples, textbooks, and historical documents. An important focus will be on determining the author's purpose and the function of the text. Your child will learn to analyze how writers use details to support ideas, how a text is organized to best present an argument, and how to find information that is explicitly stated as well as how to draw inferences. The topics covered in the Reading Informational Text (RI) include:

- Using text evidence to complete and support analysis of a text
- Determining the main idea of and provide an objective summary of a text
- Analyzing the structure of an informational text
- Determining an author's purpose
- Evaluating an argument and identify evidence and reasoning used to support a claim

Using Text Evidence

When analyzing an informational text, sixth graders will evaluate how an author uses evidence, explanations, and details to support his or her ideas. Your child will learn to evaluate a text and use evidence from the text to support his conclusions. Reading with purpose is one important strategy that students should learn. When readers know why they are reading a text, it is much easier for them to understand that text. The text that follows has been annotated by a reader whose main purpose is to learn why there will never be a permanent settlement on Antarctica. Notice that the notes point out the reasons.

Antarctica

Very little
land that is
not covered
with ice

The southernmost of earth's seven continents is the home of the South Pole. Antarctica is a landmass of about 5.4 million square miles. All but 2 percent of the continent is covered by ice that is at least 1 mile thick. There are no forests, rivers, or native populations. In fact, it is unlikely that any human laid eyes upon the continent before 1820. The first person to set foot on the continent was likely Henryk Bull, who walked onto the frozen land in 1895.

Could never
grow crops or
raise animals
in such cold
temperatures

Antarctica is the coldest place on earth. A record low temperature of minus 133.6°F has been recorded and the land beneath the ice is permanently frozen. It is impossible for plants to take root or grow in the interior. On most summer days, the temperature stays below 32°F, which is the temperature at which water freezes.

The reason for these extremely cold temperatures is Antarctica's location. At the bottom of the planet, the continent is mostly hidden from the sun's direct light. Because Antarctica is in the southern hemisphere, winter is May through August, and during most of this time, the sun never rises. The continent is in complete darkness. During the summer, December to March, the sun never sets, but is always low in the sky. Most of the sun's warmth is reflected by the thick white ice.

Even when it
is sunny, most
of the heat
is reflected
away.

Four months
with no
sunlight

Notice that the reader ignored some interesting points about the history of the exploration of Antarctica and focused only on the points related to the purpose he established before reading. Notice also that the reader made an inference to support his conclusions. In the excerpt that follows, the reader combined the information in the text with his own knowledge to conclude that one could not grow crops or raise animals where the land is permanently frozen.

Antarctica is the coldest place on earth. A record low temperature of -133.6°F has been recorded and the land beneath the ice is permanently frozen.

Reading with purpose, interacting with the text, and trusting her own knowledge as a basis for making inferences are three of the most important skills your sixth grader will develop this year. You can support these efforts at home by offering different ways for your child to gather schema, or background knowledge. Teachers cannot provide all of the personal experiences and understanding of the world that a typical sixth grader brings to a reading. But parents can initiate conversations and create opportunities to help their children acquire general knowledge. If, for example, the student had no idea how crops are grown, he could not have inferred the reasons why a permanent settlement is unlikely in Antarctica.

Determining Ideas and Summarizing the Text

Finding the main points of a text and writing a summary can be challenging for sixth graders, especially when working with longer texts that have many details. The Common Core uses the term *gist* to refer to this idea, and this term is often found in assessments. The gist is the central point of a paragraph or a longer passage. When a passage makes several points, the summary will include several gists.

The most effective way to find the gist of a section of text is to identify the following (if they exist):

- Who?
- What?
- Where?
- When?
- Why?
- How?

In the following table, a student would use these questions to establish the gist of the first paragraph.

The southernmost of earth's seven continents is the home of the South Pole. Antarctica is a landmass of about 5.4 million square miles. All but 2 percent of the continent is covered by ice that is at least 1 mile thick. There are no forests, rivers, or native populations. In fact, it is unlikely that any human laid eyes upon the continent before 1820. The first person to set foot on the continent was likely Henryk Bull, who walked onto the frozen land in 1895.

FINDING THE GIST	
Question	**Answer**
Who?	Henryk Bull walked on Antarctica in 1895
What?	Antarctica, a continent of 5.4 million square miles with no vegetation or native inhabitants
Where?	Southernmost
When?	First sighted in 1820
Why?	98% covered in ice at least 1 mile thick
How?	N/A

Once these details on the paragraph are collected, the reader can combine them into a short summary that captures the main points.

Antarctica, a 5.4 million square mile, uninhabited landmass almost entirely covered in ice, is the home of the South Pole and the southernmost continent on the planet. It was first spotted in 1820, and 75 years later, Henryk Bull was the first person to walk on it.

The summary captures the main points of the first paragraph in two dense sentences. If the student were to summarize the entire text, she would create a gist statement for each paragraph and then combine them.

Analyzing the Structure of an Informational Text

Your child will learn to identify and analyze text structures that show relationship. The most common text structures he will review include:

- Compare and contrast
- Cause and effect
- Problem and solution
- Order and sequence

Compare and Contrast

Sometimes a writer will look for similarities and differences between two people, places, or things. When a writer looks for similarities, he compares.

When he looks for differences, he contrasts. A good way to analyze a compare and contrast text is to use a Venn diagram.

Read the following short text:

Both seals and sea lions are sea mammals. Sea mammals are warm-blooded and give birth to live babies, rather than lay eggs. Both animals are also pinnipeds, which is Latin for fin-footed. Both have flippers instead of legs and feet. Seals have small furry front flippers with claws on each tiny toe. Sea lions have large skin-covered flippers that have no fur or claws. Sea lions are much noisier than seals. Sea lions bark and squawk, while seals make soft grunting noises.

In this text, the author has pointed out ways that sea lions and seals are similar and ways they are different. Using a Venn diagram, the reader can sort these characteristics to better analyze the text.

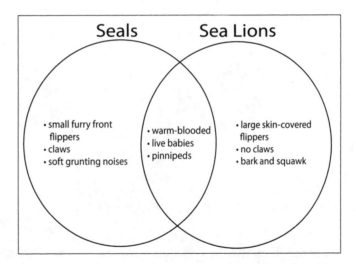

This Venn diagram helps the reader understand and identify the similarities and differences between the animals. When studying a compare/contrast text, several keywords and phrases help focus the analysis:

- Different from
- Same as
- Compared to
- As opposed to

- Although
- Like/unlike
- Either/or

Cause and Effect

A text that shows a causal relationship explains how one situation leads to another. Often the text will list several causes and have a single effect. Review the following text:

Almost anyone who has a brother or sister has experienced sibling rivalry. There are several reasons why siblings sometimes do not get along. For example, sometimes an older sibling may resent that he or she is held to a different set of rules than a younger sibling. While, in other instances, a younger brother or sister might feel upset because an older sibling has more privileges.

A good way to analyze cause and effect is with a graphic organizer.

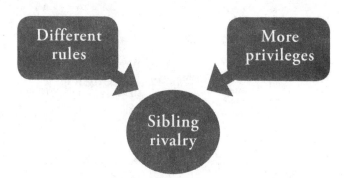

In the diagram, the passage shows two causes that have been described as leading to sibling rivalry. When analyzing a cause/effect text, the reader should look for certain keywords and phrases:

- Because
- Since
- As a result of
- For this reason

Problem and Solution

A problem and solution essay, as it suggests, identifies a problem and one or more ways to solve that problem. Review the following text:

Many students find they don't get the high grades they're capable of because they procrastinate or put off completing assignments. For those who worry that procrastinating may get in the way of their success, there are several strategies that can help. For example, some people set up a timer and push themselves to work on a project or assignment for a specific amount of time before they can take a break, which is also timed. Others break assignments into specific tasks, and reward themselves after completing each task. Still others use a to-do list that includes every step in every assignment and feel motivated by the opportunity to cross tasks off their list.

The first step is to identify the problem. The reader can annotate as she reads to pick out that procrastination is the problem. Using a graphic organizer can help pinpoint the solutions that directly address the problem.

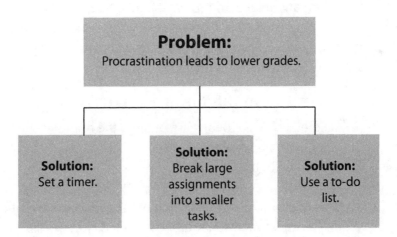

In this graphic organizer, the reader has identified the main point of the problem and the main point of each of the solutions. When reading a problem/solution essay, students should look for the following keywords and phrases:

- Problem
- The question is

- Answer
- A solution

Order and Sequence

Order and sequence are most often used in essays that give instructions or directions, such as how to complete a task. Students may be given an informative essay that provides directions and then demonstrate that they understand that specific step-by-step activities should be performed. Review the following short text:

Maracas are traditional percussion instruments usually made from gourds. They are popular with Latin American musicians. To make your own maracas you'll need two empty plastic bottles with screw-on caps. Collect small objects such as pebbles, beans, or rice, making sure that you have a mix of items to create an interesting sound. Once you've added the items to the bottles, replace the tops. Maracas are generally decorated with colorful painted designs. Use poster paints to cover the plastic bottle and add decorations.

When annotating an order/sequence text, a reader can simply highlight and number each step. Doing so allows a reader to easily access the information. Questions on these types of texts vary. Using the example of the maracas text, a question might be:

WHEN SHOULD THE TOP OF THE BOTTLE BE REPLACED?

1. Before pebbles or beans are put into the bottle.
2. After the bottle is painted.
3. Before the bottle is painted.

This question and others like it require readers to think about order and sequence and how events are connected. Keywords for order/sequence reading include:

- First, second, third . . .
- Before, after
- Next
- Then

Determining an Author's Purpose

Every text is written with an audience and a purpose in mind. The author of an editorial in the *New York Times* is writing to persuade a college-educated audience. The author of a young adult novel is writing to entertain a middle-school audience. Your child will learn to find and analyze clues in a text that reveal the author's purpose, or why the author wrote the text.

Your sixth grader will learn that authors write informational texts for several reasons:

- To persuade
- To inform or explain
- To entertain

Understanding specific features of each purpose will help a reader determine the author's intent.

To Persuade

When an author writes to persuade, she wants the reader to agree with her point of view, take some action, or even buy or sign up for something. Advertising, political speeches, and newspaper editorials are examples of persuasive writing. Persuasive writing uses specific kinds of appeals, or ways to convince the reader to agree with the writer's point of view. These appeals include:

- Logos, or an appeal to logic. The writer uses statistics, facts, and information from research to prove that his or her point is correct.
- Ethos, or an appeal to the credibility of the writer. The writer explains why he is qualified to make the argument, and why he should be trusted or believed.
- Pathos, or an appeal to emotion. The writer uses ideas, imagery, or concepts that cause the reader to respond emotionally and want to act in response to those emotions.

Review the following example of persuasive writing, which has been annotated to highlight the different appeals.

There is a crisis in America. Thousands of people who need organ transplants must wait months or even years for a suitable organ to become available. Every day more than a dozen people on organ transplant waiting lists die because a suitable match was not found in time. As one of the top transplant surgeons in the United States, I appeal to each and every American to register as an organ donor. It costs nothing to register, and doing so will not impact your life in any way. When you pass away, your organs will be harvested and transplanted, saving up to twenty lives! Imagine if one of those lives were your mom, your brother, or your best friend. Every person waiting for an organ transplant is someone special to his or her family and friends. Won't you help? Register today.

Notice that the reader of the passage has annotated the call to action. A persuasive text will suggest specifically what the reader should agree to, believe, or do.

To Inform or Explain

When an author writes to inform, his goal is to teach a lesson, explain a concept, or provide instructions. Some examples of writing to inform include:

- Nonfiction books, such as biographies
- Textbooks
- Encyclopedias and other reference books
- News stories or magazine articles
- Recipes, instructions, or directions

Information in a text that is intended to inform is organized in a logical order. Main points might be explained in order of time, in order of importance, or in a spatial order. Spatial order is useful when giving instructions, because it explains things as they relate to others. An example would be, "Press the red button that is to the left of the steering wheel."

To Entertain

Informational texts can also be intended to entertain, such as a retelling of a funny situation. When its primary purpose is to entertain, informational text often takes a fictional form. This type of fictional writing may be based on true stories or events, although it may not accurately portray the actual facts. This type of informational entertainment can be presented in a variety of forms, including short stories, novels, jokes, and poetry.

Evaluating an Argument

The last key skill in the Reading Informational Text (RI) strand for your sixth grader is evaluating an argument. An argument is a work that makes a claim and supports it with evidence. An argument has two main parts:

- The claim—what the writer wants to prove
- Reasons and evidence—the support the writer uses to prove his claim

Review the following essay:

In many schools students are required to wear uniforms. School officials believe that uniforms are economical, help students stay focused, and reduce incidents of bullying. While those points may be true, there are many reasons why students at Wilson Middle School should not be required to wear uniforms.

School uniforms take away students' right to express their individuality. Research has shown that students begin to develop their adult personalities in late childhood and early adolescence. During this time children need opportunities to make choices and decisions. Being allowed to choose what to wear to school each day is a crucial step in each child's development and should not be taken away.

In addition to being able to choose their own clothing, students need to realize that there are differences among people, and that it is important to respect and honor those differences. If everyone dresses alike, students don't get to practice working and studying in an environment where everyone is different. Being denied that opportunity could hurt them later in life as college students or in their future careers.

Finally, many students are concerned about fair trade and the conditions of the workers who make the products they buy. Unless the school administration can guarantee and prove that all school uniforms are manufactured by workers who enjoy good working conditions and make a fair wage, some students will have to violate their own code of ethics in order to follow school rules. It is unreasonable to expect students to ignore strongly held beliefs.

In conclusion, while there may be benefits in some schools to wearing school uniforms, none of the problems the administration referenced are widespread here at Wilson Middle School. Requiring school uniforms could interfere with students' opportunities to mature appropriately and may even violate some students' personal beliefs. Wilson Middle School should not, under any circumstances, implement school uniforms.

When a reader evaluates an argument, the first step is to determine what the issue is and what the author's position is on that issue. In this essay, the issue is whether or not students at Wilson Middle School should wear uniforms. The author's position is that students should not be required to wear uniforms.

Once you know the position, you can evaluate the claims the author makes to support that position. Each claim will be supported with reasons and evidence. The first claim is that uniforms take away students' right to express their individuality. The author supports that claim with evidence: students need to make decisions such as what to wear to school, as doing so is an important part of growing into an adult.

The second claim in this essay is that students learn to respect differences when everyone is dressed in their own clothes. The author's reason for this claim is that in the students' futures, as college students and workers, they will have to be able to function in environments where everyone is not the same.

Finally, the writer makes a third claim that students who care about the conditions of workers may have to violate a moral belief to purchase the required clothing. The reason used to support this claim is that the school may not be able to prove that the workers who manufacture the uniforms are treated fairly.

In the conclusion the writer restates the thesis and summarizes the three main points, ending with his very clear stance on the issue.

Once the reader has gone through each claim and noted the evidence or reasons the writer has provided, the next step is to evaluate that evidence. For example, in the third paragraph, the claim is that the school may not be able to prove that the workers making the uniforms have good working conditions. This evidence is not particularly strong. First, the school *may* be able to prove that the working conditions are acceptable. Second, even if the school cannot prove it to be so, the working conditions may still be acceptable. There are many variables in this reason. This claim could be strengthened with more evidence. For example, if the writer knew that most school uniforms produced for American schools come from a specific manufacturer that utilizes child labor in undeveloped nations, the claim would be well supported.

For each of the claims, the reader should review and evaluate the specific evidence and reasons, and then ask critical questions to test the validity of the evidence. This evaluation can be completed through annotations while reading the text. Note the sample annotations in the following paragraph:

> What sort of proof would be required? If they don't have proof, that doesn't mean that conditions are poor.

> Are there specific standards here? What are good working conditions? What are fair wages? This seems vague.

Finally, many students are concerned about fair trade and the conditions of the workers who make the products they buy. Unless the school administration can guarantee and prove that all school uniforms are manufactured by workers who enjoy good working conditions and make a fair wage, some students will have to violate their own code of ethics in order to follow school rules. It is unreasonable to expect students to ignore strongly held beliefs.

> What kind of evidence could support this?

> Would students have to prove that they have these strongly held beliefs?

The more your child practices evaluating arguments and persuasive texts, the easier she'll find it to do so. Eventually similarities among misleading arguments will begin to emerge. As she moves into the higher grades, she'll begin to notice different types of logical fallacies used in arguments. This type of analysis calls on your child's ability to think critically. For even the most successful student, this can be challenging at first. Students have been conditioned to accept what is written in a text as fact, and so your child might need help to build the confidence she needs to become an evaluative and critical reader.

Helping Your Child Succeed

Your child can become a strong critical and analytical reader if he practices reading with a critical, analytical eye. The only way your child will become a strong critical and analytical reader is if he works with challenging texts that require him to continually improve his skills. Provide opportunities for your child to look beyond the concrete details on the page and to draw conclusions, consider motives, and make predictions. You can help your child dissect his reading assignments and discuss the material. If your child is reading a novel for class, for example, ask him about the elements of the plot, help him understand the story it tells, and encourage him to consider how the novel is constructed. When reading informational texts, even encyclopedias or textbooks, encourage critical thinking by asking questions about the author's purpose and the structure of each text.

In the 6th grade readers begin to seriously consider the idea that a text is something that has been produced by another person with a specific intent. Children understand the idea of authorship from an early age, but critically evaluating authorship only comes about through the work of textual analysis. As always, the best way for your child to learn these skills is to deliberately practice them.

Practice Exercises

These exercises will help your child practice the skills covered in this chapter. They are similar to the types of questions she will encounter on standardized tests.

Making Inferences

Read the following short passages and respond to the questions that follow.

1. As Martin walked down the street, he noticed that most people were carrying closed umbrellas. Although he had not seen a weather report, what could Martin infer?
   a. That it was going to rain later that day.
   b. That there was a sale on umbrellas at a local store.
   c. That he was late for work.
2. When he got home, Pete took off his muddy boots and left them on the front steps. He would get them later and clean them off. He went directly into the bathroom and took off his dirty overalls, changing into clean jeans

and a T-shirt. He'd spent a long day in the fields, but he was satisfied that he had accomplished quite a bit. What kind of work does Pete most likely do?

    a. An attorney

    b. A bus driver

    c. A farmer

3. Mary rushed through the door and called out, "I'm here! I'm sorry! I'm here!" Her mother appeared in the doorway to the kitchen, looked at her watch, and glared at Mary. "Well hurry up, then," she said. "Don't make us wait any longer than you already have." From this passage you can infer that . . .

    a. It is Mary's mother's birthday.

    b. Mary is late.

    c. Mary's mother was worried she had been hurt.

4. A little boy is sitting with his mother in a doctor's office. He leans listlessly against his mother, and when she gives him a cup to sip some water he slowly pushes it away. After a while he begins to whimper and puts a hand to his neck. What can you infer from this situation?

    a. The boy is tired.

    b. The boy has hurt his hand.

    c. The boy has a sore throat.

5. Margie climbed the two steps and walked out onto the narrow board. She looked down into the pool. It seemed so far away now that she was on the board. She saw her parents and brother watching her. "I have to go through with it," she thought. She gently bounced on her feet a couple of times and put her hands over her head. Based on this passage, you can infer that what probably happens next?

    a. Margie begins to cry.

    b. Margie dives into the pool.

    c. Margie heads down the ski slope.

Identifying the Author's Purpose

Read each of the following and determine the author's purpose.

1. The owl and the pussycat went to sea / In a beautiful pea-green boat. / They took some honey and plenty of money / Wrapped up in a five-pound note.

    a. Inform

   b. Persuade

   c. Entertain

2. Take advantage of this one-time offer and receive three books for the price of two. This is a limited-time offer. Act now!

   a. Inform

   b. Persuade

   c. Entertain

3. Henry Brady is 58 years old and has one of the most unique jobs in the world. He is a professional whistler. Not many people know about professional whistlers, but it is a real career and one that is in demand for movies, commercials, and even songs you hear on the radio.

   a. Inform

   b. Persuade

   c. Entertain

4. In 1974 an eccentric millionaire named Stanley Marsh bought ten vintage cars, all manufactured between 1949 and 1963. Marsh buried the cars, headlights down, into the sand of a desert outside the city of Amarillo, Texas. Today the area is known as Cadillac Ranch, and visitors still park and hike into the desert to see the strange attraction.

   a. Inform

   b. Persuade

   c. Entertain

5. "Winter" by Mother Goose

Cold and raw the north wind doth blow,

Bleak in the morning early;

All the hills are covered with snow,

And winter's now come fairly.

   a. Inform

   b. Persuade

   c. Entertain

CHAPTER 6

Grade 6—Writing, Speaking, and Listening

In the 6th grade your child will learn to communicate ideas in writing and in conversations with others, including peers and adults. The writing, speaking, and listening standards cover all components of communication, and are designed to help your child develop the skills she needs to be successful in future grades, college, and the workplace. By providing constructive support, opportunities for practice, and thoughtful guidance, you can help your child become a confident and effective communicator.

What Your Sixth Grader Will Learn

The writing standard covers three types of writing: persuasive, explanatory, and narrative. Writing instruction focuses on using vivid, specific details to support ideas, and writing concisely. The goal is for student writers to use precise, descriptive details to create efficient, clear texts. Your child will continue to build on the writing process she learned in grades 4 and 5, and will approach writing as a project that requires planning and revision. The speaking and listening standard has two main areas of focus: the skills needed to be an active collaborator and contributor to discussion, and engaging in meaningful conversations that lead to learning. Finally, she'll begin developing presentation skills and learn about the different contexts or situations for sharing information.

There are three types of essays your child will learn to plan and write. She'll also begin to learn about conducting academic research, a skill she will use throughout her K–12 and college experience. Finally, she will begin to practice the skills she'll need to be an effective part of a group of colleagues or collaborators.

There are four main focus areas in the Writing standard:

- Writing arguments to support claims
- Writing informative/explanatory texts
- Writing narratives to develop real or imagined experiences
- Conducting research to build and present knowledge

In addition, your child will focus on the following topics in the Speaking and Listening standard:

- Being a collaborative participant in a range of discussions
- Presenting claims and information to others

Writing Arguments

In elementary school, your child learned about persuasive writing. Both persuasive and argumentative writing require a thesis statement or main claim. They differ in that persuasive writing relies on emotion and personal opinion, while argumentative writing relies on logic and factual evidence. Argumentative writing may use an emotional appeal, but it is more balanced than persuasive writing, especially because argumentation includes a counterargument, or an acknowledgement of an opposing viewpoint. It can be helpful to think of argumentative writing as similar to proving a point in a courtroom. It is methodical, logical, and relies on credible or trustworthy evidence. There are several assessed components to argumentative writing in the 6th grade.

Introduce a Claim

The claim is also called the thesis. It is the main point the writer intends to prove. A claim for an argumentative essay must be a debatable point of view on an issue. For example, the sentence that follows is a fact, not a claim:

More than 30 percent of American children and adolescents are overweight or obese.

The sentence states a fact that can be readily supported with credible evidence. There are dozens of studies and years of research and statistics that support this statement. There is no reasonable counterargument, or point of view that disagrees with this.

The next sentence, however, *is* an argumentative claim:

Vending machines in public schools should not sell junk food, because doing so will lead to obesity and poor eating habits among children.

This sentence is a claim because it argues that something should or should not be done. It provides a reason why the action should be taken. There is at least one reasonable counterargument:

Vending machines in public schools should offer junk food because students appreciate variety, and selling these items can raise money for field trips and special programs schools could not otherwise afford.

A writer could reasonably be expected to support either side of the issue. This is a debatable point. Notice, also, that both stances combine the claim and a "because statement." The "because statement" is the reason for the claim and is crucial to an effective thesis.

Support Claim with Evidence, Using Credible Sources

Your sixth grader will learn about conducting academic research using online sources, his school library, and the public library. He will learn to take evidence from his sources to provide support for the points he makes in his writing. The following are examples of strong evidence, for either the argument or the counterargument:

More than 20 percent of American adolescents are clinically obese.

In-school vending machines provide up to $10,000 per year in additional revenue to school districts.

The following are examples of weak evidence, based on opinion or personal narrative:

In my school we have several vending machines and there aren't really any overweight students.

Most kids don't eat school lunch anyway.

The first example is a personal observation, but there isn't any actual data or facts to support a claim. The second example is a very broad generalization. The second example could be more credible if the writer included a statistic, such as, "55 percent of students in grades six through twelve report that they choose not to eat school lunch."

Clarify Relationships Among Claims

In the 6th grade your child will be expected to use words and phrases called transitions to make connections between ideas. Transitions improve the logical flow of an essay. Review the following examples. In the first example, two ideas are presented, but there is no connection between them:

In many schools vending machines offer a selection of healthier snacks as well as junk food. Some offer whole-grain pretzels, which contain about 108 calories per serving.

In the next example, a transition is used to tie these ideas together and show the reader how the information is linked:

In many schools vending machines offer a selection of healthier snacks as well as junk food. For example, some offer whole-grain pretzels, which contain about 108 calories per serving.

In the second example, the reader learns that the writer considers the whole-grain pretzels to be an example of a healthier snack choice.

There are many different kinds of transitions that can show different relationships between ideas. Here are some of the most common:

COMMON TRANSITION WORDS AND PHRASES	
Type of transition	**Word or phrase**
For emphasis	in fact
	to emphasize
	again
To compare	similarly
	likewise or like
	just as
To contrast	although
	however
	on the other hand
To elaborate	for example
	additionally (in addition)
	further (furthermore)
To show order	first, second, third, etc.
	next, afterward
	finally

Maintain a Formal Style

Formal academic writing may be new to your sixth grader. In the earlier grades, he was encouraged to write about his own experiences using informal language and to use first person pronouns (I, me, we, us). Now he'll be expected to write using formal language and third person pronouns (he, she, they, them) unless he is specifically assigned a personal narrative or story.

Informal style is conversational and is written as a child might speak.

I think kids are getting obese because we have vending machines in the cafeteria that sell junk foods.

Formal style is more precise, avoids slang, is written in the third person, and does not mention what the writer thinks or feels.

Vending machines in school cafeterias sell junk foods that may lead to obesity in children.

When your child writes a formal essay, encourage him to state his feelings and beliefs but back them up using facts that he can support with evidence.

I think Leavenworth, Washington is the most beautiful town in America.

Leavenworth, Washington is the most beautiful town in America. A recent article in *Forbes* magazine, which highlights the village's unique Bavarian architecture, confirms this.

In the first example, the writer has expressed a feeling or belief. In the second, he has made a claim that can be supported with evidence.

Ending an Argument

The end of an essay is just as important as the beginning. The conclusion should accomplish three things:

1. Restate the thesis
2. Summarize the most important evidence
3. Leave the reader with a closing thought or a call to action

In conclusion, the rise in childhood obesity is caused, in part, by the junk food sold in school cafeteria vending machines. Vending machine snacks are usually high in calories, fat, and sugar. When students buy these junk foods, instead of bringing a healthy lunch from home or eating a school meal, they are filling their stomachs with empty calories, which can lead to overeating and weight gain. Contact your school today and demand all junk foods be removed from school vending machines.

Writing Informative/Explanatory Texts

It's likely that your sixth grader already has experience with informative and explanatory writing. This type of writing describes or explains. A report on a president, an essay comparing and contrasting dogs and cats, and a research paper that studies the effects of global warming are all examples of informative writing. This type of text can take many forms:

- Definition
- Compare/contrast
- Cause/effect
- Biographical/historical

An informative/explanatory essay usually requires outside research, but not always. For example, your child may be asked to explain a task that is familiar to her, such as how to make her bed or brush her teeth.

Your child's teacher will likely present her with several "mentor texts," or examples of effective explanatory writing. Mentor texts serve as models for student writers because they provide a pattern that is easy to follow.

Your child may be asked to write in response to a prompt. The following is an example of a prompt your child might encounter:

Think of two different modes of transportation. Some examples might include a car, a train, a bus, a plane, a bicycle, and the like. Now choose two and compare and contrast them. How are they similar? How are they different?

In your essay be sure to:

- Introduce your topic and choose an organizational strategy such as definition, classification, comparison/contrast, or cause and effect
- Develop the topic with relevant facts, definitions, concrete details, quotations or other information or examples
- Use transitions to clarify the relationships among ideas
- Use precise language to inform or explain your topic
- Maintain a formal style
- Provide a concluding statement or section that follows the explanation

There are several assessed components to an informative/explanatory text:

The Introduction

The first step in writing an informational text is to determine a controlling idea. This is also called a thesis. The thesis should provide information about the topic. Here is an example thesis for an essay that is based on the prompt just described:

Although riding a bike and riding a bus are both ways to get to school, they differ in cost, the exercise they provide, and safety.

The controlling idea does two things:

- It responds directly to the prompt.
- It lists specific categories that will be used to organize the essay.

Once the controlling idea is in place, your child can write the rest of the introduction. The purpose of the introduction is to hook the reader, provide necessary background information, and present the controlling idea, usually in that order. The following is a sample introduction for this essay prompt:

Imagine a warm spring morning. The sun is shining; the birds are chirping. It's time to go to school. What's the best way to get there? Although riding a bike and riding a bus are both ways to get to school, they differ in cost, the exercise they provide, and safety.

This example used a description as a hook. Other strategies for beginning an essay include:

- A quotation from a famous person
- A startling fact
- A humorous comment
- An anecdote or real-life incident
- A figure of speech

In earlier grades your child may have learned to begin an essay with a question or a sound effect such as, "Vroom! The big yellow bus pulled up to our driveway." In the 6th grade, writing becomes more formal and these strategies are not encouraged. At this grade level, the introduction should provide a very clear idea of what the essay will be about, though it should never include phrases such as "in this essay . . ." or "this essay will . . ."

Format

Another element to consider at the beginning of a writing assignment is the format. Your child may be asked to use headings, graphics such as charts or tables, and citations for outside sources. Her teacher will likely provide specific requirements for formatting, or the teacher may abide by a style guide such as MLA or APA.

QUESTION

What is a style guide?
A style guide is a set of very specific standards for the formatting of a document. The purpose is to ensure consistency with all work within a field. The two most commonly used style guides in schools are the MLA (from the Modern Language Association) and APA (from the American Psychological Association).

General formatting usually includes:

- 1-inch margins at the top and bottom and at either side of the paper
- A serif font such as Times New Roman
- A font size, usually 12 or 14 point
- Requirements for a title page or a reference page, depending on the project

Body Paragraphs

Once the introduction and the formatting are in place, your child can develop her essay with information she knows and, sometimes, with information from research. This information is organized by categories into separate paragraphs, each with a topic sentence.

The controlling idea used in the transportation example appears in the introduction and includes three categories of information:

- Cost
- Exercise
- Safety

Introducing the categories of information in the introduction or controlling idea will strengthen your child's paper and give him the opportunity to demonstrate his ability to create categories, which is a grading criterion.

Each body paragraph should include a topic sentence, which identifies the category of information, and concrete examples, definitions, or details that elaborate on the information in the topic sentence. Here is an example of a topic sentence for the first category of information in this essay:

Riding a bike is a less expensive way to get to school than taking the bus.

The supporting details for this paragraph should be specific. It is not enough, for example, to simply say that biking is cheaper than riding a bus. The student writer might include details such as:

- The comparative maintenance costs of buses and bicycles.
- The average cost of gas, compared to the fact that no gas is burned.

- The initial cost of a bicycle compared to the initial cost of a bus divided by the average number of riders.

The strongest essay will include at least three body paragraphs, each covering a different category that has already been introduced in the thesis. A good way to plan an essay is to outline it first, based on the thesis. The criteria established in the thesis can be used to create an outline. For example:

1. Introduction
2. Riding a bicycle to school is less expensive than taking the bus
   a. Supporting detail (perhaps the fuel costs of the bus compared to maintenance of a bicycle)

Your child's teacher may ask him to cite his sources if he uses outside research to write information in the body paragraphs. While the teacher will determine what style the citations should take, some basic guidelines should be followed.

For example, whenever a writer uses text from a source, word for word, that text must be placed inside quotation marks. The following text is from a source on school bus maintenance:

"The cost of operation includes fuel, maintenance, and the cost of the driver" (Sims, 2014).

Notice, also, that the writer has cited the source using the author's last name and the year the information was published. This citation will coordinate with another citation at the end of the essay. Again, your child's teacher will likely have a very specific requirement for citing sources. The Common Core standards do not require a specific style, only that sources are cited.

Transitional Words and Phrases

Like the argumentative essay, the informative essay is strengthened with transitional words and phrases between paragraphs. These transitions connect ideas so that the reader understands how the writer intends to connect information. The following transitions are particularly effective for cause/effect, compare/contrast, and chronological essays:

COMMON TRANSITION WORDS AND PHRASES	
Type of transition	**Word or phrase**
To show similarity	just as
	both
	also
	similarly
To show difference	on the other hand
	however
	unlike
	on the contrary
To show time order	first, second, third . . .
	before, after, later
	next
	prior to, following
Cause/effect	as a result
	thus
	for this reason
	since/because

Use Precise Language

Precise language is clear and specific. It can include descriptive language, and is writing that uses the best word for the purpose of the writing. In writing intended to inform or explain, precise vocabulary is very important. Imagine an essay intended to explain how to start a vegetable garden, and then consider the following two sentences:

Put the seeds in the ground where it is sunny most of the day.

Plant tomato seeds in two inches of soil where they will receive at least four hours of direct sunlight per day.

Notice that in the second sentence the writer used "soil" instead of "the ground." In addition, "most of the day" was replaced with "four hours of direct sunlight."

Take a look at the following sentences and consider how they could be made more precise:

- The boy ate a sandwich.
- I don't feel well.
- The dog made a sound.

Each of these sentences can be made more precise as follows:

- John ate a peanut butter and jelly sandwich.
- I have a headache and a sore throat.
- Buster, a golden retriever, barked fiercely.

In each of the revisions the writer added information about the subject to make the information more specific. The goal of informative/explanatory writing is for the reader to understand a topic as well as the writer does. The only way to achieve this goal is to use precise language.

Getting into the habit of using precise language is something you can practice with your child every day. Ask for follow-up information when your child makes a statement that is vague or not fully detailed. Doing so will remind him of the importance of precision. In his writing point out the most vague terms, words like *thing* or *stuff*, that don't tell the reader anything about a subject.

Another important aspect of using precise language is domain-specific vocabulary. Your child should have access to domain-specific information so that he can write about a subject using the words that are unique to that subject. The following sentences, which are about cars, lack domain-specific language:

A liquid from a container in the front of the car sprays onto the glass in front of the driver.

A tube comes out of the car and is where bad air from burning fuel is released.

Now review the following revisions that use domain-specific language:

Washer fluid from a reservoir under the hood of a car is sprayed onto the windshield.

The exhaust pipe, which extends from beneath the trunk of the car, releases carbon monoxide and other gases produced when gas is burned in the engine.

Almost every subject has domain-specific vocabulary. Imagine writing about fish without mentioning gills, or writing about space exploration without using the word *astronaut*. Using terms unique to a subject make writing more precise, interesting, and informative.

As in argumentative writing, informational/explanatory writing uses a formal style. There are specific characteristics of formal writing. The obvious characteristic is that a formal style avoids slang, text-speak, or writing shortcuts. If your sixth grader is accustomed to texting or communicating via social networking, she may have developed some habits in writing that are not appropriate for formal writing at school. Some of the most common errors resulting from frequent texting/social media use include using the letter *u* instead of the word *you*, using & instead of *and*, and including *lol* in a text to indicate when a writer is trying to be humorous. Encourage your child to proofread carefully for these types of errors; she may notice them in a quick read of a text.

Formal writing includes other important characteristics as well, some of which can be difficult to remember, especially for a writer who is new to using a formal style. Formal writing does not use contractions. So instead of *can't* your child should write, *cannot*. Instead of *they're*, she should use *they are*, and so on. If your child has typed his or her essay, a good way to search for contractions is to do a search for apostrophes and then revise any contractions that appear.

Formal style is also impersonal, meaning it does not feature first or second person pronouns. The writer never refers to herself, nor does she refer to the reader by using the pronoun *you*. Formal writing also avoids slang, which can be difficult because your child may not realize that some terms are slang, such as *kids* for children or *cops* for police officers. The following are examples of informal language:

When you're a kid you can't drive.

If you're worried about a noise outside your house, you should call a cop.

Here the same sentences have been rewritten using formal language:

Children are not allowed to drive.

Someone worried about a noise outside his house should call the police.

Notice that the first and second pronouns have been revised, contractions have been spelled out, and slang has been replaced with the more formal terms.

Provide a Concluding Statement

Every strong essay ends with a conclusion. In shorter essays this conclusion might be a single sentence that wraps up the main points. For a longer essay, the conclusion could be a full paragraph. There are several strategies for a strong conclusion:

- **A brief summary of the main points.** This kind of conclusion can be based on the topic sentences of the body paragraphs, and repeats the main points of the paper.
- **A call to action or question.** In the example of the essay comparing and contrasting riding the bus or a bicycle, the writer might end with a question that challenges the reader to consider what type of transportation would work best.
- **Relate the topic to other situations.** This is also called universalizing. In this type of conclusion the writer applies what he hopes the reader has learned from this essay to other topics. For example, the conclusion to the essay comparing biking and riding the bus might compare other types of fuel-burning transportation to alternative solutions, such as walking instead of driving a car.

It is important that the conclusion is definitive, and that it clearly states the importance of the topic. The writer should avoid apologizing for the paper. Young writers especially tend to end their papers with some sort of disclaimer such as, "Although I'm not an expert . . ." Try to encourage your child to claim his expertise in the subject he is writing about.

Finally, the conclusion should not bring in any new information. If there is additional information needed to support the topic, it should be in its own paragraph before the conclusion. A strong outline will help your child organize what he wants to say before he writes. The most common reason why new information pops up at the end of a paper is that something occurs to the writer just as he's finishing.

Writing Narratives

Narrative writing tells a story. The story can be completely fictional (made up), a retelling of a story the writer knows well, or a retelling of a real event. Anyone who has ever listened to a middle school student tell a story of something that happened with his friends knows that children at this age find it challenging to create a well-organized narrative that follows a logical timeline. There are several criteria that are assessed in narrative writing.

Engaging the Reader

Young writers often want to establish some mystery and hold back crucial details about a story with the well-meaning assumption that doing so will engage the reader. However, this technique can often confuse the reader, and should be discouraged, especially for developing writers of narratives. The first paragraph of a narrative should include the following information:

- The setting, including time and place
- Information about the main characters and their relationships to each other
- An introduction of a problem or conflict

Writing a narrative can also challenge young writers because it requires a clearly defined conflict or problem. Many young writers will write long descriptive essays assuming that they are sharing a narrative, but, in fact, the piece will not have a narrative structure. The problem or conflict in a narrative does not have to be life shattering, but it does have to exist. For example, an appropriate problem might be that a main character was eager for her birthday party and worried that her best friend might not get home from vacation in time to attend. The narrative could follow the character through the day leading up to the birthday party and the arrival of her friend. In this case, the conflict or problem is the anxiety the character is experiencing. It is resolved when her friend arrives. A descriptive essay might just describe the party, and could even use a time order, but would not be a narrative.

Also keep in mind that a narrative uses dialogue, pacing, and description. The old adage "show, don't tell," is particularly appropriate for narrative writing. Your child should try to create characters and events that seem realistic, or plausible, even if the story is set in an unrealistic time or place. Encourage your child to develop his characters and to give them a voice. Consider the following examples:

Little Red Riding Hood wanted to get to her grandmother's house quickly.

"I have to hurry," said Little Red Riding Hood. "Grandma is waiting for me."

In the second example the reader gets a sense of the character and that she feels the need to hurry. In the first example it isn't clear if the character or the narrator believes she needs to hurry.

Consider the following example:

Joshua woke up half an hour late.

Now consider these two revisions, both using dialogue:

Joshua woke up. "Oh no!" he exclaimed. "My alarm didn't go off. I'm a half hour late!"

Joshua woke up. "Oops," he thought. "I'm going to be a half hour late."

The first revision indicates Joshua is upset about being late. In the second example, he considers that being late is a mistake but isn't in a panic. When your child is writing his narrative, ask him questions about the characters and what they might say or think during important events in the story. Encourage him to write in the voice of the character, and, as he develops his narrative writing skills, to use different voices for different characters.

Pacing is another important aspect of narrative writing. A story is basically a series of scenes. There is an opening scene, several scenes that develop the plot, a climax, and a resolution scene. In between these scenes the writer uses words and description to explain the passing of time or the moving of the characters from one place to the next. Consider the following example:

Little Red Riding Hood set off that morning with a basket of goodies for her grandmother. She knew she had to get out of the forest quickly. She was at the door to her grandmother's house.

Obviously this is an exaggerated example, but it demonstrates how missing information can interfere with pacing. The reader has little sense of the time that passes between events. Words and phrases that indicate the passing of time or distance build the reader's anticipation and interest in the story as it develops. Pacing builds tension, which is important for any kind of narrative. The previous example could be revised as follows to add some indication of pacing:

Little Red Riding Hood set off that morning with a basket of goodies for her grandmother. After she'd walked for several hours, she noticed it was beginning to get dark. She knew she had to get out of the forest quickly. She walked for another thirty minutes and found herself at a familiar clearing. She crossed the clearing, and climbed a small hill. She was at the door of her grandmother's house.

In the second example the reader gets a sense of the passing of time and of specific actions and distances covered. This pacing helps the reader understand the story with more detail. Pacing is often accomplished with the use of transitional words and phrases.

Transitional Words and Phrases

Just as in argumentative and explanatory writing, transitions are crucial to narrative writing to move the story from one point to the next. Two types of transitions especially helpful for narrative writing are those used to show the passing of time and those used to show spatial relationships.

COMMON TRANSITION WORDS AND PHRASES	
Type of transition	Word or phrase
To show time	soon
	later
	then
	by the time
	eventually
	before/after
	until/since
To show spatial relationships	near, far
	farther, closer
	up, down, right, left
	in front of, behind
	nearby, beside

Whenever a character moves within a setting, using spatial transitions helps orient the reader. Combined with strong descriptive language, transitions can make a scene or story seem much more realistic.

Precise Language and Descriptive Details

Narrative writing also relies on precise language. Precision is developed using very clear and vivid details. It takes practice for a writer to determine what kinds of details are most important to a narrative, and the best way to practice is to describe real scenes or events. Encourage your child to vividly describe events from her own life. For example, suggest she write a paragraph about eating breakfast. A less vivid or precise paragraph might look like this:

I put cereal in the bowl and added milk.

While that sentence describes what happened, it is lacking the vivid details that bring the reader into the scene.

I picked up the box of Fruity-O's cereal and shook it. There was just enough for breakfast in the box. I tipped the box over my bowl and smiled as the rainbow colored O's tumbled out. I reached in and picked out a marshmallow, then reached for the gallon jug of milk Mom had just plunked onto the table. Glug, glug, I poured the milk into my bowl until a bit ran over and puddled on the red and blue plaid placemat.

The revision adds more detail, pacing transitions, and sound effects to bring the scene to life. The reader can visualize what is happening and what the narrator is doing in the scene. In narrative writing, the best details are sensory details.

As your child is writing, encourage her to think about what she would see, hear, smell, taste, or touch if she were in the story. These types of sensory details add realism to a story, and will help your child write more clearly. Vivid, sensory details successfully "show" rather than "tell" what is going on. For example, saying something smelled gross is far less vivid than writing that something had an "acrid odor that burned your nostrils." Describing a kitten's ear as "soft" is less vivid and descriptive than saying it is "velvety." Help your child get into the habit of making comparisons and explaining experiences to develop her ability to use vivid language.

Provide a Conclusion

Every good narrative has an ending. The ending ties up the loose plot lines and resolves the conflict. The conclusion of a narrative might also include a moral or a reflection on the event. The writer can share what he learned from the experience, or how he might have done something differently. If there is a lesson or an epiphany, it should be something authentic. Every narrative doesn't have to end with a life-changing observation. Start from the point of view that there is something to learn from almost every experience.

Conducting Research

In the 6th grade your child will learn to access different kinds of resources to find information for her writing. There are several important skills required for effective research:

- Assessing the credibility of sources
- Paraphrasing or quoting from sources
- Avoiding plagiarism

Using outside sources such as credible websites, textbooks, and encyclopedias will give your child the experience of learning independently through his own research. He'll develop a research question, or the information he wants to discover, and use multiple sources to answer that question. This is an important critical thinking skill that encourages active learning. Instead of being told what to learn, remember, or focus on, your child will have the opportunity to decide what he most wants to know, and then set out in search of that information.

Assessing the Credibility of Sources

There are several factors to consider when reviewing a source. The first thing to consider is the type of source. Online sources can be credible, but the Internet is full of commercial websites, amateur websites, and blogs, all of which don't necessarily provide reliable information written by experts. The most reliable websites are those that end in *.gov* or *.edu*, but websites ending in *.com* are not necessarily unreliable. Help your child evaluate reliable *.com* websites. Have conversations about credibility factors such as appearance, timeliness, and the named authors. Most writers would consider websites such as *WebMD.com* or *CNN.com* reliable, as they are named authorities, the content is updated frequently, and there is no obvious bias.

Some websites may appear to be credible, but aren't. For example, *Wikipedia* seems to offer a wide range of information. What some people don't know, however, is that Wikipedia is an open resource, which means that any registered user can edit the content. There is always the possibility that someone has edited a Wikipedia page with inaccurate information just as your child is accessing it for research. Despite the dangers in using

Wikipedia as a credible source, it certainly can be a valuable learning tool. At the bottom of most pages is a list of sources, and many of those sources are credible and can be used for research.

To learn about the background of a source, help your child find an About link on the website. This link will usually lead to information about the publishers and writers. You and your child should be able to review the credentials of the writers, which is very important. For example, if your child is doing research on weather systems and has found a website that seems interesting, but there are no scientists associated with the website, then the credibility might be questionable.

Young researchers sometimes have trouble determining the difference between sponsored links, ads, and actual informative websites. A very important skill you can help your child hone is using search engines critically. Point out the sponsored links that appear at the top of search results and explain how companies pay the search engine for this placement. Also point out the ads or links that appear in the margins, which are also paid links and may not be the best sources for academic research.

Paraphrasing or Quoting from Sources

There are two ways to use information from sources. To start, review the following excerpt from an article called "Spiders" written by Jill Mountain in 2014:

> There are more than 50,000 species of spiders in the world. Some, like the giant huntsman spider, can grow to over a foot long. Others, like the Patu marplesi, grow to no more than one tenth of one inch in length. The vast majority of spiders are harmless to humans, but some, like the tarantula, are dangerous, and their venomous bites can cause severe pain, or even death. Despite all of these differences, all spiders have some characteristics in common.

Sometimes a writer chooses to copy information directly from a source. This is called a quote or quotation from the source. The information copied directly from the source must be inside of a pair of quotation marks and should include a citation. An in-text citation is a short reference that lets the reader know the name of the writer. Here is a quote from the passage:

"The vast majority of spiders are harmless to humans . . ." (Mountain, 2014).

Notice that the writer didn't use the whole sentence. Instead she used an ellipsis (. . .) to indicate that there is more to the sentence. See also that after the quote, the writer included a parenthetical reference to the original author.

Sometimes, a writer might want to use information from a source but put it in her own words. Review this example:

The tarantula, unlike most spiders, is dangerous and can hurt or kill a human (Mountain, 2014).

This writer put the information about tarantulas in her own words, but she still cited the original source. It is very important to give credit to the authors who provide information used in academic writing, and it's a good habit that you can help your young writer develop. Your child's teacher will likely provide more detailed information about how he or she would like to see sources cited.

Avoiding Plagiarism

Plagiarism is a term used to describe the act of using the work of others as your own. When a writer copies the work of another writer from a book, magazine, another paper, or any kind of Internet source without including a citation, it is considered plagiarism. While all students make mistakes when they are learning about academic research and writing, in later grades plagiarism can lead to consequences such as a zero on the assignment.

ESSENTIAL

Many schools now use plagiarism detection software such as Turnitin (TII). TII is an online program that compares student writing to a huge database of Internet sources and student papers from schools and colleges all over the country. If your child has been given access to a TII account to check her own work, keep in mind that the goal is not to get to zero percent match on any paper that requires outside sources. Usually teachers accept a match of less than 20 percent to outside sources, as long as all sources are cited and all direct quotes are indicated with quotation marks.

There are some very effective ways to avoid plagiarism:

- **Keep track of sources.** Sometimes when using many different sources, it can be easy to lose track of where information comes from. This can lead to using information without giving a credit to the source. To avoid this, try to have your child read from a source while using a worksheet or document to summarize the information from that source. Your child can use the document as he writes to confirm where the information originated so that it can be properly cited.
- **Encourage your child to keep notes on sources separate from the draft of a paper.** Some student writers keep copied notes within the same document of a paper they are writing. That practice can lead to inadvertently copying information from a source without the proper citation.
- **Have your child paraphrase or put information into his own words whenever possible.** Have him use direct quotes only for specific facts, statistics, or authoritative sources. Otherwise, encourage him to make the information his own.
- **Always use a citation.** Don't worry about over-citing. But if you discover that almost every sentence in your child's essay needs a citation, ask him to think about how to add more original information.

Outside sources can be of great value, but they must be used responsibly. Encourage your child to use research as a tool to make his own ideas more detailed, but not as a substitution for his own ideas.

Being a Collaborative Participant

In the 6th grade your child will be asked to discuss topics with others. Some typical topics will include class readings and specific skills. For example, the teacher might ask your child and others in the class to discuss the characteristics of an effective argumentative essay. A teacher might do this as a way to assess how well students understand that type of writing. Or your child and the other students may be given a reading assignment and be asked to come to class prepared to discuss the text. Being an effective participant requires preparation, listening, and the ability to express ideas clearly.

Preparing for a discussion requires that your child read any assigned text carefully and annotate it (perhaps using sticky notes). Doing so will help him recall interesting points he can bring up, questions he has, or information related to a question posed by the teacher. Also help your child identify a purpose for reading. Usually the teacher will provide questions or let students know what they will be doing with the text. That information should direct the reading. For example, review the following excerpt:

> There are more than 50,000 species of spiders in the world. Some, like the giant huntsman spider, can grow to over a foot long. Others, like the Patu marplesi, grow to no more than one tenth of one inch in length. The vast majority of spiders are harmless to humans, but some, like the tarantula, are dangerous, and their venomous bites can cause severe pain, or even death. Despite all of these differences, there are some characteristics that all spiders have in common.

If the purpose of reading this text is to determine what can happen if someone is bitten by a dangerous spider, your child might underline or highlight, "their venomous bites can cause severe pain, or even death." That information would be useful in a discussion about dangerous spiders.

If, however, the purpose of the discussion is to better understand the different kinds of spiders in the world, the student might underline or highlight, "more than 50,000 species" and "The vast majority of spiders are harmless to humans."

Once your child is prepared for a class discussion with an understanding of the topic, he must also be able to listen effectively to others. Class discussions can be teacher-led, but they are often conducted among the students themselves, with the teacher acting as the facilitator. Many students get into the habit of waiting for a question, answering a question, and moving on. In a collaborative discussion, students must build upon what others have said and use effective listening skills. These skills can be developed and practiced at home. The following behaviors are important for being a good listener:

- **Have your child face the speaker.** When another person is speaking, your child should face the speaker directly so that he can observe movements and facial expressions.

- **Encourage your child to focus on what the speaker is saying, not on how he will respond.** Sometimes people listen solely for the opportunity to respond. Help your child get into the habit of waiting for someone else to finish speaking before chiming in. Encourage him to hear the entire message and pause before saying something in return. Waiting ensures the listener doesn't miss important information, and pausing gives the listener time to process information before going on.
- **Encourage your child to ask questions.** It is okay if a listener doesn't understand everything a speaker says. Sometimes a speaker will invite questions; other times he will pause when he is finished. Instruct your child to ask for clarification or more information before responding.

In some instances your child's teacher may assign students to a particular discussion group and give each student a role in the conversation, such as to ask questions, confirm understanding, record main points, and so forth. If your child reports that he is part of such a discussion group, encourage him to practice completing all of the roles so that he can have the full experience of a class or group discussion.

Finally, class discussion is intended to be collegial. When a discussion is collegial, it means that all members of the discussion group are responsible for the outcome and for participating. Discussions in your child's classroom have a purpose, and each student is responsible for helping the group achieve that purpose. Encourage your child to be an active participant, but not to overwhelm. Ask him about others in his discussion group, and if there are students who are quiet or seem shy. Addressing those students is an opportunity for your child to improve the quality of his class discussion experience.

Presenting Claims and Information to Others

In the 6th grade your child will be asked to present information to the class, either as an individual or as part of a group. For some children, the idea of standing up in front of the class can be frightening. One good way to overcome a fear of public speaking is to be thoroughly prepared.

QUESTION

What if my child is paralyzed by the idea of public speaking?
When your child practices her speech at home, offer a lot of praise. As she's developing confidence, ignore missteps, hesitations, and the like. Praise her for making the effort. If it seems that your child might not be able to overcome her fear of making a presentation, consider contacting the teacher to see if she can present privately, before or after school.

Class presentations will be based on work your child has already completed and will be the culmination of research or analysis of a text. Everyone struggles when they are speaking "off the cuff" or without preparation. So the most important first step is to be thoroughly prepared. If your child has a class presentation scheduled, encourage her to leave plenty of time to gather information, make speaking notes, and practice.

Encourage your child to practice his presentation in front of you. If you have access to the assignment or grading rubric, try to evaluate him as he practices and highlight areas for improvement. When speaking in front of a group, your child should pay attention to the following:

- **Volume**—Be sure your child is speaking loud enough to be heard. Encourage your child to keep her chin up and look out toward the audience, even if it is to a wall at the back of the room.
- **Pace**—When a child knows a topic well and has practiced a presentation several times, she may begin to speak very quickly. Encourage her to pace her words at a natural speaking rate, pausing before and after important ideas.
- **No reading**—While using index cards or notes is a good way to remember important ideas, encourage your child to try to memorize what she intends to say. Reading in front of a group is very different from simply speaking.
- **Body language**—Help your child relax enough while speaking so that he uses natural gestures and movements. Standing stiffly behind a podium, or waving his arms in an exaggerated way, can detract from his ideas.

Your child may be required to use visuals in his presentation. The most common presentation platform is PowerPoint, which is part of the Microsoft suite of software products. If your child is required to use PowerPoint, it is likely he has had some instruction for using it. Children find PowerPoint to be a lot of fun. They can insert transitions, sound effects, and use different kinds of images within the slide show. Help your child create visuals that are an effective complement to his presentation:

- **Limit text**—Remind your child that the audience will be listening to her. The words on a PowerPoint slide should cover just main points that she will elaborate on. Limit each slide to three or four lines of text with no more than five to seven words.
- **Transitions**—There are a lot of options for transitions, but some can slow down a presentation. If using a software program like PowerPoint, encourage your child to use one or two "wow" transitions, and stick with quick movements from one slide to the next for the majority of the presentation.
- **Text size and color**—Be sure that the text can be read several feet away and that there is contrast between the text color and the background. Avoid fonts like script that can be difficult to read.
- **Images**—Usually there should be no more than one image to a presentation slide and it should be directly related to what the speaker is saying while it is on the screen.

Encourage your child to practice her presentation while using the actual slide show so that she has a good sense of when to change slides and what information to stress on each slide.

FACT

There are several online presentation tools that are fun to use and easy to learn. Consider reviewing Prezi.com, Animoto.com, Haiku Deck, or Google Slides. All of these programs offer tutorials and give users the ability to incorporate text and images. Presentations made with these software programs can be saved online, meaning that your child should be able to access them easily in the classroom.

When your child is working on a presentation with a group, it is likely he will have a specific role in the process or will be assigned a component of the presentation to complete. While group work can be challenging, you can support your child by asking questions about the different roles each student has, what your child's role is, and offering opportunities for your child to work with her group outside of school if necessary.

Practice Exercises

The following exercises cover the skills in these learning strands. They are similar to questions your child might encounter on a standardized test.

Transitions

Read each of the following sentence pairs and determine the transition that would best fit.

1. Cats are quickly becoming more popular than dogs. In some northeastern states, twice as many people own cats than dogs.
   a. In fact
   b. Because
   c. Next
2. Spread peanut butter on two slices of bread. Spread jelly on top of the peanut butter.
   a. Furthermore
   b. Later
   c. Next
3. Even though it may be tempting to cheat on small assignments, doing so can lead to lower grades overall. Being caught cheating can result in a zero on a major assignment.
   a. However
   b. Since
   c. Furthermore
4. In many communities, local youth groups volunteer to maintain parks. Senior centers set up volunteer groups that focus on maintaining beaches and playgrounds.
   a. Similarly
   b. Although
   c. On the other hand

5. Many families look forward to weekends together. Students often have hours of homework to complete every weekend.
   a. Again
   b. For example
   c. However

Using Precise Language

Rewrite each of the following sentences.

1. The person taking money gave us things to get into the movie.
2. We rode to the concert.
3. The boat traveled to the other country.
4. He didn't finish his assignment because he was thinking about other things.
5. She bought some clothes at the store.
6. I need a tool to get that nail into the wall.
7. We put on the clothes we wear to the beach and went there.
8. I have to read a book for my class right after lunch.
9. The astronauts landed on a planet.
10. They have two pets with clever names.

Using Formal English

Rewrite the following sentences using only formal English.

1. That movie was really funny; it made me LOL.
2. Mom told me to bite my tongue and not say anything.
3. My dad joked that my mom was over the hill at her last birthday.
4. That was an awesome party, yo!
5. Hey. You alright?
6. I dunno when we'll be there.
7. I have no clue what the assignment is.
8. Nope. My project's not done yet.
9. Sorry, I have a frog in my throat. Keep coughing.
10. Oh he's got a heart of gold; he's a good person.

CHAPTER 7
Grade 6—Language

Language skills are the building blocks of literacy. The Common Core language skills include grammar, punctuation, sentence structure, vocabulary, and descriptive language. Sixth graders build on skills they have already developed, and learn new skills that help them become more confident and effective writers. Keep in mind that the purpose of studying these conventions is to help students become effective communicators. This chapter reviews the language skills that sixth graders are expected to master and provides clear explanations of each of those skills.

What Your Sixth Grader Will Learn

Even though the language standard has very similar categories from year to year, the content is very different. The content in each grade is very specific and builds upon content mastered in prior grades.

There are four categories of study in the language standard:

- Conventions of grammar
- Knowledge of language and style
- Vocabulary
- Figurative language

The conventions of grammar section for grade 6 of the Common Core focuses almost exclusively on pronouns and how to use them most effectively, including how to find and correct usage errors. The focus is always on the clarity of writing, because the goal of the Common Core language strand is to help students understand what they read and write so that, in turn, others can understand what the students have written. Students will learn to identify and use pronouns in the proper case, subjective, objective, and possessive, as well as learn the definition and correct use of intensive pronouns. Students will be taught to recognize when pronouns are used incorrectly or result in vagueness, and correct these errors. Finally, in what is an ongoing focus in the standards, students will continue to develop the ability to discriminate between standard and nonstandard English.

Having a broad knowledge of language is important when considering writing style. Most readers recognize when an essay or even a paragraph is made up of short, choppy sentences, and most readers agree that writing that uses the same sentence pattern over and over again is dull. When students learn different sentence structures, their writing becomes much more interesting. Moreover, they find it easier to write effective texts that explain, describe, or argue a point.

Acquiring and using vocabulary is an important part of learning to be a better reader and writer. Your sixth grader will learn several different strategies for determining the meaning of an unknown word. For example, he or she will learn to use the context in which the word is used to figure out meaning. The context refers to the sentence or paragraph where the unfamiliar word appears, and provides clues to meaning. In addition, sixth graders study Greek and Latin suffixes and prefixes, which provide hints about the meaning of a word.

Finally, your child will learn how to most effectively choose and use reference materials, both online and in print, to determine the meanings of unfamiliar words. Having multiple strategies helps students build confidence in learning and using new vocabulary. Being able to acquire and confirm the definition of a new word makes it much more likely that a student writer will actually use the word in his or her own work.

Adult readers and writers know that language can be complicated and that meanings can be fluid. Your sixth grader will learn and practice interpreting figurative language so that he or she can better understand literary texts that develop ideas through comparisons and other relationships. These skills are built upon the foundation of skills that students acquired in grades K–5, and are intended to help them continue their development as readers and writers.

Conventions of Language: Grammar

Conventions of grammar for your sixth grade student focus on pronouns. The standard assumes your sixth grader has already learned about other parts of speech, such as nouns, prepositions, and verbs, so that he can understand how to use different types of pronouns in different types of sentences. If you find your child is struggling with identifying the other parts of speech, you can support his grammar study by offering some practice in picking nouns, verbs, and prepositions out in sentences. Since research shows that students learn grammar most effectively when it is modeled for them in speech and writing, rather than correcting errors in your child's speech and writing, offer models or restatements that correct the error.

Pronoun Case

Pronouns are words that take the place of nouns. Most students are familiar with pronouns like I, me, we, us, he, she, it, they, them, etc. These words can replace nouns so that writing is not repetitive. For example, instead of writing, "Tim took Tim's dog for a walk," one can write, "Tim took *his* dog for a walk." The pronoun *his* takes the place of Tim's. There are three cases of pronouns:

- Subjective
- Objective
- Possessive

Subjective Pronouns

Subjective pronouns serve as the subject of a sentence or act as the subject of a verb. In the following sentence, *I* is the subjective pronoun:

I rowed the boat.

The pronoun *I* takes the place of the noun, the speaker's name. The verb is *rowed*. The pronoun *I* is the subject because it is performing the action, *rowed*.

The subjective pronouns are:

- I
- you
- he, she, it
- we
- they

Subjective pronouns can be singular, and refer to one person or thing. They can be plural, and refer to two or more people or things. The pronoun *you* can be singular or plural. In the following sentences, the subjective pronoun is *italicized*:

She received a new bicycle for her birthday.

They planned the party.

It is in your mailbox.

Objective Pronouns

An objective pronoun is the object of a verb or a preposition. In the following sentence, the verb is <u>underlined</u> and the objective pronoun is in **bold** type:

Mom <u>hugged</u> **me**.

Mom is the subject. She is performing the action. The action is *hugged*. The recipient of the action, or, in this case, the person who received the hug, is *me*. When an objective pronoun is the object of a verb, it receives the action of that verb.

The objective pronouns are:

- me
- you
- him, her, it
- us
- them

Like subjective pronouns, objective pronouns can be either singular or plural. And, as with subjective pronouns, the objective pronoun *you* can be singular or plural.

In the following sentences, the verb has been underlined and the objective pronoun is italicized:

Mom *trusts them* to be home on time.

I didn't want my video game system, so I *sold it*.

The teacher *asked us* to stop talking.

Objective pronouns are also used with prepositions.

FACT

Prepositions describe relationships between other words in a sentence. There are hundreds of prepositions, but some of the most common are: *about, above, below, after, before, in, inside, outside, for, from, of, into, onto, to, with, within,* and *without*. In this sentence, "Go to school with him," the preposition is *with*, and the object of that preposition is *him*.

When an objective pronoun is used as the object of a preposition, the sentence describes the relationship between the pronoun and a noun or another pronoun in the sentence. In the sentence that follows, the preposition has been underlined and the objective pronoun is *italicized*:

I like that movie; my favorite actor is in *it*.

In this sentence, the preposition *in* shows a relationship between the actor and *it*, which is the movie. The pronoun *it* is the object of the preposition.

Possessive Pronouns

Possessive pronouns show ownership. They are usually used with a noun, but can be used alone to describe a noun.

The possessive pronouns are:

- my, mine
- your, yours
- his, her/s, its
- our, ours
- their, theirs

Often a possessive pronoun is placed before a noun to show possession. In the following sentences, the possessive pronoun is *italicized* and the noun it describes is underlined:

I think that is *my* bicycle.

You should make sure that is *your* book.

She forgot *her* coat.

We found *our* cat.

They surprised *their* grandmother.

Notice, also, that in these sentences, the possessive pronoun agrees with the subject pronouns used. For example, in the first sentence the subject is *I*, so the possessive pronoun is *my*.

Possessive pronouns can also stand alone and refer back to a noun. When that happens, the pronoun is preceded by a verb. In the following sentences, the verb is underlined and the possessive pronoun is *italicized*:

I think that bicycle is *mine*.

You should see if that book is *yours*.

Mary told me that coat is *hers*.

The cat we found is *ours*.

They confirmed the car is *theirs*.

Intensive Pronouns

Intensive pronouns are used to emphasize the subject of the sentence or to point out and overstress exactly who is completing the action. Here are some examples (in **bold**):

I **myself** prefer basketball to football.

You **yourself** must clean your room.

The president **himself** visited our school today.

The intensive pronouns are:

- myself
- yourself
- himself, herself, itself
- ourselves
- themselves

FACT

The intensive pronouns are also used as reflexive pronouns. Reflexive pronouns are objects, or receivers of the action of the verb. For example, "I bought *myself* a new car." In this sentence, *myself* receives the new car. You can remove an intensive pronoun without changing the meaning of a sentence.

Shifts in Pronouns

Pronouns must agree with the **antecedent** in number and person. The antecedent is the noun a pronoun refers to. In this sentence, "*Bob* said *he* was going to be late," the pronoun is *he* and it refers to the noun, *Bob*, which is the antecedent.

Pronouns Agree in Number

When a pronoun takes the place of a singular noun, the pronoun must be singular. When a pronoun takes the place of a plural noun, the pronoun must be plural.

ESSENTIAL

The indefinite pronouns *everybody, anybody, each, neither,* and *someone* are singular. Always use a *singular* pronoun to replace them. For example, "*Each* student should turn in *his* homework."

Consider the following sentences. In sentence one the pronoun agrees in number. In sentence two the pronoun does not agree.

1. The student placed her book on the desk.
2. The student placed their book on the desk.

Since *student* is singular, meaning there is just one student, the pronoun must also be singular, *he* or *she.*

ALERT

Sometimes when the gender of the antecedent isn't clear, writers substitute a plural pronoun, *them* or *their,* which is an error. While it may seem awkward, the correct pronoun choice in such a case is to use both masculine and feminine, such as *him or her, his or hers,* or *he or she.* For example, "*Each* student put *his or her* paper on the teacher's desk."

Pronouns Agree in Person

First person pronouns include *I, we, me,* and *us.* The second person pronouns are *you, your,* and *yours.* The third person pronouns are *he, she, it, him, her, his, hers.* It can be confusing to the reader to switch the person of a pronoun within the same sentence. For example:

When a *student* is absent from class *you* should make up *your* work quickly.

In this sentence, the antecedent is *student*, which is the third person (meaning it can be replaced by a third person pronoun like *he* or *she*). But the pronouns in the sentence, *you* and *your*, are second person pronouns. This is an example of disagreement. Here is the corrected sentence:

When a *student* is absent from class *he or she* should make up *his or her* work quickly.

Recognizing and Correcting Vague Pronoun References

Vague pronoun references can occur when there are several nouns in a sentence and it isn't clear which noun the pronoun refers to. That is, the reader can't tell which noun is the antecedent. For example, in this sentence:

When the *teacher* handed *Sally* the test *she* smiled.

It is not clear who *she* is in this sentence, or who was smiling. The sentence must be revised so that it is clear to whom the pronoun refers.

The *teacher* smiled when *she* handed Sally the test.

Sally smiled when the teacher handed *her* the test.
Another common vague pronoun error is the use of *they* to refer to some unknown person or group.

At Lynbrook Elementary *they* require students to report to class by 8:00 A.M.

They close the gates to the park at dusk.
It is not clear in either sentence who *they* are. There is no antecedent in the sentence, and there is no context or information from other sentences. The following sentences correct the error:

At Lynbrook Elementary *teachers* require students to report to class by 8:00 A.M.

City workers close the gates to the park at dusk.

In both cases, specific nouns replace the vague pronouns.

Punctuation—Commas, Dashes, Parentheses

In 6th grade, punctuation instruction is focused on commas, parentheses, and dashes when they are used to set off nonrestrictive or parenthetical expressions. In other words, these punctuation marks are used to separate information that is not crucial, but may be valuable or interesting, from the main part of the sentence.

ALERT

In setting off nonessential information, commas, dashes, and parentheses fulfill similar functions, but with different emphasis. The dash emphasizes the information, parentheses deemphasize the information, and the comma is neutral.

Commas to Set Off Parenthetical Expressions

Parenthetical expressions are words or phrases that are used for emphasis, to qualify a sentence, or to transition from one idea to the next:

For example, there are 25 students in this grade who rent musical instruments.

The families of these students are less likely to renew private music lessons, *as a result.*

Most students, *in my opinion*, enjoy playing in the school band.

In the three previous examples there would be no change to the meaning of the sentence if the parenthetical expression were removed. Notice that the parenthetical expression can occur at the beginning, in the middle, or at the end of a sentence. When it occurs in the middle of a sentence, it should be offset by a comma before and after the phrase.

Commas to Set Off a Nonrestrictive Expression

A nonrestrictive expression provides information about a noun or subject in a sentence, but can be omitted from a sentence. The information usually provides clarification, explains who or what something is, or refers to information that was provided earlier. Here are some examples:

Timothy, *who joined the team late in the season*, surprised everyone and scored the winning goal.

The coach commended Jane, *who played in all nine innings*, for her stamina.

Notice that the nonrestrictive expression usually adds details about a noun in the sentence. That noun does not have to be the subject, as the following sentence illustrates:

We visited the art museum, *which was remodeled last summer.*

In the previous example, the nonrestrictive expression provides more information about the art museum, which is not the subject of the sentence. Note that like the parenthetical expression, the nonrestrictive expression is always set off by commas.

Dashes to Set Off Nonrestrictive Expressions

Dashes are used to set off nonrestrictive expressions with emphasis. A dash shows that the thought or idea in a sentence has been suddenly interrupted. These examples demonstrate the kind of information that should be set off with a dash:

My little brother—*he's such a pain*—took my bike without my permission.

The coach—*he is never happy*—was not pleased when we lost the game.

Notice also that the information set off with dashes could be a standalone sentence. Imagine someone speaking and pausing to make these pronouncements.

Parentheses to Set Off Nonrestrictive Expressions

While the comma is neutral, and the dash yells, the parentheses, in a way, whisper the nonrestrictive expression. The purpose of parentheses is to add information but not distract the reader from the main purpose of the text. The least important information is parenthetical information. Review these examples:

Calvin (*who lives on Mott Street*) offered to walk my dog until my cast comes off.

Mom made chocolate cake (*my favorite*) for dessert last night.

I get As (*most of the time*) in math.

In each of these sentences, the information in parentheses is interesting but not crucial to the purpose of the text.

QUESTION

How can a student tell what degree of emphasis a writer intended in a nonrestrictive clause?
The simple answer is, a student can't. Knowing when and why commas, dashes, or parentheses are used to offset nonrestrictive expressions is important in writing, but is not necessary for identifying errors in the writing of others. It is most important to understand *where* one of these three conventions would fit in one's own writing.

Knowledge of Language and Style

In the 6th grade, students practice writing longer texts and varying their sentence patterns to maintain the interest of the reader and to most effectively move from one idea to the next. In English, writers can use three sentence patterns:

- Simple sentences
- Compound sentences
- Complex sentences

Using examples of all three types of sentences makes a text interesting and engaging.

Simple Sentences

A simple sentence portrays a single thought that is expressed with little more than a subject and a verb. That is, a simple sentence tells who the subject is and what the subject is doing. Here are some examples:

Margot lost her umbrella on the train.

This sentence is a single idea. The subject is *Margot*; the action is *lost*.

Our dog Duke brings in the paper every morning.

Again, this sentence is a single idea. *Duke* is the subject, and the action is *brings*.

Compound Sentences

A compound sentence combines two or more simple sentences using punctuation and/or a conjunction. When these simple sentences are combined into a compound sentence, each is referred to as an independent clause. A compound sentence consists of two or more independent clauses.

Here are some examples of compound sentences:

Margot lost her umbrella on the train, so she bought a new one at the station.

In this sentence, there are two independent clauses. The first is italicized; the second is underlined. Notice how there is a comma before the *coordinating conjunction* that joins these two clauses.

Our dog Duke brings in the paper every morning, yet he refuses to fetch a ball or a stick.

In this sentence, there are two independent clauses. The first is italicized; the second is underlined. Notice how there is a comma before the *coordinating conjunction* that joins these two clauses.

Complex Sentences

Complex sentences include an independent clause (which is a simple sentence) and one or more subordinate clauses. A subordinate clause includes a noun and a verb, but it doesn't make sense on its own. A subordinate clause usually begins with a word that indicates it relies on other information to make sense. Here are some examples of subordinate clauses on their own, and then used with independent clauses to make sense:

Because he failed the test

In this clause, there is a subject, *he*, and there is a verb, *failed*, but it starts with the word *because*, which indicates it is *dependent* on other information to make sense. If the subordinate clause is added to an independent clause, it becomes part of a sentence that makes sense:

Because he failed the test, Simon accepted extra help after school.

Here is another example of a subordinate clause on its own:

After we ate dinner

In this clause there is a subject, *we*, and there is a verb, *ate*, but the sentence begins with *after*, which indicates it depends on other information to make sense. Added to a simple sentence, it makes sense:

After we ate dinner, we went to the movies.

Vocabulary Acquisition

In the 6th grade, students are instructed to use context clues to determine the meanings of unfamiliar words. They also study and use their knowledge of common Greek or Latin suffixes, prefixes, and root words to investigate and understand unfamiliar words. Finally, they continue to use reference materials when they cannot determine the meaning of a word using other strategies.

Using Context Clues

There are four different types of context clues:

- Synonyms
- Antonyms
- Examples
- Explanations

In each type, the writer provides information that explains a term. Readers use this information to develop a working definition so that the sentence makes sense.

Synonym Context Clues

The author can help readers understand a text by including a familiar word that has the same or similar meaning as an unfamiliar word. Words that have a close or identical meaning are known as *synonyms*. Here are some examples:

The store displayed the spring *apparel*, or clothing, in the front window.

In this sentence, the vocabulary word *apparel* is explicitly explained with a synonym (*clothing*) that immediately follows it. The synonym context-clue may not always be as immediate, as in the following sentence:

Justin felt *inept* on the ski slopes and worried that the other skiers would notice how unskilled he was.

In this example, the synonym occurs later in the sentence, but it still provides a definition for the word.

Antonym Context Clues

Antonyms are words that have opposite meanings; for example, *happy* and *sad* are antonyms. In sentences that use antonym context clues, the reader will usually find a cue that there will be a contrast between two or more ideas. Take a look at this sentence:

Underline her sister, who was an *inept* skier, Marissa was *very skilled* and skied the most challenging slopes.

In this sentence, the writer included the cue *unlike* to let the reader know there will be a contrast in the sentence. Further dissecting the sentence, the reader knows that Marissa is *unlike* her sister. Since her sister is *inept* and Marissa is *very skilled*, the reader can make an inference that *inept* means unskilled.

Here is another example of an antonym context clue:

Mr. Jenkins had a reputation for being *aloof*, but *Thomas* found him *friendly and warm*.

In this example, the cue that there will be a contrast is the conjunction *but*. The reader knows that what comes before the conjunction will be contrasted or be different from what comes after it. If Thomas found Mr. Jenkins *friendly and warm* and that is the different from *aloof*, the reader can conclude that *aloof* must mean *unfriendly* and *cold*.

Other cues that indicate contrast, and that there may be an antonym context clue, include:

- although
- besides
- however
- to the contrary
- unlike
- yet
- on the other hand
- instead

Explanation Context Clues

Explanation context clues add more information that explains, but doesn't explicitly define, what a word means. The context could be a description of a situation, details that can lead to an inference, or other information. Here is an example:

That slice of pizza is *immense; I don't think I can eat that much.*

In this example, the context clue follows the unfamiliar word and explains how the writer feels about it. In this case, the writer notes that he or she can't eat that much pizza. The reader can make a logical inference that it must be a lot of pizza, and that *immense* must mean *very large.*

Here is another example:

The Mojave Desert is an *arid* climate because it *seldom rains* and there are *no underground water sources.*

In this sentence, the context clue explains reasons why the desert is *arid.* The reader can make an inference that a climate where it seldom rains and where there are no underground water sources is likely *very dry.*

Example Context Clues

As the name suggests, example context clues provide examples of the unfamiliar word. Review the following sentence:

In the early twentieth century, many middle class households employed *domestic servants,* such as *maids, cooks,* and *nannies* for their children.

In this example, the term *domestic servant* is unfamiliar. The phrase "such as maids, cooks, and nannies" provides the reader a way to develop a definition. Using these examples the reader can determine that domestic servants are people who work in the homes of their employers. Here is another example:

Students often decide what *occupation* to pursue when they are in high school, and choose college programs to become, for example, *doctors, teachers, lawyers,* or *accountants.*

In this example, the word *occupation* is unfamiliar. The examples of different professions, such as doctors, teachers, lawyers, or accountants, help the reader determine a definition. In this case the reader can draw the conclusion that an occupation is a job.

Using Greek and Latin Affixes

In grades 1–5 and in grade 6, students study common Greek and Latin affixes and use them to help understand new words. There are hundreds of affixes from both languages. Some of the most common studied in grade 6 include:

COMMON GREEK AND LATIN AFFIXES		
Affix	**Meaning**	**Examples**
–ann	year	annual
–frig	cold	frigid
–chron	time	chronology
–neg	deny	renege
–lum	light	illuminate
–son	sound	sonar
–bibl	book	bibliography
–cred	believe	credible
–foli	leaf or page	portfolio
–pyr	fire	pyrotechnics
–equ	fair, same	equal
–dyn	power	dynamite
–cog	to know	recognize
–port	to carry	transport

In the following sentence, an unfamiliar word is used:

The climate there is *frigid*.

Since the affix *frig* means *cold*, the reader can conclude that the word *frigid* also means cold. In addition, the reader can draw a connection to a more familiar word, re*frig*erator, which he or she knows is used to keep food cold.

In the following sentence, the reader can use knowledge of two different affixes to determine a definition:

Sandra brought her *portfolio* to the meeting.

The reader knows that *port* means to carry, so the word is something that can be carried. The reader also knows that *foli* can mean pages or leaves. The reader makes an inference that in this case, it is likely that pages are meant, and determines that a *portfolio* is something used to carry pages. The dictionary defines a portfolio as a "large, thin, flat case for loose sheets of paper."

Consulting Reference Materials

While using context clues and word roots are excellent strategies for understanding unfamiliar words, they are not always available. Readers who are uncertain of a word meaning should use reference materials to confirm the meaning, even after using clues. Reference materials will provide the meaning of words when there are no context or word-part clues.

All sorts of dictionaries and reference materials are available to readers. Those with e-reader devices, for example, can often simply tap on an unfamiliar word within a text and get a pop-up window with its definition. Word processing programs, similarly, offer a dictionary look-up function.

ESSENTIAL

Reliable online dictionaries include: Merriam-Webster (*www.m-w.com*), Dictionary.com (*www.dictionary.com*), Macmillian (*www.macmillandictionary.com*), and Oxford Dictionary (*www.oxforddictionaries.com*)

When using a reference to determine the meaning, the reader should know what part of speech the word is in the context of the sentence. If there are several definitions, the reader can then use other clues in the sentence to determine the definition that applies. For example, consider a reader who has come upon the following sentence:

She applied for *asylum* and was relieved when it was granted.

The dictionary offers two definitions of *asylum*:

1. (noun) Protection granted to someone who has left his or her native country.
2. (noun) A psychiatric hospital.

The reader should consider the context of the sentence in the larger text. In this case, it is more likely that definition one is applicable, as the subject *applied* or asked for *protection* and was relieved when it was granted.

In some cases to determine meaning it is important to discern the part of speech where the unfamiliar word is being used. Review the following sentence:

My grandfather claims he *courted* my grandmother for two years before they were married.

The dictionary offers several definitions of *court*:
1. (noun) A meeting presided over by a judge that makes decisions in civil and criminal cases.
2. (noun) An area marked out for ball games such as tennis or basketball.
3. (verb) Pursue romantically with the intention of marrying.

In this sentence, *court* is used as a verb, and the only reasonable definition that can be applied is definition three.

Using and Understanding Figurative Language

In the 6th grade, students generally study the following types of figurative language:

- Similes
- Metaphors
- Personification
- Onomatopoeia
- Alliteration

While figurative language is most frequently found in poetry, it is also common in both fiction and nonfiction texts. Comparisons, such as similes and metaphors, are particularly useful to help readers understand settings and descriptions.

Simile

A simile is a comparison between two things using either *like* or *as*. This is probably the easiest kind of figurative language to recognize. Review the following examples:

"The girls meantime spread the table, set the children round the fire, and fed them like so many hungry birds . . ." *Little Women* by Louisa May Alcott.

In this example, the children are being compared to hungry birds. Readers who are familiar with birds can imagine how birds sometimes chirp, and can be fragile and a bit nervous or shy. This comparison calls on sensory details such as what one sees and hears. Similes are also common in song lyrics, as in this example "Camptown Races":

I bet my money on a bob-tailed nag/Somebody bet on the bay/They fly along like a rail-road car/Doo-dah! doo-dah!/Running a race with a shooting star.

In this lyric, the horses, the nag, and bay are being compared to rail-road cars that are racing stars to show that they are moving very fast.

Metaphors

Metaphors also make comparisons between two things, but there is no cue-word, such as *like* or *as*, to help the reader. A well-known metaphor is this often-quoted excerpt from William Shakespeare's *Hamlet:*

"All the world's a stage, and all the men and women merely players."

In this metaphor, Shakespeare compares life to a performance. The world is a stage and everyone is an actor.

Usually a metaphor will state simply that one thing *is* another thing, as in these examples:

"A good conscience *is* a continual Christmas." *Benjamin Franklin*

"Conscience *is* a man's compass." *Vincent van Gogh*

Other times, however, the comparison is more subtle, and the writer assumes the reader will understand what is being compared. For example, the term *Big Bang* is often used to refer to the formation and expansion of the universe. The term is a metaphor that compares the universe to an explosion.

Here is another example:

"Fill your paper with the breathings of your heart." *William Wordsworth*

In this example, the author makes a comparison that is intended to stress the importance of true emotion in writing. This comparison compares words to the "breathings of your heart," but doesn't mention *words*. The reader has to make an inference based on his or her background knowledge.

Finally, there are more common metaphors that have become figures of speech used in everyday conversation:

He was afraid to go into the pool because *he was a chicken*.

The highway is *a parking lot* during rush hour.

I experienced *a rollercoaster* of emotions.

In each of these examples, a comparison is being made to provide information. For example, if the highway is a parking lot, the reader understands that the cars are not moving, or that there is a traffic jam.

Personification

When writers give human characteristics to things that are not human, it is called personification. For example, if someone observes trees bending in the wind, he or she might remark that they are *dancing*. Personification makes note of an actual behavior or action, and applies a human explanation. That is, personification is a way to explain or elaborate on something that is happening.

In the following example, the writer notes what is happening to his car, and applies human traits as a way to make the description more vivid:

My old car moaned and complained as it pulled itself to the top of the hill.

An old car might make several different noises, and have several mechanical problems while climbing a steep hill. This use of personification compares it to a person as a way to express those problems in a more interesting and vivid way.

In the following sentence, the writer uses personification to describe the sounds in her house:

The wind whistled and the windows returned a scratchy song.

In this example, both the wind and the windows are personified to express the sounds they make.

Onomatopoeia

Onomatopoeia is a word that is intended to mimic the sound associated with that term. For example, a *cuckoo* clock is a clock that makes a distinctive sound, *cuckoo*. Other examples include *buzz*, which is the sound a bee makes, and *flip-flops*, which are sandals that make that sound when the wearer walks in them. All animal sounds—*meow, woof, oink*, and *moo*—for example, are onomatopoeia. Finally, comic book exclamations, such as *bang, pow*, or *oomph* are also examples.

Alliteration

Alliteration is the repetition of a beginning consonant sound. It is common in poetry but is also used in prose to draw attention to an idea. Alliteration is common in advertising as well, as it is memorable.

In poetry, alliteration highlights sounds, often in ways intended to add dimension to a poem. For example, in "The Building of the Ship," poet Henry Wadsworth Longfellow uses alliteration of *S* and *W* to highlight the strength of the boat and the churning water of the sea:

Build me straight, O worthy Master!
Stanch and *strong*, a goodly vessel,
That shall laugh at all disaster,

And *with wave* and *whirlwind* wrestle.

Alliteration assesses consonant *sounds* not just the letters. A frequent mistake students make when looking for alliteration is to identify only letters. In the last line of this poem, the word *wrestle* also begins with W, but this is not alliteration, because the word begins with the "R" sound, not the "W" sound of *with*, *wave*, and *whirlwind*.

In the next example there *is* alliteration, even though the consonants are not the same:

Photographers frequently capture kangaroos in the wild.

Helping Your Child Succeed

Multiple studies have shown that reading regularly leads to improved writing, grammar, and vocabulary skills. Provide opportunities for your sixth grader to read every day, and make time to interact and discuss what he is reading. Reading and talking about texts doesn't have to be a formal event. E-mail your child interesting articles, clips of magazine articles, or even share a favorite poem. Talk about individual words in a text, especially if they are unfamiliar or could have multiple meanings. Strategize with your child to find the definition. Having the opportunity to use vocabulary skills in authentic, real-world situations is not only good practice, it also shows your student why these skills are important.

When your child is writing for school assignments, help him remember to apply the language skills he is learning to his own writing. Sixth graders often find it difficult to transfer skills from one subject to another. For example, if your sixth grader is writing a report for social studies, he might need support and reminders to use varied sentence patterns to make the writing more interesting. Your knowledge of what your sixth grader is learning is crucial to helping him apply those skills across the curriculum and ultimately master them.

Finally, try to draw attention to the figurative language you encounter in everyday life. For example, you can point out that business names like Dunkin' Donuts and Bed Bath & Beyond are examples of alliteration. You might note that the Rice Krispies mascots (Snap, Crackle, and Pop) have names that are examples of onomatopoeia. Or you might ask your child to use personification to describe the waves at the beach or the snow piling up in the backyard.

Practice Exercises

These exercises will help your children practice the skills covered in this chapter. They are similar to the types of questions she will encounter on standardized tests.

Pronoun Practice

Choose the correct pronoun for each of the following sentences.

1. (We/us) students wish we had less homework.
2. Everyone should turn in (their/his or her) homework before leaving class today.
3. Either Robert or (I/me) will play goalie in tomorrow's game.
4. My brother said, "You and (I/me) are going to shovel snow in the morning."
5. The students didn't seem to know where (they/them) should go when the fire alarm rang.
6. The governor (hisself/himself) attended our graduation ceremony.
7. That is Amy's backpack; it belongs to (hers/her).
8. Timothy said he lost (his/him) homework and would have to turn (it/them) in tomorrow.
9. One of the librarians parks (his or her/their) car in that parking spot.
10. The substitute teacher gave (us/we) a quiz.

Shifts in Pronouns Practice

Read the following sentences and choose the best word to replace the underlined word.

1. I was very hungry, but didn't eat the potato chips because they could make *you* sick.
   a. us
   b. me
   c. them
2. When a student has been absent from school *you* should try to make up missed work as soon as possible.
   a. he or she

b. they

c. them

3. A marathon runner must drink plenty of water; *they* should plan to drink at least a liter of water before the race.

   a. you

   b. one

   c. he or she

4. Tim refuses to attend extra help. He doesn't realize that getting help on concepts he doesn't understand will help *you* be more successful.

   a. them

   b. he

   c. him

5. Although I enjoy playing hockey, it is a dangerous sport and sometimes *you* get injured.

   a. they

   b. I

   c. me

Indefinite Pronoun Agreement Practice

Choose the correct indefinite pronoun for each of the following sentences.

1. Everybody on the boys' basketball team keeps (their/his) equipment in the locker room.

2. Anybody who is late for class must put (their/ his or her) name on the list by the door.

3. Each of my aunts called me (themselves/herself) to wish me a happy birthday.

4. Someone left (their/his or her) phone on the bus, so I gave it to the bus driver.

5. Neither my brother nor his friend Rob will let me borrow (their/his) skateboard.

Vague Pronoun References

Rewrite the following sentences to correct the vague pronoun reference.

1. Many students like either math or history, but it has always been my favorite subject.
2. Lisa complained to her mother that she didn't like the cake she made.
3. Both Faith and Kim are good at basketball, but she is a better volleyball player.
4. Jimmy told his brother he should talk to his teacher.
5. Bob told his dad he found his missing watch.

Use Commas to Set Off Parenthetical and Nonrestrictive Information

Rewrite the following sentences using commas correctly.

1. That movie in my opinion is one of the best of the year.
2. Aiden who is an excellent hockey player volunteered to coach the youth league.
3. This dog for example has learned to open the door and dial the phone.
4. In other words I am really looking forward to the game.
5. My favorite song which is playing on the radio right now came out last year.

Dashes to Set Off Nonrestrictive Expressions

Rewrite the following sentences, using dashes to set off nonrestrictive expressions.

1. The new *Hunger Games* movie it is my favorite so far is showing at the plaza cinema.
2. My aunt Mary she's a wonderful lady volunteers at the hospital three days a week.
3. My dog Duke he's the greatest dog was a gift from my grandparents.
4. Lake Wautaska the jewel of the northeast is a popular tourist spot.
5. My favorite TV show it is so exciting is on tonight.

CHAPTER 8

Grade 7—Reading

Seventh grade reading instruction builds on what students learned in grade 6. The 7th grade curriculum assumes your child has mastered or is approaching mastery of those topics. In the 7th grade your child will read more informational texts than literary texts. Even some of the novels or longer literary texts will be based on actual events or facts, which provide opportunities for your child to read supporting nonfiction information. By 8th grade, 55 percent of your child's reading in school will be informational texts.

What Your Seventh Grader Will Learn

There are two sets of reading standards for grades K–12. The Reading Literature (RL) standards provide guidance for reading literature. The Reading Informational Text (RI) standards provide guidance for reading informational texts. In the 7th grade, students use the technique of "read as evidence" to support their conclusions about their reading. Much emphasis is placed on independently finding meaning in a literature and informational text, and on proving that a conclusion is valid by supporting it with information the author provides.

In the 7th grade, your child's teacher will encourage conversations among students. During these conversations, the hope is that students will debate and discuss what an author is saying and why the author is making a particular point. It is likely that your child will have many independent discussion experiences. Some parents worry that these conversations, which aren't led by the teacher, can lead to misinterpretation or misunderstandings. That may be the case at first, but also keep in mind that these conversations are usually bookended with mini-lessons on how to annotate a text, determine an author's point or bias, and other skills. In other words, these conversations are practice sessions rather than instruction.

ESSENTIAL

Active reading and annotating texts in the 7th grade should be done with purpose. Remind your child to ask himself, "Why am I reading this?" before reading. Write the purpose on a sticky note or at the top of a page before reading.

When the Common Core standards were first released, there was much concern regarding the amount of time teachers would need to spend on a single excerpt or short text. For example, in New York, the state published a lesson that focused for several days on the Gettysburg Address, which might seem like too much time to spend on a 272-word text. The rationale for lessons like this is to support the practice of close reading. The goal is for students to get away from just *covering* a text and instead spend time understanding how it is constructed. While this degree of focus won't be appropriate for everything your child reads, you should expect that teachers will spend a lot more time on each whole-class text. Instead of teachers explaining why a speech or novel is important, they will now guide students toward understanding the relevance and potential meaning of the text independently.

Reading Literature

In the 7th grade, your child will read examples of literature from many different genres, including realistic fiction, historical fiction, and science fiction and/or fantasy. He will also read poetry, including contemporary and classic works. Analysis of poetry and drama will be an important focus. The topics covered in the Reading Literature (RL) standard include:

- Using text evidence to support analysis.
- Determining a theme or central idea and how it is developed over the course of a text.
- Writing an objective summary of a text.
- Analyzing how elements of a story or drama interact.
- Analyzing the impact of rhymes and repetition of sounds on a verse or stanza of poetry.
- Analyzing how a drama's or poem's structure contributes to meaning.
- Analyzing how an author develops and contrasts points of view of different characters or narrators.
- Comparing and contrasting a fictional portrayal of a time, place, or character with a historical account of the same period.

Using Text Evidence to Support Analysis

Analysis is a close, almost technical reading of a text. Usually, analysis results in the reader making some sort of claim related to the text. For example, the reader might claim that the narrator is biased against a particular character, that a character is motivated by relationships with other characters, or that the setting has a specific effect on that story. To complete a close analysis, your child should be familiar with a few important terms related to the study of literature:

Character: The characters are the people who populate a story. Readers analyze characters by considering the following:

- The characters' actions
- The characters' thoughts and words
- What the characters look like
- What the characters say or think about each other

Foreshadowing: An author may foreshadow or hint at what will come later in the story or poem. Close, analytical reading looks for clues to the climax or conclusion along the way.

Narrator: The narrator tells the story. Sometimes the narrator is part of the story (first person), while other times the narrator is more of an observer (third person).

Plot: The sequence of events or story line in a narrative, drama, and sometimes a poem. Review Chapter 5 for more information on elements of plot, including exposition, rising action, climax, falling action, and resolution.

Setting: The time and place in which the story occurs.

Symbolism: An author can refer to objects that she expects will result in some sort of emotional response or understanding from the reader. For example, a flag can be a symbol of patriotism.

To begin an analysis, readers should set a purpose for reading the text. For the following excerpt, the focus will be what the text tells the reader about the characters and the setting. The following is a passage adapted from *Treasure Island*. The text is annotated to demonstrate how active reading can help students work through analysis questions.

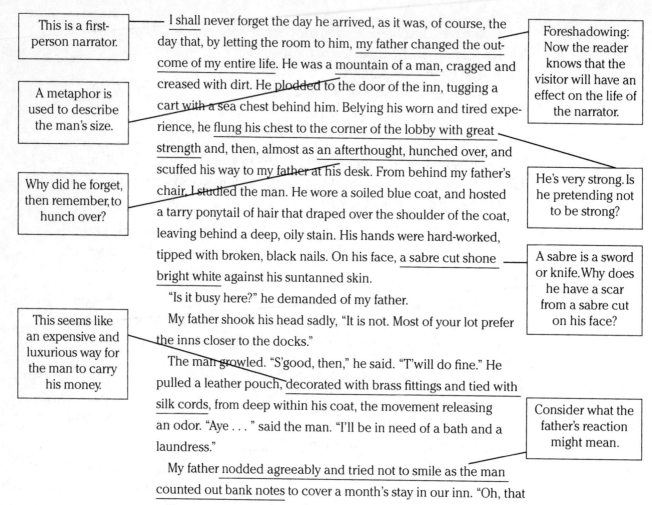

This is a first-person narrator.

A metaphor is used to describe the man's size.

Why did he forget, then remember, to hunch over?

This seems like an expensive and luxurious way for the man to carry his money.

Foreshadowing: Now the reader knows that the visitor will have an effect on the life of the narrator.

He's very strong. Is he pretending not to be strong?

A sabre is a sword or knife. Why does he have a scar from a sabre cut on his face?

Consider what the father's reaction might mean.

I shall never forget the day he arrived, as it was, of course, the day that, by letting the room to him, my father changed the outcome of my entire life. He was a mountain of a man, cragged and creased with dirt. He plodded to the door of the inn, tugging a cart with a sea chest behind him. Belying his worn and tired experience, he flung his chest to the corner of the lobby with great strength and, then, almost as an afterthought, hunched over, and scuffed his way to my father at his desk. From behind my father's chair, I studied the man. He wore a soiled blue coat, and hosted a tarry ponytail of hair that draped over the shoulder of the coat, leaving behind a deep, oily stain. His hands were hard-worked, tipped with broken, black nails. On his face, a sabre cut shone bright white against his suntanned skin.

"Is it busy here?" he demanded of my father.

My father shook his head sadly, "It is not. Most of your lot prefer the inns closer to the docks."

The man growled. "S'good, then," he said. "T'will do fine." He pulled a leather pouch, decorated with brass fittings and tied with silk cords, from deep within his coat, the movement releasing an odor. "Aye . . . " said the man. "I'll be in need of a bath and a laundress."

My father nodded agreeably and tried not to smile as the man counted out bank notes to cover a month's stay in our inn. "Oh, that will do. I thank you, sir."

Now that you've read and annotated the text, consider the following questions, which are typical analysis questions:

1. How does the narrator react to the new guest?

In questions like this, which ask the reader to determine an emotion experienced by a character, it is very important to use evidence to develop a point. The narrator captures many details about the man's appearance, so it is accurate to note that he is **curious**. The best responses to questions like this use two or more descriptors. Notice that the narrator describes himself he studies the new guest. This tells

as being "behind his father's chair" when he studies the new guest. This tells the reader that, perhaps, the narrator is nervous or a bit afraid of the man. So it would be reasonable to amend the first description, and respond, "The narrator was curious about, and a bit afraid of, the man. The narrator notices many details about the guest, including his clothing, his hair, his hands, and even a scar on his face. He writes, however, that he stayed behind his father's chair as he looked at the man. It is reasonable to assume that he was a bit afraid of the man and wanted to be a bit hidden."

2. What is the description of the man who is checking into the inn?

This question, like the preceding question, should be supported with text evidence. Rereading the text with the purpose of gathering details about the man reveals several physical characteristics, as well as a bit about his personality. Review the following passage from the text and notice the annotations:

> He's a large man, wrinkled and dirty.

To bely is to show that something isn't true. So, is he pretending to be worn out and tired? Why?

He was a mountain of a man, cragged and creased with dirt. He plodded to the door of the inn, tugging a cart with a sea chest behind him. Belying his worn and tired appearance, he flung the chest from the cart to the corner of the lobby with great strength and, then, almost as an afterthought, hunched over, and scuffed his way to my father at his desk.

> Why is he pretending to be weaker than he is?

Notice how this sample response uses text evidence:

"The man is large, older, and very dirty. The narrator believes that he is pretending to be tired and weak, because the man is able to throw a heavy trunk across the room, and then, 'almost as an afterthought, hunched over.' That quote tells me that hunching over and scuffing were things he was doing on purpose so that the narrator and his father would have a certain impression of him."

Notice how the writer uses text evidence to support his claims. The writer's main claim is that the man is trying to deceive the narrator's father. It isn't clear yet why he might be doing so.

3. Why do you think the man has chosen this inn?

This is a "hypothesize" question, and there are really no wrong answers, only answers that are not well supported. Review the following sample response and explanation to see how a writer can use text evidence to support such an analysis:

"The man has chosen this inn because it is not very popular with other people like him. He is likely a sailor, as he has a sea chest. The narrator's father tells him that others like him prefer the inns 'closer to the docks,' which is where other sailors would likely want to stay. When the man learns that the inn is not busy, he responds, 'S'good' and 'Twill do fine,' which means he is happy that there won't be many other guests. The man is likely hiding from someone. He has a leather pouch of money and has paid far in advance, which means he has a lot of money. It may be that he has stolen money and doesn't want to be caught."

In this response, the writer used details from the text to complete a thorough analysis of the character. Notice how the writer makes inferences and uses the text to support them, such as the fact that the man is likely a sailor, and that he does not want to see other people.

It takes time to master the ability to make this type of analysis, and requires multiple readings of the same text. One of the most challenging aspects of close reading for 7th grade students is that they are seventh graders; that is, it may be difficult to motivate them to read through a text a second or third time to find evidence.

Determining the Theme or Central Idea of a Text

Your child learned how to identify the theme of a text in the 6th grade. In the 7th grade she will apply analysis to her study of theme to determine how different aspects of the text help develop the theme or central idea. To do so, your child must consider:

- What the author wants to say about the subject of the text.
- An observation, lesson, or moral that can be taken from the text and applied to life in general.

The theme must be a statement that can be supported by text evidence. Returning to the excerpt adapted from *Treasure Island*, consider the following statement as a possible theme, "People sometimes ignore signs of danger when they are in need." This theme statement can be supported with several details from the text. First, what are some signs that the man who arrives at the inn might be dangerous?

- He throws his chest in a way "belying his worn and tired appearance . . ." He is pretending to be someone weaker than he is. He doesn't want the innkeeper to know he is a strong, powerful man.
- He is pleased that few people stay at this inn, and says, "S'good, then," when he hears most sailors stay somewhere else.
- He has a scar from a sabre on his face. A sabre!

Obviously this man is powerful and is hiding from someone; it is not a stretch to consider him dangerous. There is a second part to the theme, as well. Evidence is needed to support that "people," namely the narrator's father, ignore signs of danger when they are in need. How does the reader know the father is in need?

- When the man asks if many people stay at the hotel, the father shakes his head "sadly" and says, "It is not." He's sad that there aren't more guests. The reader can infer that the father is saying that his business is suffering. He may be in need.
- The father "tried not to smile" when the filthy, scary-looking man counted out enough money to pay for his room for a month. The father is ignoring quite a few details about this man and thanks him enthusiastically.

Even though the reader has not read the entire novel, there is enough evidence in this excerpt to support this theme statement.

Writing an Objective Summary of a Text

In the 7th grade, your child will continue to develop her skills in this area. The texts she reads will likely be more complex, and the plots may include subplots and even distracting details such as red herrings. A red herring is a fact or detail that appears to be a clue in a mystery, but is actually intended to mislead the characters (and the reader) or distract them from meaningful details that can solve the mystery. The goal of the reader remains the same: to identify key information and to develop a summary that captures the most important points.

An objective summary recounts the main idea and most important details of a narrative, using only the information provided in the text. A summary is much shorter than the original text and may omit many details.

There are several strategies to help students learn how to summarize a narrative text. A helpful mnemonic is C-PETE.

C—Character
P—has a Problem
E—which Escalates
T—until a Turning point
E—when it Ends

Read the story that follows:

Once upon a time there was a prince who wanted to marry a princess; but she would have to be a real princess. He travelled all over the world to find one, but nowhere could he get what he wanted. There were princesses enough, but it was difficult to find out whether they were real ones. There was always something about them that was not as it should be. So he came home again and was sad, for he would have liked very much to have a real princess.

One evening a terrible storm came on; there was thunder and lightning, and the rain poured down in torrents. Suddenly a knocking was heard at the city gate, and the old king went to open it.

It was a princess standing out there in front of the gate. But, good gracious! What a sight the rain and the wind had made her look. The water ran down from her hair and clothes; it ran down into the toes of her shoes and out again at the heels. And yet she said that she was a real princess.

Well, we'll soon find that out, thought the old queen. But she said nothing, went into the bedroom, took all the bedding off the bedstead, and laid a pea on the bottom; then she took twenty mattresses and laid them on the pea, and then twenty eider-down beds on top of the mattresses.

On this the princess had to lie all night. In the morning she was asked how she had slept.

"Oh, very badly!" said she. "I have scarcely closed my eyes all night. Heaven only knows what was in the bed, but I was lying on something hard, so that I am black and blue all over my body. It's horrible!"

Now they knew that she was a real princess because she had felt the pea right through the twenty mattresses and the twenty eider-down beds.

Nobody but a real princess could be as sensitive as that.

So the prince took her for his wife, for now he knew that he had a real princess; and the pea was put in the museum, where it may still be seen, if no one has stolen it.

Using the C-PETE strategy, determine the main points of this story. Begin by answering these questions:

- Who is the main character?
- What is his problem?
- How does it escalate?
- What is the turning point?
- How does the story end?

Here is an objective summary based on the C-PETE strategy:

"A prince wanted to marry a princess, but no matter how hard he looked, he couldn't find a woman who was a real princess. One night a young woman showed up in the middle of a storm seeking shelter and claiming to be a princess. The Queen tested her by placing a pea in her bed, as only a real princess would feel such a small thing. The princess felt the pea, proving that she was really a princess, and the prince took her for his wife."

Notice that the summary is much shorter than the original text and that it is objective; that is, it does not express judgments or opinions.

Elements of Drama

In the 6th grade your child learned about the elements of plot, from the exposition to the resolution. She will continue to use that knowledge and those skills of analysis in the 7th grade, and she will extend her understanding of fictional prose to drama (plays) and some types of narrative poetry. In the 7th grade, your child will learn about the following elements of drama:

Acts: The divisions of a play, somewhat like chapters in a novel. Acts do not have to be chronologically ordered. Long periods of time can elapse between acts, and acts can go back in time.

Comedy: A type of drama intended to entertain the audience; a comedy may or may not be funny, but it always has a happy ending.

Dialogue: The words spoken by actors playing characters in a play.

Playwright: The author of a play.

Props: Objects the characters use in the play. Props can include the characters' costumes.

Set: The stage on which the play is performed and all of the furnishings and props on the stage.

Stage directions: Instructions the playwright includes in the play to tell the actors how to move on the set.

Soliloquy: A long speech delivered by one actor; a monologue usually tells the audience about the character's feelings.

Tragedy: A play in which a hero experiences a downfall or great failure. This type of play does not have a happy ending.

Analyzing Drama

Analyzing drama is much like analyzing other types of literature. It is likely that when your child reads drama in her 7th grade classroom, the teacher will assign roles to different students, so it will be a class-reading experience. When reading in a group setting or reading a drama independently, readers should answer the following questions in order to complete an analysis. Remember that an analysis of a drama is based on the entire play. There are instances when students are asked to analyze passages from a play and consider how they work with the rest of the text. When analyzing a specific passage, the reader should ask the following questions:

- Who are the characters?
- What is the main issue the characters are discussing?
- How does each character's motives or wants change how they view the issue being discussed?
- Does it seem like the playwright wants you, the audience, to support a specific character? Which one?
- How is the passage related to the rest of the play?

The C-PETE strategy also can be applied to a play. The challenge of a play is that no narrative fills in the blanks. The analysis must therefore be based almost entirely on dialogue, which makes it even more important that your child be able to apply good annotation and analysis practices when reading a play.

Rhymes and Repetition of Sounds

In the 6th grade your child learned that poetry is divided into stanzas. Stanzas divide a poem into meaningful thought divisions.

Review the following poem, "O Captain! My Captain!" by Walt Whitman. Whitman wrote this poem after the assassination of Abraham Lincoln. The "Captain" in the poem is Lincoln.

> O Captain! my Captain! our fearful trip is done,
> The ship has weather'd every rack, the prize we sought is won,
> The port is near, the bells I hear, the people all exulting,
> While follow eyes the steady keel, the vessel grim and daring;
>> But O heart! heart! heart!
>>> O the bleeding drops of red,
>>>> Where on the deck my Captain lies,
>>>>> Fallen cold and dead.
>
> O Captain! my Captain! rise up and hear the bells;
> Rise up—for you the flag is flung—for you the bugle trills,
> For you bouquets and ribbon'd wreaths—for you the shores a-crowding,
> For you they call, the swaying mass, their eager faces turning;
>> Here Captain! dear father!
>>> This arm beneath your head!
>>>> It is some dream that on the deck,
>>>>> You've fallen cold and dead.
>
> My Captain does not answer, his lips are pale and still,
> My father does not feel my arm, he has no pulse nor will,
> The ship is anchor'd safe and sound, its voyage closed and done,
> From fearful trip the victor ship comes in with object won;
>> Exult O shores, and ring O bells!
>>> But I with mournful tread,

Walk the deck my Captain lies,
        Fallen cold and dead.

This poem has three stanzas. Students might be asked to consider how each stanza expresses an idea related to the whole. Let us review and annotate the first stanza to answer the following questions:

1. Since the captain is Lincoln, what does the ship symbolize?
   The ship likely symbolizes the United States. The captain lies on the deck, and the ship is near port, which could mean that the end of the Civil War was near, but the captain has died. Now the crew is worried because the ship has no leader.

2. Explain how the metaphor of a ship is carried through the entire poem.
   This type of extended analysis requires that your child read the poem in its entirety *and* consider the different components independently. The reader should read with the purpose of following the metaphor of the ship. Other details may seem interesting, but it is important to maintain focus. Keep in mind that reading with a purpose is the best way to read closely.
   Stanzas also help balance the rhyme of a poem. There are two basics types of rhyme in poetry:
   End Rhyme: Rhyme that occurs between words at the ends of lines in a stanza.
   Internal Rhyme: Rhyme that occurs within a single line of a poem.
   Review the following stanza, which is annotated to show both end rhyme and internal rhyme:

"Done" and "won" rhyme. This is end rhyme: The words appear at the end of the lines.

O Captain! my Captain! our fearful trip is done,
The ship has weather'd every rack, the prize we sought is won,
The port is near, the bells I hear, the people all exulting,
While follow eyes the steady keel, the vessel grim and daring;
    But O heart! heart! heart!
      O the bleeding drops of red,
        Where on the deck my Captain lies,
          Fallen cold and dead.

"Near" and "hear" rhyme. This is internal rhyme: The words appear in the same line.

When completing an analysis of a poem, seventh graders will mark and analyze the rhyme scheme. The rhyme scheme is the pattern of end rhyme used in a poem and is marked using letters. The following stanza is annotated for rhyme scheme:

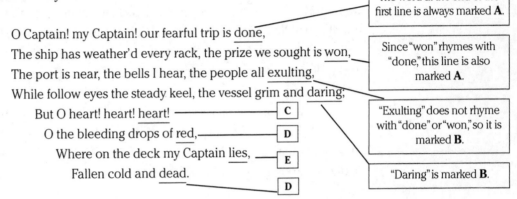

O Captain! my Captain! our fearful trip is done,
The ship has weather'd every rack, the prize we sought is won,
The port is near, the bells I hear, the people all exulting,
While follow eyes the steady keel, the vessel grim and daring;
  But O heart! heart! heart! ——————— **C**
   O the bleeding drops of red, —————— **D**
   Where on the deck my Captain lies, —— **E**
    Fallen cold and dead. ————————— **D**

The word at the end of the first line is always marked **A**.

Since "won" rhymes with "done," this line is also marked **A**.

"Exulting" does not rhyme with "done" or "won," so it is marked **B**.

"Daring" is marked **B**.

Review the rest of the poem. Do the other stanzas follow the same rhyme scheme?

Most middle school students are less than thrilled when it is time to study poetry. But that may in part be because they haven't developed the tools to really understand the poetry they are studying. Encourage your child to invest the time it takes to understand a poet's purpose and message, as doing so can bring new understanding, and even offer new insights into historical and important political or social trends.

Practice Exercises

These practice exercises are meant to assess skills in ways similar to what your child may encounter on standardized tests.

Reading Literature

Read this passage and answer the questions that follow.

With just an hour to go before the birthday party, Sandra began to panic. She still had to frost the cake, decorate the dining room, and wrap the gifts. More than anything she wanted her mom's birthday to be special. She wiped her forehead and sighed, wondering where her little brothers were.

They promised to help her set up for the party, but they were nowhere to be found. Sandra called up the stairs, "Tim? Robby?" No answer. She pulled the cake out of the refrigerator so that it wouldn't be too cold to frost, then went into the dining room. Sandra gasped. The dining room was a mess. Plastic wrap was strewn all over the chairs and table. A pile of uninflated balloons lay in the corner. Packing tape was stuck on the walls, and some of it had pulled off the paint. She sat down in a chair and began to cry. Her mom would be back in an hour and Sandra knew there was no way she would get the room cleaned up in time. Just then, her little brothers came running into the room, laughing. "What have you done!" Sandra bellowed. Timmy stuck out his tongue. Robby knocked over a chair and they were off again. As they raced out of the room, Sandra noticed they had the wrapping paper trailing behind them.

1. Who is the protagonist of this story?
   a. Tim
   b. Robby
   c. Sandra
2. What kind of conflict is present in this story?
   a. Character versus self
   b. Character versus character
   c. Character versus society
3. What is Sandra planning for?
   a. A party for her brothers
   b. A party for her mother
   c. To have her friends over later
4. What part of the story is missing?
   a. Exposition
   b. Resolution
   c. Rising action
5. What causes a complication in this story?
   a. Tim and Robby are missing.
   b. Tim and Robby haven't wrapped the presents.
   c. Tim and Robby make a mess in the dining room.

Symbolism

Read the following passages and identify the meanings of key symbols.

1. Emily is writing a story about a wise animal who teaches others a valuable lesson. Which animal should she choose for her main character to symbolize wisdom and knowledge?
   a. A horse
   b. A cat
   c. An owl

2. The teacher handed each student a brainstorming worksheet. On each worksheet there were six lightbulbs. The students were to write their brainstorming notes within the lightbulbs. On this worksheet, the lightbulbs symbolize:
   a. Energy
   b. Electricity
   c. Ideas

3. The soldiers lay down their guns and put up a white flag. They sent a message to the enemy that they wanted to stop fighting and find a way to resolve their problems without violence. In this excerpt, the color white symbolizes:
   a. Marriage
   b. Innocence
   c. Peace

4. In an essay for her English class, Lisa compared her grandmother to a tree. She noted all the important lessons she learned from her grandmother, and wrote how much she appreciated being able to spend time with her. In Lisa's essay, the tree likely symbolizes:
   a. Nature
   b. Changing seasons
   c. Wisdom

5. The evil Dr. Maddread wrapped his cape around his bony shoulders. He laughed bitterly to himself as he watched his neighbors through the window. "They seem happy enough now," he said. "Just wait until I put my plan into action!" Based on what you know about Dr. Maddread, what color should his cape be?
   a. Brown
   b. Black
   c. White

CHAPTER 9

Grade 7—Writing, Speaking, and Listening

In the 7th grade your child will continue learning how to write argumentative, explanatory, and narrative essays. For example, in writing argumentative or persuasive essays, she will acknowledge that valid, opposing points of view may exist, and she will write not only to prove her own point, but to clarify her disagreement with an opposing point of view. In addition, new components of each type of writing will be introduced. The Speaking and Listening standard will help your child continue to develop her collaborative skills, specifically by providing her opportunities to respond to the ideas of others, or acknowledge different points of view in speaking and listening, just as she did in writing. Finally, in presenting information to a small or large group, your child will continue to build confidence in addressing others and presenting her ideas.

What Your Seventh Grader Will Learn

In the 7th grade, the Writing, Speaking, and Listening standards encourage your child to consider different points of view, and think about ways her own views might evolve as a result of new information gathered from sources or from conversations with others. She'll also focus more closely on the concept of the audience, and begin to explore ways to ensure her intended audience has enough information to understand her point of view.

As in the 6th grade, seventh graders learn to participate in collaborative discussion. They are expected to respond respectfully to what others have to say, just as they did in prior grades. In the 7th grade, however, your child will spend time considering and asking clarification questions to better understand how the opinions of others differ from her own. She will learn and practice evaluating her point of view to incorporate new information. Finally, she will learn to use questions and redirection in group discussion to maintain her own focus and that of the group.

There are four main focus areas in the Writing standard:

- Writing arguments to support claims
- Writing informative/explanatory texts
- Writing narratives to develop real or imagined experiences
- Conducting research to build and present knowledge

In addition, your child will focus on the following topics in the Speaking and Listening standard:

- Being a collaborative participant in a range of discussions
- Presenting claims and information to others

Writing Arguments to Support Claims

Argumentative writing in the 7th grade adds new focus areas to instruction and assessment. In addition to introducing a claim, your child will learn how to acknowledge and respond to reasonable opposing claims, also called counterclaims. Seventh grade writers learn that it is reasonable to expect disagreement with a claim, and they develop the research and writing skills necessary to respond to an opposing viewpoint. There are several assessed components to argumentative writing in the 7th grade.

Introduce a Claim

The claim is also called the thesis. It is the main point the writer intends to prove. The thesis often offers the writer's point of view and the opposing viewpoint, using a clause that begins with *although*. Review the following writing prompt, and the elements of a claim and counterclaim:

What is the most important technological development or invention that has come about in your lifetime?

In the essay, your child should include:

- An introductory paragraph that introduces her claim and acknowledges a relevant counterclaim.
- Logical reasoning and detailed evidence to support her point of view and demonstrate her understanding of the topic.

The claim for an essay can also introduce a counterclaim:

Although some may argue that the hybrid automobile is the most important recent invention because of its positive impact on the use of natural resources, the development that has changed the lives of more people is the smartphone because it provides information, communication, and security to millions of individuals.

This thesis sentence provides two points of view on the same question. Both can be logically supported. The writer has formed a claim that will lead to the development of an essay to prove that while both the hybrid car and the smartphone are important, the smartphone is likely more valuable because it affects a greater number of people.

This claim or thesis "promises" the reader that the following points will be covered:

- The impact of the hybrid car on the environment.

- Details of how smartphones provide information, communication, and security.
- Some sort of comparison of the number of people impacted by the two technologies.

It will help your child to think of an argumentative essay with a counter-claim as being a friendly argument or debate.

Support a Claim

In the 6th grade your child learned how to identify credible sources and use evidence to support a point. She will continue to call on these skills in the 7th grade to support a point of view, and her goal is to be methodical in the use of credible information that directly supports her point of view. In addition, in the 7th grade your child will learn about the importance of writing logical arguments, and avoiding logical fallacies.

A logical fallacy is a flaw in reasoning. Writers can use them inadvertently in an effort to support a point of view. The most common types of logical fallacies, and the ones your child should be aware of in order to actively avoid them, are:

The Bandwagon Fallacy

The name of this fallacy comes from an idiom, "to jump on the bandwagon," which means to go along with what most people are doing. The bandwagon fallacy says that if an idea is popular, it must be correct. Here's an example: "Every day, more Americans eat French fries than tofu; so, obviously, French fries are a healthier food choice." Whenever an argument relies on the popularity of an idea, it is important to analyze it more closely to ensure the argument doesn't rely on false logic.

The Straw Man Fallacy

The name of this fallacy comes from an old story about attacking a man made of straw, or an enemy that can't fight back and is not, in fact, actually an enemy. This is the type of fallacy that emerges when writers and speakers refer to *they*, the imagined opposition who disagree with a point of view. A writer might use this fallacy as follows, "There are some who believe smartphones are overpriced toys, but they don't understand the benefits of this technology." In this sentence, the writer hasn't named this imagined opposition or provided details about the point of view. This is a weak approach to a counterargument, as it does nothing but disagree; it doesn't provide an alternative.

Ad Hominem Fallacy

The name of this fallacy comes from Latin and means "to the person." In this type of fallacy, the writer attacks the character of someone with an opposing point of view, rather than the evidence and logic of the argument. This is an example of an ad hominem fallacy: "Mr. Jones, a leading environmentalist, argues that hybrid cars produce less carbon monoxide and help improve air quality. However, Mr. Jones was fired from his last job for being rude to his coworkers, so his point of view is obviously flawed." In the example, Mr. Jones is attacked for being rude to coworkers and losing his job, two events that aren't related to whether or not he is right about air quality. This writer didn't counter the claim that hybrid cars help improve air quality; she only tried to discredit Mr. Jones.

When writing an argument it is important that evidence is concrete and specific. The best way to provide a logical argument is to use specifics. Help your child find specific information and avoid using fallacies to counter opposing viewpoints.

Make Connections Between Claims

An argumentative essay has three components: the claim, the reason, and the evidence. The following sentence is a claim and is the main point of an argumentative paper:

The smartphone is the most important invention of the twenty-first century.

The claim states the main point that the paper intends to prove. It is a claim because it is an arguable point that someone could reasonably disagree with.

The reasons for the claim provide logical support. Reasons are valid statements that support the claim. The following are the reasons for the aforementioned claim:

- Smartphones provide information
- Smartphones enable communication
- Smartphones provide security

The evidence of a claim is proof. Evidence is found through research and by reading and reviewing credible sources. Evidence is necessary to support the reasons for a claim. The first claim in this example states that smartphones provide information. Evidence for this claim could include:

- Using Wi-Fi or cellular data, smartphone users can access the Internet and use a wide range of reference and information sources including dictionaries, encyclopedias, and news and educational websites.

In a fully developed essay, the writer might go on to explain some of the most valuable sources of information that can be accessed with a smartphone. The evidence provides examples that support a particular reason.

To connect the claim, reasons, and evidence, your child will use transitional words and phrases. Transitions that link claims and reasons include:

TRANSITIONS THAT LINK CLAIMS AND REASONS	
Transition	Example Sentence
Because	Smartphones are the most important recent invention *because* they provide access to information.
Due to	*Due to* the fact that they offer users security, smartphones are the most important recent invention.
Since	Smartphones are the most important recent invention *since* they allow users to communicate with others anytime and anywhere.
In view of	*In view of* the fact that smartphones offer access to information, communication, and security, they are the most important recent invention.

Your child should also use transitions to connect evidence to reasons. Evidence usually provides a specific example of information in a reason, so the most effective transitions are those that link examples to general statements, including:

- Such as
- For example
- Like
- In particular
- Including
- To illustrate

Here is an example of a paragraph that uses transitions to create narrative cohesion between a claim, reason, and evidence:

Smartphones are one of the most import recent inventions *because* of the valuable security features they provide. *For example*, parents can activate the Find My Phone feature on their children's phones and be able to track their location using GPS technology. This technology has proven invaluable in locating lost children. *For instance*, in 2013 a group of teenagers failed to return from a hiking trip on the Appalachian Trail in New Hampshire. Search parties set out, but the teens had been hiking for more than twelve hours and rescue workers estimated that they could be anywhere within a five hundred square mile area. A quick-thinking parent used the Find My Phone app to locate her daughter's phone, narrowed down the search area, and helped rescuers find and rescue the teens within a few hours.

In this example, the writer used transitions to link the claim, the reason, and the evidence so that the reader can understand the logical connections between ideas.

Maintain a Formal Style

As a sixth grader your child learned about formal writing. He learned that it is important to avoid first and second person pronouns, and knows that personal pronouns suggest a bias, or a skewed point of view. He will have also learned that such styles might be suitable for personal opinion, but they are not appropriate for a carefully constructed, logical essay. In the 7th grade, he will continue to maintain a formal point of view and use only third person pronouns. In addition, he will be expected to be as specific as possible in his writing and avoid using pronouns that are not linked to specific names of people, places, or things. Formal writing is precise and focuses on what can be supported or proven. The following sentence uses third person pronouns but is neither formal nor precise:

> When teens ask their parents for smartphones, most usually are interested in using apps to play games.

The next sentence is a revision that improves the formality and precision:

> According to consumer surveys, 75 percent of teenagers between the ages of 13–15 want smartphones so that they can download the most popular gaming apps, such as *Angry Birds* and *Words with Friends*.

Notice that the revision uses specific information to define what is meant by *most* (75 percent), *teens* (13–15 year olds), and *games* (*Angry Birds* and *Words with Friends*). These details improve the work by making it more formal and more precise.

Using Concluding Statements

The end of an essay is just as important as the beginning. The conclusion should accomplish three things:

1. Restate the thesis
2. Summarize the most important evidence
3. Leave the reader with a closing thought or a call to action

Here is an example of a concluding paragraph that pulls together the author's main points, restates the thesis, and draws a reasonable closing statement that leaves the reader with something to think about:

> In conclusion, while hybrid cars do show promise in conserving resources and improving air quality, they have not been widely adopted and may never have a wide impact on the planet. Smartphones, however, have wide-reaching advantages and have provided millions of people with information, communication, and security. As

developers continue to add features and apps, smartphones will continue to improve the lives of everyone who owns them.

Notice that the conclusion also offers a final rebuttal or explanation for why the counterargument isn't valid before restating the thesis and summarizing the reasons. The reader is left with a clear overview of the argument, and the most compelling reason why the counterargument isn't valid.

Writing Informative/Explanatory Texts

Informative writing is also called expository writing. Its purpose is to inform or explain. Your child has been writing expository texts for several years in school. In the 6th grade she learned how to organize her thoughts and write papers to compare/contrast, show cause and effect, and describe events in history using chronological order. In the 7th grade, informative writing can take several forms, including:

- Definition
- Classification
- Compare/contrast
- Cause/effect

Your child will be asked to use facts, definitions, and concrete details to support her essay. This type of information will usually be gathered through research, or by accessing materials studied in class, such as nonfiction texts and articles.

Your seventh grader will likely learn about the definition essay for the first time this year. When writing a definition essay, your child will use examples to define a concept or idea. Here is an example of a writing prompt he might encounter for a definition essay:

The word *hero* is used to describe many different types of people in many different situations. Consider what the true definition of a hero is. Define the term *hero* and provide examples to support your definition.

There are several assessed components of a definition essay.

The Introduction

The introduction of a definition essay should provide a general definition of the term or an example of the term in use. The introduction should include a controlling idea, or thesis, that previews the definition the writer will explain. The following is an appropriate thesis statement for the aforementioned writing prompt:

A hero is someone who voluntarily puts herself in harms' way to help others, steps forward when others are afraid to do so, or overcomes personal hardship or hurdles to offer assistance to another person.

The controlling idea in the previous statement does two things:

- It responds directly to the prompt.
- It provides a very specific definition that can be explained in the essay with examples and evidence.

Once the controlling idea is in place, your child can write the rest of the introduction. The purpose of the introduction is to hook the reader, provide necessary background information, and present the controlling idea, usually in that order. Following is a sample of an introduction for the essay prompt about a hero:

Lisa Ellson was working in her yard one quiet morning when she noticed a car had stopped on the railroad tracks not far from her house. It looked like the driver had turned onto the tracks, thinking they were a road, and was trying to pull her car off the rails. As Ellson watched the driver struggle, turning one way, then the next, she heard the unmistakable sound of a train in the distance. Ellson knew that the train would be coming around a bend in the tracks, and that the engineer would not see the car. Despite a back injury that made it difficult for her to walk sometimes, let alone run, Ellson sprinted down a bank toward the car. She pounded furiously on the window, but the driver, an elderly woman, seemed frightened, and tried to get away. Ellson could feel the vibrations of the approaching train beneath her feet. She knew she had just moments to save the woman. Finally, with the train just in sight, coming around the bend, Ellson broke the window of the car, unlocked the door, and dragged the woman to safety. A moment later, the train barreled into the car, crushing it beyond recognition. Despite her disability, Lisa Ellson is truly a hero. A hero is someone who voluntarily puts herself in harms' way to help others, steps forward when others are afraid to do so, or overcomes personal hardship or hurdles to offer assistance to another person.

This example used an anecdote as a hook. An anecdote is a short story that illustrates the main point of an essay. In this case, Lisa Ellson's actions demonstrated the definition of heroism that the writer then explained in the essay.

Other strategies for beginning an essay include:

- A quotation from a famous person
- A startling fact
- A humorous comment
- A description
- A figure of speech

In earlier grades your child may have learned to begin an essay with a question such as, "Have you ever done anything heroic?" In the 7th grade, writing becomes more formal and questions are only a good choice to begin an essay when the answer is directly related to the thesis or controlling idea. That being said, it is best to avoid opening an essay with a question simply because questions can often be unrealistic and have obvious answers. The introduction should provide a very clear idea of what the essay will be about, but it should never include phrases such as "in this essay . . ." or "this essay will . . ." The thesis will provide the information about the topic.

Graphics

Another component of an expository essay is graphics, which can include images, illustrations, charts, and tables. Writers may choose to use graphics created by others and available in research resources, or they can create their own. If graphics from outside sources are used, the original author must be properly cited.

Charts, tables, illustrations, and other graphics can be valuable, but they must be explained in the body of the essay. For example, if the essay on heroes included a photo of Lisa Ellson, it would be appropriate for a caption to appear under the photo. As well, an explanation in the paragraph immediately following the photo could detail the names of the people in the picture and provide a very brief summary of the point that the photo supports, such as, "Lisa Ellson shakes hands with the elderly woman she rescued from an oncoming train on June 1, 2013."

QUESTION

What kinds of graphics are appropriate in a formal paper?
Your child should check with her teacher about the kinds of graphics that are acceptable. Students are usually encouraged to use diagrams, photos, line graphs, pie charts, and tables. However, they should avoid overly complex graphics such as info graphics or images with several different labels. Regardless, the graphic should be directly related to the topic of the paper.

Body Paragraphs

Once the introduction and the formatting are in place, your child will develop her essay with information from research. This information is organized by categories into separate paragraphs, each with a topic sentence.

In the hero example, the controlling idea includes three main points to create the definition of a hero:

- puts herself in harms' way to help others
- steps forward when others are afraid
- overcomes personal hardship or hurdles to offer assistance

Introducing the categories of information in the introduction or controlling idea will strengthen your child's paper and give him the opportunity to demonstrate his ability to address different categories of evidence, which is a grading criterion.

Each body paragraph should include a topic sentence, which identifies the category of information, and concrete examples, definitions, or details that elaborate on the information in the topic sentence. Here is an example of a topic sentence for the first category of information in this essay:

A hero is someone who voluntarily puts herself in harms' way to help others.

The supporting details for this paragraph should be specific. For example, it is not enough to simply say it is heroic to risk one's life for another person. The student writer might include details such as:

- Elaboration about careers that demonstrate this type of heroic behavior, such as firefighters or police officers.
- Research about bystander behavior and the likelihood that bystanders will step forward to help another.
- An example of another hero who stepped forward to help another person.

A strong essay will include at least three body paragraphs, each covering a different category that has already been introduced in the thesis. A good way to plan an essay is to outline it first, based on the thesis.

Citing Sources

Your child's teacher may ask him to cite his sources if he uses outside research to write information in the body paragraphs. While the teacher will determine what style the citations should take, there are some basic guidelines that should be followed.

For example, whenever a writer uses text from a source, word for word, the text must be inside quotation marks. For example, the following text is from a source about the events of September 11, 2001:

"William Rodriguez was a maintenance worker at the World Trade Center. The only person with a key to the locked stairwells, he bravely led firefighters into the building and unlocked the doors, allowing the rescue of fifteen people just before the tower collapsed" (Rosado, 2014).

Notice that the writer has cited the source using the author's last name and the year the information was published. This citation will coordinate with another citation at the end of the essay. Again, your child's teacher will likely have a very specific requirement for citing sources. The Common Core standards do not require a specific style, only that sources are cited.

Transitional Words and Phrases

Like the argumentative essay, the informative essay is strengthened with transitional words and phrases between paragraphs. These transitions connect ideas so that the reader understands how the writer intends to connect information. The following transitions are particularly effective for definition essays:

COMMON TRANSITION WORDS AND PHRASES	
Type of transition	Word or phrase
Examples	to explain
	for instance
	in detail
	for example
	namely
	such as
Emphasis	that is to say
	notably
	truly
	surely
	indeed

Use Precise Language

Precise language is clear and specific. It can include descriptive language, and it is writing that uses the best word for the purpose of the writing. In writing intended to inform or explain, using precise vocabulary is very important. Domain-specific words are words that are used in a specific field of study or when writing about a specific subject. Your child is exposed to domain-specific language most often when she reads nonfiction texts, and she will be expected to use domain-specific vocabulary for the subjects (or domains) she writes about. Review the following sentence, which might have been included in the anecdote about the train in the previous sample introduction:

Lisa Ellson knew the driver of the train would not see the car in time to stop.

The driver of a train is called an "engineer" because she drives the "engine," which pulls the train. In addition, rather than saying the train "stops," a train "brakes." Engineer, engine, and brake are domain-specific terms that should be used when writing about trains. An improved sentence, using domain-specific vocabulary, would be:

Lisa Ellson knew the engineer would not see the car in time to brake.

The second sentence is more precise because it uses domain-specific language.

Your child is likely familiar with domain-specific language for different topics. Consider how the following sentences might be improved:

- The head of the school spoke when all the students were gathered in the auditorium.
- The man in the white coat checked to see if my body temperature was too high.
- A large truck with a blade on the front cleared the snow on the road.

Each of these sentences can be made more precise using domain-specific language. For example:

- The **principal** spoke during an **assembly** in the auditorium.
- The **doctor took my temperature** to see if I had a **fever**.
- A **snowplow** cleared the road.

In each of the revisions, the writer altered the language to make the information more specific. The goal is for the reader to understand a topic as well as the writer does. The only way to achieve this goal is to use precise, domain-specific language.

Getting into the habit of using domain-specific language is something you can practice with your child every day. Point out the domain-specific language for everyday tasks and activities. It can be fun to search for the precise words for certain situations. For example, the domain-specific word for *stop light* is *traffic control signal*. When one road leads to another via an exit ramp, the domain-specific term for the connected roads is *interchange*. Encourage your child to look up domain-specific terms when he uses vague or imprecise wording in conversation or informal writing.

Maintain a Formal Style

As in argumentative writing, informative writing uses a formal style. There are specific characteristics of formal writing. The obvious characteristic is that it avoids slang, text-speak, or writing shortcuts. Your child should be aware of several specific characteristics when he writes academic essays:

- Formal writing avoids words like *maybe, might, may,* or *seems.* Instead the writer states ideas as facts, and because academic writing requires evidence, what your child writes will be factual.
- No contractions. Your child should not use contractions in his academic writing. Avoid words like *can't, won't, haven't,* and so forth.
- No slang. Be sure to review words that are commonly used, but are actually slang, such as *kid, junk food, cop,* and *cool.*
- Avoids clichés, which are phrases that are used so often that they have become commonplace. Some examples include, "don't judge a book by its cover" and "better safe than sorry." Encourage your student to use original wording instead of tired clichés.
- Avoid euphemisms, or expressions that are intended to seem nicer than more realistic word choices. For example, a euphemism for "died" is "passed away." Encourage your child to write realistically.

Review the following sentences with your child and consider how to revise them so that the writing is more formal:

Mr. Simmons was let go from his last job and is now between jobs.

It isn't cool to be rude to cops.

Here the same sentences have been rewritten using formal language:

Mr. Simmons was dismissed from his job and is now unemployed.

It is not acceptable to be rude to police officers.

Notice that euphemisms and slang words have been replaced with more precise terms. In the second sentence, the contraction has been spelled out.

Provide a Concluding Statement

Every strong essay ends with a conclusion. In shorter essays, that conclusion might be a single sentence that wraps up the main points. For a longer essay, the conclusion could be a full paragraph. There are several strategies for a strong conclusion:

- **A brief summary of the main points.** This kind of conclusion, which can be based on the topic sentences of the body paragraphs, repeats the main points of the paper.
- **A call to action or question.** In the example of the essay defining a hero, the writer might summarize the characteristics of a hero as they have been explained in the essay.
- **Relate the topic to other situations.** This is also called universalizing. In this type of conclusion the writer applies what he hopes the reader has learned from this essay to other topics. For the definition essay about heroism, the writer might finalize the essay by noting specific professions or situations that consistently call for heroism as a way to apply the definition to the greater world.

It is important that the conclusion be definite—that it ends with a clear idea of the importance of the topic. Also, the conclusion should not bring in any new information. If there is additional information needed to support the topic, it should be in its own paragraph before the conclusion. A strong outline will help your child organize what he wants to say before he writes.

Writing Narratives

A narrative essay re-creates an experience in time order. A narrative essay is not only a story, but an essay that communicates a main idea, a lesson, or a moral. The story can be completely fictional, a retelling of a story the writer knows well, or a retelling of a real event. Before writing the narrative essay, writers must start with an outline. Otherwise, there is a risk of creating a rambling narrative that doesn't get to the point. Several criteria are assessed in narrative writing:

Engaging the Reader

The first paragraph tells the reader why the story is important, interesting, or what lesson it teaches. The first paragraph of a narrative should include the following information:

- The purpose and context. This includes the who, what, when, and where of the essay. In other words, the characters and setting.
- Point of view and characters. In the introduction your child should introduce her narrative voice. For example, the narrative voice might use the first person (I) to look back at an event in the past, such as, "I was just six years old when I learned the meaning of friendship."
- An introduction of a problem or conflict.

Writing a narrative can also challenge young writers because it requires a clearly defined conflict or problem. Review the following example:

I was just six years old when I learned the meaning of friendship. I had been recruited to be a flower girl in my aunt's wedding, and I was afraid I would do something wrong that would ruin the ceremony. When I shared my feelings with my family, they assured me nothing could go wrong. On the day of the wedding, when everything seemed to go wrong, my cousin Amy showed me what it meant to be a good friend.

The problem in this narrative could be something as simple as the narrator spilling ice cream on her dress just before the ceremony or misplacing the basket of flowers she was to carry. Regardless, the real crux of the story is how "Amy" showed her friendship.

Through narrative elements such as dialog and description, as well as pacing that shows an authentic passage of time from one event to the next, a narrative tells a believable, engaging story. While it is important to "show, not tell" in all types of writing, this is particularly relevant in a narrative, as the goal is to bring the reader into the story and to make it seem realistic. Keep in mind that there is such a thing as too much description. Young writers, especially, can get caught up in very detailed descriptions of irrelevant aspects of a story. Your 7th grade writer will work on learning which details are crucial to a narrative, and which details are not.

1. All of the wedding guests were seated and waiting for the ceremony to start. There were a lot of people.

2. A ruby-red carpet ran down the center aisle of the room. Along each side of the carpet, gold fringe fluttered onto the highly polished floor. On each side of the carpet, and just inches from the gold fringe, were twelve rows of white wooden chairs. The chairs were decorated with gold designs on the back, and each had brass hinges that connected the legs and the seats. In each of the seats sat a wedding guest. I overheard a lady say they had to add two more rows of seats. She said, "Every single person who was invited is here. Imagine! There are 240 people out there!"

3. I looked into the room where the ceremony was to take place. On either side of a long, ruby-red carpet were rows of chairs filled with guests. I overheard a lady standing near me say, "Everyone who was invited is here. Imagine! There are 240 people out there!" I gulped. There were 240 guests, and all of them would be looking at me.

In the first example, there is not enough detail to understand the narrator's uneasiness about walking down the aisle as the flower girl in the wedding. The second example offers a tremendous amount of detail, but little of it is relevant to the main point of the narrative, namely that the narrator is nervous about walking out in front of so many people. The third example offers an effective balance of detail and narrative. The point is that there are 240 wedding guests and the narrator will have to walk down the aisle in front of them.

A story is not completely realistic. That is, it doesn't include every single detail in every single moment of a character's life. Instead, it provides a series of scenes. Each of these scenes serves a specific purpose. The story usually begins with the opening scene, which establishes the main character, the setting, and may introduce the problem. Then there are several scenes that build the plot. The main character deals with problems and meets other characters. Strong writers use descriptions that help the reader understand that time is passing during and between these scenes without having to describe every single thing a character does or says.

Consider the following example:

> I looked down at my rose-pink dress and watched the chocolate ice cream bounce and stain its way from the neck to the hem. I was afraid to walk out in front of everyone. My cousin Amy offered to switch dresses with me. I walked out and wasn't embarrassed. She was a good friend.

Obviously this is an exaggerated example, but it demonstrates how missing information can interfere with pacing. The reader has little sense of the time that passes between events. Words and phrases that indicate the passing of time or distance build the reader's anticipation and interest in the story as it develops. Pacing builds tension, which is important for any kind of narrative. Each of the events previously described should be described in detail to give the reader a sense of the time that passes. For example, notice how the following paragraph builds tension in the story:

> Waiting in the dressing room I heard the unmistakable sound of an ice cream truck. No one seemed to be paying attention to me, and I was sure no one would even notice that I was gone. I dashed out the side door and across the plush green lawn up to the street. I jumped up and down, hoping the driver would see me. He did, and when he pulled over I dug in my little satin purse for the money my mother had tucked in there this morning. "A large chocolate cone," I said, feeling very grown up. The driver smiled and said, "Well, don't you look nice, all dressed up." I smiled and held out my hand to take the ice cream. As he drove away I waved before I started back toward the building and my responsibility as a flower girl. Just as I reached the side door, my foot slipped on a loose brick on the sidewalk. I stretched out my

arms to regain my balance, and watched in horror as the chocolate ice cream fell from the cone and onto the front of my rose-pink dress. I felt frozen as I watched one scoop, and then another, bounce on the neck, the waist, and finally the hem of my dress, leaving a trail of chocolate all along the way down.

In this paragraph, the writer has used description, dialogue, and pacing to create a single scene of the narrative. This paragraph creates the problem: the narrator has spilled ice cream on her dress just before she is supposed to walk down the aisle in a wedding party. The reader can picture the girl buying the ice cream, tripping, and watching the ice cream spill. In addition, the writer has slowed down the action, describing how the ice cream slowly moves down the length of the dress.

Transitional Words and Phrases

Just as in argumentative and explanatory writing, transitions are crucial in narrative writing to move the story from one point to the next. Two types of transitions are especially helpful for narrative writing, and they are those used to show the passing of time and those used to show spatial relationships.

COMMON TRANSITION WORDS AND PHRASES	
Type of transition	**Word or phrase**
To show time	soon
	later
	then
	by the time
	eventually
	before/after
	until/since
To show spatial relationships	near, far
	farther, closer
	up, down, right, left
	in front of, behind
	nearby, beside

Whenever a character moves within a setting, writers can help orient the reader by using spatial transitions. Combined with strong descriptive language, transitions can make a scene or story seem much more realistic.

Precise Language and Descriptive Details

Narrative writing also relies on precise language. Precision is developed using very clear and vivid details. It takes practice for a writer to determine what kinds of details are most important to a narrative, and the best way to practice is to describe real scenes or events. Encourage your child to vividly describe events from her own life. For example, suggest she write a few sentences about going to the movies. A less vivid paragraph might look like this:

We paid for our tickets, bought some popcorn, went to the theater and sat down.

While that sentence describes what happened, it is lacking the vivid details that bring the reader into the scene, such as in the following:

There's no mistaking a movie theater. As soon as we pushed through the glass doors we were met by the smell of fresh popcorn and the sound of video games and movie trailers blaring from screens all along the walls. We made our way to the ticket counter, weaving around clusters of teenagers who were waiting for friends or just chatting. At the counter, I said to the clerk, "Two tickets for *Frozen*, please." The woman pressed several buttons on the computer panel in front of her, and with a buzz and a snap, two tickets popped up from a slot in the counter.

The revision adds more detail, pacing transitions, and sound effects to bring the scene to life. The reader can visualize what is happening and what the narrator is doing in the scene. In narrative writing, the best details are sensory details. Sensory details describe sounds, sights, tactile sensations, smells, and tastes. When your child is practicing his narrative writing, help him find opportunities to describe what he's experiencing with his senses and to use vivid language to do so. For example, saying that something tastes "bad" is much less precise than saying something tastes "sour." Describing a sound as "annoying" is less vivid than describing a sound that is like ragged metal scraping across concrete. Continue to help your child make comparisons between experiences to find more and more precise ways to describe those experiences.

Provide a Conclusion

Every good narrative has an ending. The ending ties up the loose plot lines and resolves the conflict. The conclusion of a narrative might also include a moral or a reflection on the event. The writer can share what he learned from the experience, or how he might have done something differently. If there is a lesson or an epiphany, it should be something authentic. Every narrative doesn't have to end with a life-changing observation. Start from the point of view that there is something to learn from almost every experience.

Conducting Research

In the 7th grade your child will complete short research projects to answer a research question. He will learn to access multiple sources to find information. There are several important skills required for effective research:

- Developing a research question
- Choosing relevant sources
- Using sources appropriately

Using outside sources will give your child the experience of learning independently through his own research. He'll develop a research question, or the information he wants to discover, and use multiple sources to answer that question. This is an important critical thinking skill that encourages active learning. Instead of being told what to learn, remember, or focus on, your child will have the opportunity to decide what he most wants to know, and set out in search of that information.

There are several characteristics of a strong research question:

- It is a question that requires research to derive an answer. "What is the capital of California?" is not a good research question. Certainly someone who doesn't know that it is Sacramento might have to look it up, but that doesn't constitute research.

- It is interesting and requires analyzing different sources. Research questions can be based on the study of any subject. For example, "What were the causes of WWII?" is an interesting research question. The writer can learn a lot from conducting research on this question, and there are many sources offering different points of view.
- It is relevant beyond the writer's experience. The question, "Why can't I have a cell phone for my birthday?" is not relevant beyond the writer's life or experience. However, the question, "What is the best age for a person to have her first cell phone?" is relevant and there is likely quite a bit of information available on the topic.
- It asks about a clear and specific concept or idea. For example, the question, "What causes war?" is too broad, while, "What were the causes of WWII?" is specific.

Once a research question is in place, your child can begin locating sources to help him develop his essay.

Assessing the Credibility of Sources

There are several factors to consider when reviewing a source. The first thing to consider is the type of source. Online sources can be credible, but the Internet is full of commercial websites, amateur websites, and blogs, all of which don't necessarily provide reliable information written by experts. The most reliable websites are those that end in *.gov* or *.edu*, but websites ending in *.com* are not necessarily unreliable. Help your child evaluate reliable *.com* websites. Have conversations about the credibility factors such as appearance, timeliness, and the named authors. Most writers would consider websites such as *WebMD.com* or *CNN.com* reliable, as they are named authorities, the content is updated frequently, and there is no obvious bias.

Some websites may appear to be credible, but aren't. For example, *Wikipedia* seems to offer a wide range of information. What some people don't know, however, is that Wikipedia is an open resource, which means that any registered user can edit the content. There is always the possibility that someone has edited a Wikipedia page with inaccurate information just as your child is accessing it for research. Despite the dangers in using Wikipedia as a credible source, it certainly can be a valuable learning tool. At the bottom of most pages is a list of sources, and many of those sources are credible and can be used for research.

To learn about the background of a source, help your child find an About link on the website. This link will usually lead to information about the publishers and writers. You and your child should be able to review the credentials of the writers, which is very important. For example, if your child is doing research on weather systems and has found a website that seems interesting but no scientists are associated with the website, then the credibility might be questionable.

Young researchers sometimes have trouble determining the difference between sponsored links, ads, and actual informative websites. A very important skill you can help your child hone is using search engines critically. Point out the sponsored links that appear at the top of search results and explain how companies pay the search engine for this placement. Also point out the ads or links that appear in the margins, which are also paid links and may not be the best sources for academic research.

Paraphrasing or Quoting from Sources

There are three ways to use information from sources. To start, review the following excerpt from an article called "Causes of WWII" written by Jill Mountain in 2014:

The causes of World War II can be traced back to the end of World War I and the Treaty of Versailles. The Treaty of Versailles included the terms of the end of WWI and held Germany almost exclusively responsible for the war. The main points of the treaty were:

- War Guilt Clause: This part of the treaty asserted that Germany would accept blame for starting the war.
- Reparations: Germany was responsible for paying billions of dollars to repair damage caused by the war.
- Territorial Clause: Parts of Germany were taken away from Germany and assigned to other countries.
- Disarmament: Germany was no longer allowed to have an air force; they were allowed six naval ships. The size of their army was reduced.

These were very harsh consequences, and the people of Germany were not happy. Germany was suffering from a depressed economy. The citizens were poor and there were few jobs. As a result, there was not a lot of revenue, or income from taxes, going to the government. To pay back the tremendous war debt, the government began to print more and more money. To keep up with the debt payments to other countries, Germany was printing money day and night. By 1923, 300 paper mills and 150 different printing companies were working 24 hours a day, seven days a week to print more money. The result was hyperinflation, which means that the money became less and less valuable. An item that cost 1 Mark (the German currency somewhat equivalent to a dollar) in 1914 cost 726 billion Marks in 1923. People who lived on fixed incomes, such as retired people, sold their homes and furniture to get enough money to buy food. People were forced to spend money as soon as they received it because it would be worth even less in just 24 hours.

Sometimes a writer chooses to copy information directly from a source. This is called a quote or quotation from the source. The information copied directly from the source must be inside of a pair of quotation marks and should include a citation. An in-text citation is a short reference that lets the reader know the name of the writer. Here is a quote from the passage:

"By 1923, 300 paper mills and 150 different printing companies were working 24 hours a day, seven days a week . . ." (Mountain, 2014).

Notice that the quoted material didn't use the whole sentence. Instead, the writer used an ellipsis (. . .) to indicate that there is more to the sentence. After the quote, notice that the writer included a parenthetical reference to the original author.

Sometimes, a writer might want to use information from a source but put it in her own words. Review this example:

Paper mills and printing presses ran day and night to produce more money (Mountain, 2014).

The writer put the information about printing money in her own words, but she still cited the original source. It is very important to give credit to the authors who provide information used in academic writing, and it's a good habit that you can help your young writer develop.

Finally, there are times when a writer wants to summarize information from a long source into one or two succinct paragraphs:

> Because the German government didn't have any tax revenue to pay its war debt, it decided to print money. The government printed so much currency that eventually the German Mark was nearly worthless (Mountain, 2014).

The writer has written the summary in his own words and put together the main point of the passage (that Germany suffered from hyperinflation). Note that the source is cited even though the writer has only used the main idea of the paragraph.

Your child's teacher will likely provide more detailed information about how he or she would like to see sources cited.

Avoiding Plagiarism

Plagiarism is a term used to describe using the work of others as your own. When a writer copies the work of another writer from a book, magazine, another paper, or any kind of Internet source without including a citation, it is considered plagiarism. While all students make mistakes when they are learning about academic research and writing, in later grades, plagiarism can lead to consequences such as a zero on the assignment.

ESSENTIAL

There are several free online plagiarism checkers. Encourage your child to check his own work before submitting it to the teacher. Students who are new to using research often struggle with using sources appropriately. Checking your child's work at home will help him see where he has used sources appropriately, and, if he has used them inappropriately, where he should edit his work.

There are some very effective ways to avoid plagiarism:

- **Keep track of sources.** Sometimes when using many different sources, it can be easy to lose track of where information comes from. This can lead to using information without giving a credit to the source. To avoid this, try to have your child read from a source while using a worksheet or document to summarize the information from that source. Your child can use the document as he writes to confirm where the information originated so that it can be properly cited.
- **Encourage your child to keep notes on sources separate from the draft of a paper.** Some student writers keep copied notes within the same document of a paper they are writing. That practice can lead to inadvertently copying information from a source without the proper citation.
- **Have your child paraphrase or put information into his own words whenever possible.** Have him use direct quotes only for specific facts, statistics, or authoritative sources. Otherwise, encourage him to make the information his own.
- **Always use a citation.** Don't worry about over-citing. But if you discover that almost every sentence in your child's essay needs a citation, ask him to think about how to add more original information.

Outside sources can be of great value, but they must be used responsibly. Encourage your child to use research as a tool to make his own ideas more detailed, but not as a substitution for his own ideas.

Being a Collaborative Participant

In the 7th grade your child will be asked to discuss topics with others. Some typical topics will include class readings and specific skills. For example, the teacher might ask your child and others in the class to discuss the character traits of a character in a story. Or your child and the other students may be given a reading assignment and be asked to come to class prepared to share opinions on a writer's main point. Being an effective participant requires preparation, listening, and the ability to respond to and build upon the ideas of others.

Preparing for a discussion requires that your child read any assigned text carefully and annotate it (perhaps using sticky notes). Doing so will help him recall interesting points he can bring up, questions he has, or information related to a question posed by the teacher. Also help your child identify a purpose for reading. Usually the teacher will provide questions or let students know what they will be doing with the text. That information should direct the reading. For example, review the following excerpt:

> These were very harsh consequences, and the people of Germany were not happy. Germany was suffering from a depressed economy. The citizens were poor, and there were few jobs. As a result, there was not a lot of revenue, or income from taxes, going to the government. To pay back the tremendous war debt, the government began to print more and more money. To keep up with the debt payments to other countries, Germany was printing money day and night. By 1923, 300 paper mills and 150 different printing companies were working 24 hours a day, seven days a week to print more money. The result was hyperinflation, which means that the money became less and less valuable. An item that cost 1 Mark (the German currency somewhat equivalent to a dollar) in 1914, cost 726 billion Marks in 1923. People who lived on fixed incomes, such as retired people, sold their homes and furniture to get enough money to buy food. People were forced to spend money as soon as they received it because it would be worth even less in just 24 hours.

If the purpose of reading this text is to determine the conditions endured by citizens of Germany after WWI, your child might develop the following points:

- The citizens were poor and couldn't find work.
- Because of hyperinflation, even if they could find work, the money they earned was nearly worthless.
- Those who couldn't work had to sell their possessions to buy food.

If, however, the purpose of the discussion is to define hyperinflation, your child might identify these points:

- The German government printed so much money that the currency became worthless.
- Something that cost 1 mark in 1914 cost over 700 billion marks in 1923.

Once your child is prepared for a class discussion with an understanding of the topic, he must also be able to listen effectively to others and respond to his classmates. In the 7th grade, class discussions will frequently be student-led and student-centered. Many students get into the habit of waiting for a question, answering a question, and moving on. In a collaborative discussion, students must build upon what others have said and use effective listening skills. These skills can be developed and practiced at home. The following behaviors are important for being a good listener:

- Have your child face the speaker. When another person is speaking, your child should face the speaker directly so as to observe movements and facial expressions.
- Encourage your child to focus on what the speaker is saying, not on how he will respond. Sometimes people listen solely for the opportunity to respond. Help your child get into the habit of waiting for someone else to finish speaking before chiming in. Encourage him to hear the entire message and pause before saying something in return. Waiting ensures the listener doesn't miss important information, and pausing gives the listener time to process information before going on.
- Encourage your child to ask questions. It is okay if a listener doesn't understand everything a speaker says. Sometimes a speaker will invite questions; other times he will pause when he is finished. Instruct your child to ask for clarification or more information before responding.
- Repeat a point the prior speaker has made before adding his or her own information. For example, if one student responds to a question about the causes of hyperinflation by saying, "The German government printed money almost nonstop," the next student might respond by repeating and adding to that statement. "Yes, the German government printed money almost nonstop; in fact, hundreds of paper mills and printing presses operated 24/7 to produce money."

In some instances your child's teacher may assign students to a particular discussion group and give each student a role in the conversation, such as to ask questions, confirm understanding, record main points, and so forth. If your child reports that he is part of such a discussion group, encourage him to practice completing all of the roles so that he can have the full experience of a class or group discussion.

Finally, class discussion is intended to be collegial. When a discussion is collegial, it means that all members of the conversation are responsible for the outcome and for participating. Discussions in your child's classroom have a purpose, and each student is responsible for helping the group achieve that purpose. Encourage your child to be an active participant, but not to overwhelm the conversation. Ask him about others in his discussion group, and if there are students who are quiet or seem shy. Addressing those students is an opportunity for your child to improve the quality of his class discussion experience.

Presenting Claims and Information to Others

In the 7th grade your child will be asked to present information to the class. This will usually be an individual activity. In the 6th grade your child may have presented as part of a group, but now he will be required to work independently.

QUESTION

How much help should I give my child on his presentation?
Especially when presentations require digital media, such as Power-Point, it can be tempting to provide a lot of help in designing a professional presentation. Try to limit your help to technical support and constructive feedback. If you're familiar with this software, show your child its key features, and offer pointers on working with font sizes and contrast. But you should let your child create the content itself.

Class presentations will be based on work your child has already completed and will be the culmination of research or analysis of a text. Everyone struggles when they are speaking "off the cuff" or without preparation. So the most important first step is to be thoroughly prepared. If your child has a class presentation scheduled, encourage her to leave plenty of time to gather information, make speaking notes, and practice.

Encourage your child to practice his presentation in front of you. If you have access to the assignment or grading rubric, try to evaluate him as he practices, and highlight areas for improvement. When speaking in front of a group, your child should pay attention to the following:

- **Volume**—Be sure your child is speaking loud enough to be heard. Encourage your child to keep her chin up and look out toward the audience, even if it is to a wall at the back of the room.
- **Pace**—When a child knows a topic well and has practiced a presentation several times, she may begin to speak very quickly. Encourage her to pace her words at a natural speaking rate, pausing before and after important ideas.
- **No reading**—While using index cards or notes is a good way to remember important ideas, encourage your child to try to memorize what she intends to say. Reading in front of a group is very different than simply speaking.
- **Body language**—Help your child relax enough while speaking so that she uses natural gestures and movements. Standing stiffly behind a podium, or waving his arms in an exaggerated way, can detract from his ideas.

Your child may be required to use visuals in his presentation. The most common presentation platform is PowerPoint, which is part of the Microsoft suite of software products. If your child is required to use PowerPoint, it is likely he has had some instruction for using it. Children find PowerPoint to be a lot of fun. They can insert transitions, sound effects, and use different kinds of images within the slide show. Help your child create visuals that are an effective complement to his presentation:

- **Limit text**—Remind your child that the audience will be listening to her. The words on a PowerPoint slide should cover just main points that she will elaborate on. Limit each slide to three or four lines of text with no more than five to seven words.
- **Transitions**—There are a lot of options for transitions, but some can slow down a presentation. If using a software like PowerPoint, encourage your child to use one or two "wow" transitions, and stick with quick movements from one slide to the next for the majority of the presentation.
- **Text size and color**—Be sure that the text can be read several feet away and that there is contrast between the text color and the background. Avoid fonts like script that can be difficult to read.

- **Images**—Usually there should be no more than one image to a presentation slide and it should be directly related to what the speaker is saying while it is on the screen.
- **Cite sources**—depending on your child's teacher's directions, your child may have to include a reference page for her presentation. This can usually be accomplished by citing sources on a final slide in the deck, or by providing the teacher with a paper reference page on the day of the presentation. Be sure your child is keeping track of her sources as she researches and writes her presentation.

Encourage your child to practice her presentation while using the actual slide show so that she has a good sense of when to change slides and what information to stress on each slide.

When your child is working on a presentation with a group, it is likely he will have a specific role in the process, or will be assigned a specific component of the presentation to complete. While group work can be challenging you can support your child by asking questions about the different roles each student has, what your child's role is, and offering opportunities for your child to work with her group outside of school if necessary.

Practice Exercises

These exercises will help your child practice the skills that have been outlined in this chapter. The questions are similar to those he will likely encounter on standardized tests.

Transitions

For each of the following sentence pairs, choose the transition that would best link them.

1. The annual St. Patrick's Day parade should be moved to the Sunday before St. Patrick's Day. Many families have complained that children's sports schedules make it difficult to attend on a Saturday.
   a. Since
   b. In particular
   c. Such as

2. Many local groups participate in the annual parade. The Boy Scouts, Girl Scouts, and local dance teams all march every year.
   a. In view of
   b. Because
   c. For example
3. The parade was moved from Sunday to Saturday back in 1993. Many families complained that the parade conflicted with religious services.
   a. Likewise
   b. To illustrate
   c. Because
4. It could be possible to meet the needs of families who have commitments to sports on Saturdays and those who attend religious services on Sundays. The parade could be moved to a later time on either day.
   a. In view of
   b. In particular
   c. To illustrate
5. Many communities have found a way to maintain the weekend parade and include most of the community. Sunnyvale, Seabrook, and Portland all have evening parades on the Saturday before St. Patrick's Day.
   a. Such as
   b. Due to the fact
   c. In particular

Formal versus Informal Language

Rewrite the following in formal English.

1. I thought I should write you an e-mail cuz I can't figure out this homework and need your help.
2. The homework I mean is the one you said shouldn't take more than half an hour.
3. You were wrong! I've been working more than a hour and it's still too tough for me.
4. Get back to me. Give me hints. Give me a hand!
5. Okay, thanks, bye.

CHAPTER 10

Grade 7—Language

In the 7th grade your child will begin to learn the more complex nuances of language, including phrases, clauses, and different types of sentences. These new skills are introduced on the foundation of prior years' instruction. For example, students entering the 7th grade should have an understanding of the components of complete sentences, which is crucial to understanding the difference between a phrase and a clause. As with language study in all of the preceding grades in the Common Core, the purpose of teaching these different aspects of language is so that students can become competent and confident communicators.

What Your Seventh Grader Will Learn

As in grade 6, the language standard uses categories that focus on words, sentences, and vocabulary. There are four categories of study in the Language standard:

- Conventions of grammar
- Knowledge of compound, complex, and compound-complex sentences
- Vocabulary acquisition
- Using and understanding figurative language

The grammar section focuses on phrases and clauses, how to use them to create varied sentence structures, and how to identify and correct usage errors. The focus is on writing clear, informative sentences, as the purpose of the Language strand is to facilitate academic communication skills.

Your child will learn to explain the function of phrases and clauses, independent of specific writing tasks. When she has mastered that understanding, she will be tasked with developing compound, complex, and compound-complex sentences using both phrases and clauses correctly. Your seventh grader will also learn about punctuation this year, with a specific focus on using commas to separate a series of adjectives, and learning the correct order that adjectives should appear.

Word Focus

Your seventh grader will learn about the importance of precision in writing. The focus is on choosing precise vocabulary, recognizing and correcting overly wordy writing, and avoiding redundancy. These skills are assessed when students are asked to review texts that are not written with precision. Students' own writing will also be evaluated for precision.

Vocabulary skills are a continued focus in the 7th grade. As in prior grades, your child will learn to use context to determine the meaning of a word, and the relationship between a word's function and its possible meaning. Additional Latin and Greek affixes are introduced, which provide students with new ways for understanding unfamiliar words. As in prior grades, your seventh grader will learn to make use of reference materials to understand definitions and pronunciations of unfamiliar words.

Students begin to explore some of the more complicated nuances of language in the 7th grade. For example, they learn that authors often make allusions to other texts or events that they assume are part of readers' general knowledge. Your seventh grader will practice identifying and understanding allusions to biblical stories, mythology, and well-known literary texts.

Finally, students pursue precision in vocabulary by considering nuances of meaning and connotations of words. That is, he will learn that the meaning of a word can sometimes go beyond the dictionary definition because of the context of the sentence and the writer's intent.

Conventions of Grammar

Your seventh grader's grammar study will focus on the use of phrases and clauses. Phrases and clauses are strings of words, and both can include nouns, pronouns, verbs, adjectives, and adverbs. A clause includes a subject and a verb, whereas a phrase may include nouns and verbs, but not a subject-verb relationship. This section will explain these two types of word groupings and provide examples so that you can help your child understand the differences between them.

Phrases

A phrase is a group of words that does not include a subject-verb combination. It cannot be a sentence on its own in any situation. A phrase is used to modify or add information to another part of a sentence. The following is an example of a phrase:

beside the fast-moving river

This group of words does not have a subject (a noun) that performs an action. A subject and verb can be added to a clause to create a complete sentence:

The tree grew beside the fast-moving river.

In this sentence, *tree* is the subject. The verb, or action the tree performs, is *grew*. The phrase modifies, or provides, more information about the verb.

One can ask, "Where did the tree grow?" and the answer is the phrase (in this case a prepositional phrase), "beside the fast-moving river."

There are several different types of phrases:

Noun Phrases

A noun phrase includes one or more nouns and related words, such as adjectives or other modifiers. A noun phrase functions like a noun and can be the subject of a sentence. This is an example of a noun phrase:

the fluffy brown bunny

In this phrase, the noun, *bunny*, is modified by two adjectives, *fluffy* and *brown*. In the next example, the noun phrase functions as the subject of the sentence:

The fluffy brown bunny hopped over the fence.

The phrase, *the fluffy brown bunny*, is the subject and performs an action (a verb), *hopped*.

Prepositional Phrases

A prepositional phrase begins with a preposition and ends with the object of that preposition, which is a noun, along with any words that modify the noun.

FACT

Prepositions describe relationships between other words in a sentence. There are hundreds of prepositions, but some of the most common include the following: *about, above, below, after, before, in, inside, outside, for, from, of, into, onto, to, with, within,* and *without.* In this sentence, "Put your shoes in the hall closet," the preposition is *in*, and the object of the preposition is *closet*.

for her first birthday

In this example, the preposition is *for*, and the object is *birthday*. The words *her* and *first* modify, or provide more information about the noun, *birthday*. In the following sentence, the prepositional phrase is added to a clause to create a complete sentence.

Lara received a puppy for her first birthday.

Adjective Phrases

An adjective phrase modifies, or provides more information about, a noun. An adjective phrase includes one or more adjectives and any words needed to connect or intensify those adjectives.

new bright blue

This phrase includes three adjectives, but not the noun they modify. In the sentence that follows, the phrase is included in a clause, which then makes a complete sentence. The adjective phrase modifies the noun, *bicycle*.

Chelsea has a new bright blue bicycle.

Verb Phrases

A verb phrase includes a main verb and its helping verbs, which are also called auxiliary verbs.

FACT

Auxiliary or helping verbs provide more information with an action verb. They can indicate time or condition. The helping verbs are forms of the verbs *to be*, *to do*, and *to have*. An example of a sentence using a helping verb is: She is walking to school. The main verb is *walking* and the helping verb is *is*.

The phrase that follows is a verb phrase where the main verb is *dancing*.

were dancing

In the following sentence, the verb phrase shows the action of the noun, *children*.

The children were dancing.

Infinitive Phrases

The infinitive of a verb is the basic form, preceded by *to*. For example, *to run* is the infinitive of the verb *run*. Infinitive phrases always consist of *to* + basic verb form.

> to sing
> to eat
> to dance

An infinitive phrase acts like an adjective, an adverb, or a noun in a sentence.

He forgot *to tie his shoes*.

She wants *to read* a book.

Participle Phrases

Participle phrases consist of the present participle of a verb (the base form of the verb + *ing*) or the past tense of a verb, along with any modifiers. A participle phrase always acts like an adjective, providing more information about a noun, and it is separated from the rest of a sentence with commas. Examples of the two forms of participle phrases are:

baking a cake

injured in the last game

In the sentence that follows, the participle phrases are set off by commas.

Baking a cake, Dad was busy in the kitchen.

In this example, the participle phrase, *baking a cake*, acts like an adjective that modifies, or provides more information about, Dad.

Kim, injured in the last game, could not play in the tournament.

In this example, the participle phrase, *injured in the last game*, acts like an adjective that modifies, or provides more information about, Kim.

Clauses

A clause is a group of words that contains a subject (a noun) and a verb. Some clauses can function as a simple sentence. These are called **independent** clauses. Other clauses include words that make them **dependent** on other information in a sentence in order to be a complete sentence.

Independent Clauses

When an independent clause stands alone, without a dependent clause or another independent clause, it is referred to as a simple sentence. These are examples of independent clauses:

The puppy yelped.
Jimmy laughed.

Writers can combine independent clauses to make **compound sentences**.

The puppy yelped, and Jimmy laughed.

Notice that the conjunction *and* is used to tie these two independent clauses together. Notice also that a comma is placed after the first independent clause and before the conjunction.

Dependent Clauses

A dependent clause cannot stand on its own as a sentence and make sense. A dependent clause must be combined with an independent clause in order to make sense. There are several types of dependent clauses, each of which performs a different role in a sentence. A dependent clause begins with either a **subordinate conjunction** or a **relative pronoun**.

SUBORDINATE CONJUNCTIONS		
after	although	as
before	even if	if
once	since	than

that	though	unless
when	whenever	where
whether	while	why
RELATIVE PRONOUNS		
that	who	whose
which	whoever	whomever
whom		

A dependent clause is an incomplete thought. It leaves the reader wondering, "Then what happened?" Here are some examples of dependent clauses:

because he was late for school
whose house is on the corner
though she knew she had studied

Each of these dependent clauses can be combined with an independent clause to create a **complex sentence**.

Sam missed art class *because he was late for school.*
Mrs. Johnson, *whose house is on the corner,* works at the bank.
Though she had studied, Faith was nervous about her math test.

Compound, Complex, and Compound-Complex Sentences

In the 7th grade your student will use his knowledge of phrases and clauses to construct three different kinds of sentences, with the goal of showing relationships between ideas. The three kinds of sentences are:

- Compound sentences
- Complex sentences
- Compound-complex sentences

A compound sentence combines two independent clauses using a coordinating conjunction. Many students use the mnemonic device FANBOYS to remember the seven coordinating conjunctions:

COORDINATING CONJUNCTIONS	
F	for
A	and
N	nor
B	but
O	or
Y	yet
S	so

When using a coordinating conjunction to combine two independent clauses into a single compound sentence, a comma is placed before the conjunction:

We bought tickets, and we were first in line for the movie.
Martin says he doesn't like sports, but he plays baseball, football, and soccer.
Dan doesn't play a musical instrument, nor does he sing in the chorus.

ESSENTIAL

Misplaced and Dangling Modifiers: Phrases and clauses are used to provide additional information in a sentence. Sometimes, however, phrases and clauses intended to modify nouns or verbs in a sentence are misplaced or left dangling or unconnected to the words they modify.

A complex sentence consists of at least one independent clause and two or more dependent clauses. Here is an independent clause:

Zach won the first-place trophy.

Here is a dependent clause:

Because he finished the race before all the other runners . . .

Combined, they create a complex sentence:

Because he finished the race before all the other runners, Zach won the first place trophy.

Zach won the first place trophy because he finished the race before all the other runners.

Notice that the dependent clause can be placed before or after the independent clause, depending on the context of the sentence. If it comes before, it must be followed by a comma.

A compound-complex sentence consists of a compound sentence and a complex sentence. In other words, a compound-complex sentence consists of the following:

- Two or more independent clauses
- One or more dependent clauses

Here is an example:

Because she woke up late, Kate missed her first period class, but she met with the teacher after school to go over the lesson.

In the previous sentence, there are two independent clauses:

- Kate missed her first period class.
- She met with her teacher after school to go over the lesson.

There is one dependent clause:

- Because she woke up late

There is also one coordinating conjunction (but), which is used to combine the two independent clauses.

Misplaced Modifier

A misplaced modifier is separated from the word it modifies in a way that interferes with meaning. The reader can't tell what is supposed to be modified, and as a result the sentence is awkward or doesn't make sense at all.

Frustrated that she couldn't answer all of the questions, because the test seemed very hard, Faith wished she had studied more.

Here, this sentence makes it seem as if the test is what is frustrated. Since a test would not feel frustrated, it appears that this modifier is not placed correctly in the sentence. It is more likely that Faith feels frustrated. A clearer version of this sentence might be:

Frustrated that she couldn't answer all of the questions, Faith wished she had studied more because the test seemed very hard.

The solution to a misplaced modifier error is to rearrange or revise the sentence. Most times a complete rewrite is required to establish the relationships between ideas. Unfortunately, misplaced modifier errors frequently find their way into advertising and media. In 1984 the Kellogg Company used information from a then-recent study on the effects of high fiber diets on reducing some kinds of cancer to create the following ad copy:

At last some news about cancer you can live with.

In this statement the clause "you can live with" is placed immediately after the noun *cancer*, suggesting that it is a cancer you can live with. What the advertiser likely meant was that people could live with the news, or that the news was not unpleasant since the news was that consumers could have a high fiber/low-fat diet with one of Kellogg's popular cereals. A reasonable revision of this sentence might be:

At last some news you can live with about cancer.

Dangling Modifiers

When a modifying clause or phrase doesn't have a target, or if the noun or verb it modifies is not clearly indicated in the sentence, there is a dangling modifier error.

After studying for three hours straight, the math problems finally made sense.

This sentence says that the math did the studying. Obviously, that doesn't make sense. The target or noun that is being modified is missing from this sentence. An appropriate revision would be this:

After studying for three hours straight, the student discovered that the math problems finally made sense.

Sometimes dangling modifiers, if taken literally, can conjure humorous images.

Lounging on the beach, the sun shone brightly.

In this sentence, it seems that the sun is lounging on the beach. Of course, that isn't the case. A reasonable revision would be:

Lounging on the beach, Marcia enjoyed the warmth of the sun, which shone brightly.

Using Commas

Coordinate adjectives are adjectives that appear in a series and modify the same noun.

My pretty, new, blue sweater is the same color as my eyes.

In this sentence, the three words *pretty*, *new*, and *blue* all describe the sweater. A comma between each tells the reader that they should be applied to the noun. Without the commas, a reader could misunderstand how the modifiers are to be understood. For example, one could read that it is a "new blue" sweater, meaning that the sweater features a new shade of blue.

FACT

Most native English speakers use adjectives in a specific order without realizing they're doing so. To them, it just "sounds right." There is a specific order that adjectives should be used in a sentence. That order is: opinion, size, shape, condition, age, color, national origin, material, and purpose.

Vocabulary Acquisition

In the 7th grade, students use context clues to determine the meanings of unfamiliar words. As they did in the 6th grade, they use their knowledge of Greek and Latin affixes and root words to understand unfamiliar words. Finally, they use reference materials to confirm their understanding of unfamiliar words.

Using Context Clues

In the 6th grade your child learned how to determine the meaning of an unfamiliar word using these four types of context clues, which usually appear within the same sentence as the unfamiliar word:

- Synonyms
- Antonyms
- Examples
- Explanations

In the 7th grade, your child will consider an entire sentence, paragraph, or even longer text to determine the meaning of an unfamiliar word. The strategies learned in the 6th grade will still be applied, but your child will be prepared to consider several pieces of evidence before deciding on the meaning of a word.

For example, review the following passage and notice that the word *rapscallion* is underlined. Rapscallion is the unfamiliar word that will need to be defined.

Tim's friends George and Ryan didn't mean to hurt anyone, but they couldn't help playing pranks on their teachers and parents. When the boys broke a neighbor's window, Tim's mom decided that he was not allowed to hang around with the two rapscallions anymore.

The reader needs to consider more than one sentence before determining the meaning of the underlined word. Reading just the sentence containing the word would suggest that rapscallion means vandal or troublemaker. The meaning, however, is more nuanced. A rapscallion is a mischievous person, a meaning that is only determined by including the information in both sentences.

Here is another example:

Despite his claims that he didn't really care about movie stars, when he met the famous actress, Mike was <u>besotted</u>. He stammered a bit and couldn't keep his eyes off hers. In the following weeks, he watched and rewatched all of her movies and tried to imagine a scenario when he might meet her again and ask her on a date.

In this passage, the sentence that includes the unfamiliar word doesn't provide much context. The reader can determine that Mike's feelings were the opposite of being disinterested, but the extent of his interest isn't established. If a reader stopped with the first sentence, the true meaning of the word would not be realized. It takes the next two sentences, which describe Mike's behavior during and after the meeting, to realize that Mike was infatuated with the actress.

It would seem that transitioning from one sentence to a paragraph or passage to determine meaning would be a logical next step. However, your child may find it challenging to piece together clues from multiple sentences to develop a single definition. Encourage close and active reading. Your child should ask herself what the word means at several points in the reading, and develop the confidence to change her answer when new evidence emerges. You might model this approach by thinking out loud while you read a text with her.

Greek and Latin Affixes

As in the 6th grade, in the 7th grade your child will learn the meanings of common Greek and Latin word parts and apply that knowledge to determining the meaning of unfamiliar words. There are hundreds of affixes from both Greek and Latin. Some of the most common studied in grade 7 include:

COMMON GREEK AND LATIN AFFIXES		
Affix	**Meaning**	**Example**
com-	together	community
ex- or exo-	out or outside of	exit
pro-	forward	progress
retro-	back, backward	retrospective
amo-	love	amiable

aqua-	water	aquarium
inter-	between	interrupt
magnus	big	magnify
scio	know	science
trans-	across	transportation
verbum	word(s)	verbalize

In the following sentence, the unfamiliar word is underlined:

The spies conspired to steal the secret government plans.

The reader can use his knowledge of the affix *con* to determine that the spies likely worked together, which, with the rest of the sentence is enough information to determine a meaning for *conspire*: make secret plans to commit an unlawful act.

Here is another example:

When Earth passes Mars in orbit about the sun, Mars appears to be in retrograde motion, although that is not the case.

This sentence does not offer much context other than the situation of two planets orbiting the earth, and that there is a contrast between the appearance of retrograde, and what is actually happening. Knowledge of the affix *retro*, which means backward, helps the reader understand that retrograde motion means backward motion, and that although Mars may appear to move backward at some point in Earth's orbit, that is not the case.

Consulting Reference Materials

There are times when context clues and word roots aren't enough to get a precise definition. In those situations, your child should be familiar with and confident about using different reference materials. Using a glossary in a textbook, an online reference, or a traditional dictionary are all strategies that can help a reader confirm the meaning of an unfamiliar word. In the 7th grade your student will practice selecting the best definition of an unfamiliar term based on the context of a sentence in which the word appears. For example, a student might want to confirm the definition of *retrograde* as it is used in the following sentence:

When Earth passes Mars in orbit about the sun, Mars appears to be in <u>retrograde</u> motion, although that is not the case.

The dictionary offers the following definitions:

1. (adjective): having motion that is contrary to that of similar bodies, especially the appearance of east-west motion among the stars
2. (adjective): moving or flowing backward
3. (adjective): being contrary to what is the normal order of occurrence

Since the sentence specifically mentions Earth and Mars, the reader can assume that the first definition is the most precise. This definition confirms what the reader has determined using affixes and context in the sentence. Help your seventh grader learn to use these resources with purpose and focus. Reading a list of definitions really doesn't help comprehension. Beginning with the goal of determining which definition best fits specific context builds comprehension and confidence.

Using and Understanding Figurative Language

In the 7th grade students focus on learning how to decode and understand allusions in literary and informational texts. Two common types of allusions your child will encounter include Biblical and Mythological.

Biblical Allusions

It isn't necessary that your child have an exhaustive knowledge of the Bible in order to understand common biblical allusions. Most are centered on well-known stories or quotes that have made their way into literature and popular culture.

Creation

There are a few common allusions to the creation described in the Old Testament. Most will seem familiar to parents, and none require a belief in a specific religion. Your child should have some familiarity with the Old Testament story of creation, and specifically with a couple of key quotations:

"And God said, 'Let there be light;' and there was light; and it was good" (Genesis 1:3).

This allusion refers to the creation of the sun, and the beginning of all things.

"And on the seventh day God finished the work that he had done . . ." (Genesis 2:2).

This allusion refers to the length of time it took for God of the Old Testament to create Earth and all the creatures on Earth. Writers sometimes use this to point out that a job is not so great that it can't be accomplished, since the creation of all things took just a single week.

Garden of Eden

Many poets and writers refer to pleasant natural settings with an allusion to Eden. Eden was described as a perfect garden where all plants thrived and all creatures lived in harmony. There was no pain, no struggle, and no shame among those who lived there. Adam and Eve were the first people on Earth. Eve was created from one of Adam's ribs to provide him with companionship. The couple lived pleasantly in the Garden of Eden until the devil, in the form of a snake, convinced the woman, Eve, to eat fruit from the tree of knowledge, which had been forbidden them. God learned of their disobedience and expelled them from the garden. This expulsion is referred to as "The Fall." Students should be familiar with the names Adam and Eve, the image of the serpent as a devil, the forbidden fruit, and the expulsion (The Fall).

Fallen Angels

Fallen angels are cast out of heaven and fall to Earth for crimes of ambition, disobedience, and pride. Lucifer was a fallen angel. Over time, the term *fallen angel* has been conflated with devil, and Lucifer is often a reference to someone who is selfish, ruthless, and not trustworthy.

Cain and Abel

Cain and Abel were the sons of Adam and Eve. Cain was the first human born on Earth and he committed the first murder. Cain murdered his brother, Abel. While the Bible doesn't indicate Cain's motive for killing Abel, some scholars say Cain was jealous that God seemed to favor Abel.

Noah's Ark

God pronounced that it will rain for "forty days and forty nights" and that all living things will be destroyed by flood waters. Noah was chosen to create an ark, or large boat, on which he must preserve a male and female of every species. This is how the earth will be repopulated when the rains end and the flood recedes.

Moses and the Exodus

As a baby, Moses, a Hebrew, was abandoned on a river bank. He was discovered there by the daughter of an Egyptian Pharaoh. The Pharaoh's daughter raised Moses as her own child. During this time the Egyptians had enslaved the Hebrew Israelites. One day God appeared to Moses in the form of a bush that was on fire, but didn't burn away, the "burning bush." He instructed Moses to bring the Israelites out of Egypt and to free them from their slavery. At first the Pharaoh refused to release the Israelites, so God punished him with what are called the ten plagues. The ten plagues were:

- The water of the Nile river changes into blood
- An infestation of frogs
- An infestation of lice
- Swarms of flies
- Diseases that kill the livestock
- Boils, or skin diseases
- Hail, fire, and thunderstorms
- Locusts (small flying insects that destroy crops)
- Darkness of three days with no sunlight
- Death of the firstborn children of all Egyptians

After the tenth plague Moses led the Israelites into the desert, where they wandered, homeless for forty years. During that time, Moses met with God on the summit of Mount Sinai. There, Moses received the Ten Commandments, which were a set of laws by which the people were to live.

David and Goliath

David, the future king of Israel, was challenged by Goliath. The biblical battle intended to show that the smaller warrior, David, was chosen by God, and thus was able to defeat a much bigger and stronger warrior, Goliath. The reference is not as closely aligned to the Bible as it once was, and now refers to any competition in which a smaller, weaker competitor overcomes a bigger, stronger enemy. Goliath has also become an allusion, used to refer to anything that is very large.

King Solomon

A reference to King Solomon is used to highlight wisdom. In the biblical story, two women go before the king with a single child. Both women claim to be the mother of the child. The king resolves that he will split the child in half and give one half to each woman. One of the women agrees to the proposal, while the other relents and says that her adversary can have custody of the child. The king awards the child to the woman who relents, noting that the true mother of the child would never agree to see it murdered.

Job

Job was a religious and honorable man who was very successful. Satan suggested to God that Job was only religious because God protected him from failure and heartache. To prove that Job was actually faithful, God allowed Satan to put Job through a series of terrible losses. Job's family died, he lost his money and property, and his own health declined drastically. Despite his bad fortune, Job remained faithful, and God eventually restored what he had lost. Common expressions that allude to Job include, "He has the patience of Job," or "She has endured the troubles of Job." Both are allusions to someone who is facing great hardship and sadness but remains true to his or her beliefs.

Judas

Judas was a good friend of Jesus Christ. He betrayed Jesus to the Hebrew council or Sanhedrin and collected a bounty or reward. As a result of Judas's betrayal, Jesus was crucified. The name Judas is an allusion to a good friend who turns out to be disloyal.

Apocalypse

The Apocalypse refers to the end of the world described in the last book of the Bible, Revelation. Modern references to an apocalypse are usually not religious, and instead may refer to the results of a large scale war, global warming, and the like.

Mythological Allusions

While Greek and Roman mythologies involve hundreds of characters and stories, there are a few that are used most frequently used in allusions. It will benefit your seventh grader to be familiar with these characters and stories.

Prometheus

Prometheus created mankind in the image of gods like himself. Prometheus rode his chariot to the sun to catch some fire on the end of the torch. He then presented the torch to mankind, giving them the power of fire, which he effectively stole from the sun. Zeus, who was the leader of all the gods, punished Prometheus by chaining him to a rock, where every day a vulture would eat his liver. Every night Prometheus's liver would grow back and every day the vulture attacked again.

Medusa

Medusa was a Gorgon. The Gorgons were a race of women whose hair was made of live snakes. Looking at Medusa's face could turn a man to stone.

Jason and the Argonauts

Jason's father, the king, lost his throne to his brother. The brother, Jason's uncle, agreed to return the throne to Jason if Jason brings him a Golden Fleece. Jason assembled a team, the Argonauts, and set out on a journey to find and retrieve the fleece. Jason and the Argonauts adventured through a long quest, experienced many dangers and exploits, until he finally returned with the fleece and took back the throne. This story is often used as an allusion to a long quest or to someone who overcomes many challenges to reach a goal.

Hercules

Hercules has become a symbol of great strength. In mythology he was the son of the king of the gods, Zeus. Hercules was the strongest mortal on earth. Zeus's wife was the goddess Hera. To destroy Hercules, Hera devised a series of twelve labors or trials, which included destroying terrible creatures, cleaning a giant stable, and capturing a three-headed dog. An allusion to Hercules is usually intended to make a comment about strength or perseverance, or about the size of a person.

Theseus

Theseus was sent into a large maze that was guarded by a fierce creature called a Minotaur (a creature with the head of a bull and the body of a man). No man before him had managed to escape alive, as the dual challenges of navigating the maze and killing the monster could not be overcome. Theseus was very smart. As he traveled through the maze he left behind a trail of thread. He killed the Minotaur and followed the thread to get out again.

Icarus

Icarus was the son of Daedalus. King Minos was angry with Daedalus and locked him and his son in a tower. Daedalus made wings for himself and his son Icarus so that they could safely escape. When it seemed their plan was working, and they were safely airborne and on their way to safety, Icarus, despite his father's warnings, flew too close to the sun. The wax holding the wings together melted and Icarus fell from the sky. The phrase "fly too close to the sun" is a common phrase used to refer to a foolhardy act inspired by curiosity or even bravery.

Trojan Horse

The Trojan War occurred between the Greeks and the Trojans, and began because of the most beautiful woman on earth, Helen of Troy. Helen was stolen from a Greek king and taken to Troy by Priam, the King of Troy. The Greeks surrounded the city of Troy and would not let anyone in or out for ten years. Finally the Greeks built a giant wooden horse, which they parked at the gates of the city. They gave the Trojans the impression that the horse was a gift, and then pretended to sail away. When they thought the Greeks had left, the Trojans took the horse into their city. The side of the horse opened and an army of Greeks came out and conquered Troy. The term *Trojan horse* is often an allusion to something that may seem like a gift at first but is actually a threat to one's safety or success.

Odysseus (Ulysses)

Odysseus fought in the Trojan War. After spending a decade at war, he wanted to go home to Ithaca to see his wife, Penelope, who was waiting for him. His journey home took another ten years, during which he overcame several challenges, including defeating a man-eating cyclops (creature with one eye), and avoiding the songs of the sirens (women who lured ships into rocks where they crashed, killing the sailors). Allusions refer to the siren songs, to Penelope's perseverance waiting for her husband, and, of course, to Odysseus, who refused to give up and eventually made it home.

Helping Your Child Succeed

Your seventh grader is probably not keen to have you read to him every night before bed. However, reading together and talking about language should be a part of your daily routine. Show interest in what your child has been assigned to read for school, and ask questions that give him an opportunity to share what he knows. When you hear an allusion or encounter one in a movie or television program, point it out and discuss what the writer is referring to. If necessary, do a bit of impromptu research on a smartphone or tablet while you're watching. Once your child learns the meaning of an allusion, she'll have that knowledge for a long time, and more texts will become accessible.

When reviewing your child's writing, pay attention to how she constructs sentences. Suggest and encourage revisions that make use of compound or complex sentences, and point out confusing sentences with misplaced or dangling modifiers. If (when) you hear misplaced modifier errors on television, point them out. No one is a fan of the grammar police, of course, but it can be fun to talk about how a script could have been revised, or even to discuss the role of editors in writing texts and scripts.

Practice Exercises

These exercises will help your child practice the skills in the Language standard. The questions are similar to those your child might encounter on a standardized test.

Identifying Phrases

Identify whether the italicized text is a noun phrase, a verb phrase, or a prepositional phrase.

1. The *old red car* has been parked on the street for a week.
   a. Noun phrase

b. Verb phrase

c. Prepositional phrase

2. The plane *soared silently through the blue sky.*

   a. Noun phrase

   b. Verb phrase

   c. Prepositional phrase

3. Please place your books *under your desks* until the test is over.

   a. Noun phrase

   b. Verb phrase

   c. Prepositional phrase

4. The Pilgrims *landed unexpectedly* at Plymouth Rock.

   a. Noun phrase

   b. Verb phrase

   c. Prepositional phrase

Independent and Dependent Clauses

Determine if each of the following is an independent or dependent clause.

1. Although many people are afraid of large dogs

2. Because they can appear to be vicious

3. I prefer a large dog to a smaller one

4. Because they have more stamina

5. Larger dogs make good companions for hiking

6. Also, larger dogs tend to live longer than smaller dogs

7. Delaying the grief of losing a beloved pet

8. When choosing a pet

9. It is important to consider the needs of the entire family

10. So that everyone will be comfortable with the new addition to the family

Compound and Complex Sentences

Determine if each of the following is a compound or complex sentence.

1. Although Frank Lloyd Wright became one of the most celebrated architects of his time, his contemporaries did not always take his work seriously.

   a. Compound

   b. Complex

2. Wright began his career in Chicago, and eventually worked on projects in Tokyo and New York.
   a. Compound
   b. Complex
3. Before his death, Wright completed designs for the Guggenheim museum in New York.
   a. Compound
   b. Complex
4. Frank Lloyd Wright was married, and he had six children.
   a. Compound
   b. Complex
5. Even though Wright died decades ago, people still flock to see his buildings.
   a. Compound
   b. Complex
6. Wright studied engineering at the University of Wisconsin, and he met his future mentor when he interned for him during college.
   a. Compound
   b. Complex
7. After he left college, Wright moved to Chicago.
   a. Compound
   b. Complex
8. Wright had a good job immediately out of college, but he continued to look for new opportunities.
   a. Compound
   b. Complex
9. After his career declined, Wright moved to Germany in 1911.
   a. Compound
   b. Complex
10. Before returning to the United States, he published a book of architectural drawings.
    a. Compound
    b. Complex

CHAPTER 11

Grade 8—Reading

Eighth grade reading instruction focuses on analysis, inferring meaning, and making connections between ideas. Your child will read with a critical eye and pay close attention to the author's deliberate choices. In the 8th grade your child will read more informational texts than literary texts. By the end of 8th grade the Common Core standards suggest that at least 55 percent of student reading be nonfiction reading for information. In other words, more than half of what your 8th grade child reads in school will be informational. Even some of the novels or longer literary texts will be based on actual events or facts, and provide students with opportunities to read supporting nonfiction information. You will probably notice that your child's teacher will pair a literary and informational text that share a general topic. When your child takes your state's standardized tests, he should expect to encounter more informational texts than literary, and pairing of texts for analysis.

What Your Eighth Grader Will Learn

There are two sets of reading standards for grades K–12. The Reading Literature (RL) standards provide guidance for reading literature. The Reading Information Text (RI) standards provide guidance for reading information texts. In the 8th grade your child will learn to pay close attention to how a text is constructed. That is, how the author has put together details, facts, and evidence to make a specific point.

FACT

Paired texts are two texts that consider the same subject in different ways. For example, on a test, your child might be asked to read an encyclopedia entry about Paul Revere's ride and read Longfellow's poem on the same topic. The questions that follow will consider facts from both texts as well as how the authors presented the information.

You will likely notice much more emphasis on identifying very specific aspects of what some teachers refer to as "writer's craft." Writer's craft considers the ideas of a text, how it is organized, the writer's voice, the word choice, the mood, and the purpose of the text.

One of the most frequently used words in the reading standards is *complexity*. Common Core standards not only encourage, but require students to tackle complex texts, including some that are more advanced than their current reading levels. Your child's teacher will provide her opportunities to wrestle with difficult texts independently, and will provide whole-class instruction that builds skills and strategies for close reading. Recall that your child will have developed key close reading skills in the 6th and 7th grades (see Chapter 5 and Chapter 8).

In the past, reading instruction focused on fluency. If a student could read words on a page without mispronouncing most of them, and understood how punctuation worked, she was considered a fluent reader. Those decoding skills are still important, but it is not enough for students to have just the ability to read. Understanding the main idea of a text is not enough. To be fully prepared for high school, college, and career, your eighth grader should be able to explain why a text is successful or unsuccessful in making specific points, and how the ideas in a text work together.

ESSENTIAL

There are many benefits to reading informational texts. These benefits include vocabulary development, exposure to complex and abstract ideas, and, of course, acquisition of knowledge. Encourage your child to read high-interest nonfiction texts. Beyond what your child will encounter in school, there are plenty of books and magazines dedicated to sports, video games, and other hobbies. Consider an outing to a library or local bookstore, or even browsing an online bookstore, to discover new and interesting nonfiction works. Reading informational texts is a great way to encourage your child to read and to more effectively pursue an existing interest.

Reading Literature

In the 8th grade your child will read examples of literature from many different genres. She will read prose, poetry, and drama. An important focus will be on analysis. The topics covered in the Reading Literature (RL) standard include:

- Using text evidence to support analysis
- Determining a theme or central idea and how it evolves over the course of a text through the development of characters, setting, and plot
- Writing an objective summary of a text
- Understanding how dialogue or episodes in a story reveal information about the story and its characters
- Understanding connotation and denotation
- Understanding how different types of irony are used to create effects like suspense or humor
- Noting and analyzing how common themes from myths and religious stories are addressed and "made new" in contemporary writing

Using Text Evidence to Support Analysis

In the 8th grade your child will learn to complete literary analysis, or a close reading of a work of literature, that focuses on one or more key points. The most common focus for literary analysis is one of the following areas:

Characters: Characters can be static, which means they do not change over the course of a story; or they can be dynamic, which means they experience a change as a result of the events in a story. Background or secondary characters are often static, as they are in place only to interact with the main characters. The main character, or protagonist, often undergoes a change in a story. The antagonist, or the character who works to prevent the protagonist from achieving his goal, is often static.

ESSENTIAL

Characters can be round or flat. Flat characters are, as their name suggests, two dimensional. They are not very realistic, and the only details a reader has about them are those important to the plot. Round characters, on the other hand, are complex and realistic. They are the dynamic characters in a story.

Theme: The theme of a story, novel, or even a poem is the central observation about a common idea. For example, a theme might make a comment about the nature of friendship, such as "friendship can overcome hardship." The theme is woven through the entire story. Students often find it challenging to detect the theme because it is built through different episodes and interactions in a story.

Literary elements: Your child has already studied literary elements such as simile, metaphor, personification, hyperbole, and allusion throughout her academic career. Sometimes literary analysis focuses on explaining how one or more literary elements further a plot or relate to the plot.

Setting: The setting of a story, or even a poem, consists of the time and place where the action occurs. The author will include specific details that orient the reader and give her a sense of how the story fits into a time and place. For example, a science fiction story might be set in the future on a spaceship, while a work of historical fiction might be set in the 1700s in colonial Boston. Establishing the setting is crucial to creating a story that is vivid and realistic, even if the setting itself is completely fictional.

Narrative point of view: A story can be told from the first person point of view, in which the narrator is part of the story. It can also be told from a third person point of view, in which the narrator is outside of the story, narrating the events. Sometimes third person narration includes the narrator's knowledge of the characters' thoughts. This is called an omniscient point of view.

Sometimes the narrator's omniscience includes all characters, or it can be limited to one or more characters.

Strategies to Support Analysis

To use evidence to support analysis, your child will use one of three different strategies. Information from a text can be paraphrased, summarized, or quoted directly.

Paraphrasing involves rewriting what an author has said in one's own words. The following example demonstrates how an excerpt from a text can be paraphrased. Review this original text from *Little Women*:

Margaret, the eldest of the four, was sixteen, and very pretty, being plump and fair, with large eyes, plenty of soft brown hair, a sweet mouth, and white hands, of which she was rather vain. Fifteen-year-old Jo was very tall, thin, and brown, and reminded one of a colt, for she never seemed to know what to do with her long limbs, which were very much in her way.

A paraphrase can often be as long as the original text:

Margaret, 16, was the oldest, and was attractive. She was a bit chubby and light skinned. A pretty brunette, she was very proud of her hands, which she thought were especially attractive. Jo was 15. She was slim and tall. Her skin was tan and she was gangly and awkward.

In this paraphrase, the writer has captured the main descriptive details of the original text, but used new wording. Paraphrasing is particularly effective when a writer wants to use specific details from a text to provide description.

A **summary** is a general overview of the main points of a text, and is usually quite a bit shorter than the original text. An effective summary might be:

Unlike 16-year-old Margaret, who was a bit overweight, fair skinned, and pretty, 15-year-old Jo was thin, tan, and awkward looking.

When using a **direct quotation**, the writer copies text exactly as it appears in the original literature. Quotation marks are used to indicate what has been copied from the text.

"Fifteen-year-old Jo was very tall, thin, and brown, and reminded one of a colt, for she never seemed to know what to do with her long limbs, which were very much in her way."

FACT

Whether information is paraphrased, summarized, or quoted directly, it is likely that your child's teacher will require him to include a citation. A citation shows the reader that the idea or information in a sentence is not the writer's original idea. An in-text citation usually includes the original author's last name and the publication year of the text. For example, the citation for *Little Women* would be (Alcott, 1868).

Determining the Theme of a Text

The **theme** is the central idea of a story. It can be revealed through the development of characters. As a story progresses, and moves through elements of the plot, characters encounter challenges and dilemmas. How characters deal with these dilemmas, and how they are changed by them, results in development of the central idea.

In the novel *Little Women*, for example, one theme is that making sacrifices is ethical and moral. One character, Jo, is very ambitious, as is evidenced in the following quote: "I want to do something splendid before I go into my castle—something heroic, or wonderful—that won't be forgotten after I'm dead. I don't know what, but I'm on the watch for it, and mean to astonish you all, some day. I think I shall write books, and get rich and famous; that would suit me, so that is my favorite dream."

Eventually, Jo must sacrifice her plans in order to enable and support the plans of her sisters. Her development, from an ambitious teenager to a young woman who compromises but finds happiness, supports the theme.

Setting can also support the theme. The setting of *Little Women* is New England during and after the Civil War. One of the characters travels to Europe, and Jo travels to New York to find work as a writer. In addition, the novel stretches over many years, beginning when Jo is a teenager and ending when she is in her thirties. Throughout these years, Jo makes many sacrifices. She sees her sister take a European trip she herself wanted. She sees another sister marry a man she cared for. Rather than be disappointed, she grows, over time, to see these events as sacrifices necessary to the happiness of her sisters, and that made her a stronger and more moral person. The reader grows to understand that Jo's stoicism, her ability to hide her feelings, is selfless.

In a well-written work of literature, characters are developed so that they have unique personalities and characteristics. Readers can better understand the development of a theme if they trace how a character changes from the beginning of a story to the end.

FACT

Published in 1868, *Little Women* has become one of the most popular young adult novels ever written. Louisa May Alcott aspired to be a serious writer of darker fiction for adults, but was convinced to write *Little Women* by her father, who was offered a publishing contract of his own if he could convince Louisa to write the story. Alcott wrote the novel in just ten weeks.

Writing an Objective Summary of a Text

As in the 7th grade, in the 8th grade your child will practice and apply her ability to write an objective summary of a text. The goal remains the same, which is to identify key information and develop a summary that captures the most important points.

An objective summary does not include any bias or judgment of the text. The writer does not make judgments or indicate a preference for a character. In addition, a summary does not include any information quoted directly from the text.

In the 7th grade, your child might have used the C-PETE strategy to capture key ideas from a text. Now that texts are more complex, that strategy may not be sufficient. Review the following literary nonfiction passage and follow along with the questions that, in turn, illustrate how to write an effective objective summary:

Descending to Titanic

As the submersible craft Alvin descended to thirteen thousand feet below the ocean's surface, it was eclipsed in darkness. Dr. Robert Ballard, professor of oceanography and undersea archaeologist, activated the high-intensity lights mounted to the submersible, and gazed keenly through a porthole, searching for evidence of a ship, *the* ship. This was his expedition, and with the help of Alvin's two pilots, Ballard hoped to make a historical discovery.

The submersible's lights, blindingly bright on the surface, hardly penetrated the murky water. The craft slowed to minimum speed in anticipation of encountering the wreck. Finally, Ballard made out the acute edge of a ship's bow, as distinct as a knife's blade, protruding from the ocean floor. "There," he exclaimed to the submersible pilots, gesturing enthusiastically.

The pilots deftly navigated their craft toward the shape, which was becoming less discernible in the haze of ocean silt created by the propellers. As the submersible inched forward, it became obvious that this shape in the gloom was, in fact, the front of a massive ship, and that it was very much intact, despite having been lost to the ocean for seventy-five years. Even the anchors remained in place on the bow, as if ready to be lowered when the ship reached its port.

The pilots maneuvered first over the top of the wreck, where Dr. Ballard noted that the great skylight, an iconic emblem of the ship's extravagant design, had succumbed to the pressure of the ocean, and had collapsed, providing a view directly within to the site of the famous Grand Staircase. "We should be able to launch the small remote-controlled submarine directly into the wreck by this route," noted Ballard with obvious thrill. He continued, "We'll have an unencumbered pathway deep into the structure."

The pilots negotiated the submersible around the backside of the wreckage, and then turned to survey the port and starboard sides of the ocean liner. The sides of the ship dripped with rust, but, curiously, glass remained intact in many of the windows. "Are you able to make out the name of the ship, Dr. Ballard?" asked one of the pilots.

The scientist shook his head and spoke quietly, awestruck. "No. I can't. But, gentleman, I have no doubt that we are the first human beings to lay eyes upon the HMS *Titanic* since it sank, in the early morning hours of April 15, 1912."

The objective summary should be at least one well-developed paragraph. For an original passage of this length, more than a paragraph is not necessary. The structure for such an objective summary would be:

- **Sentence 1:** The main idea of the passage; this is the topic sentence of the summary and should include the name of the work.
- **Sentences 2–4:** Three key supporting details.
- **Sentence 5:** A concluding sentence.

The topic sentence of this summary could be: "Descending to Titanic is the story of Dr. Robert Ballard's first glimpse of the Titanic."

Notice that the topic sentence includes information that is not necessarily present in the first paragraph of the original passage. It is important to remember that the summary should be written *after* the entire text has been read. Annotating during reading will assist the reader in capturing key information, but the summary will combine information taken from all parts of the text.

The three detailed sentences could be:

"Using a submersible craft and two remote-controlled robots, Dr. Ballard explored the wreck. High-intensity lights illuminated key details, such as the remains of a skylight and the site of the ship's grand staircase. The ship was remarkably intact; in fact, there was still glass in some of the windows."

These three sentences capture the concrete details in the passage and pull them together to show how they are related. The summary should end with a concluding sentence:

"Although he could not make out the name of the ship on the rusty hull, Dr. Ballard had no doubt that it was *Titanic*."

Revealing Information Through Dialogue

Dialogue consists of the words that a character says. It is expressed as an exchange of conversation between two or more characters. Dialogue can impact a story in one of several ways:

- It helps tell the story by revealing details and motives.
- It provides important information about characters including age, education, and social status.
- It is an opportunity for characters to reveal what they're thinking, especially when the narrative voice does not include their thoughts.
- It can be used to highlight conflict between characters.

Review the following adaptation of *The Time Machine* by H.G. Wells. In the following excerpt, the protagonist, who is known only as "the Time Traveler," attempts to tell his friends about his adventures of traveling through time.

The Time Traveler explained, "When I returned, when I came back through time, I noticed shadows of people, seemingly walking backwards, first very rapidly, then more and more slowly, until I came to a stop, once again, here in my laboratory. Then I collected myself, washed my face, changed my suit, and opened the door to find you here for our dinner."

The doctor smiled softly, and after a sniff said. "It certainly is a remarkable story."

"No," said the Time Traveler. "I cannot expect you to believe it. Assume that I'm lying then."

The newspaper editor stood up. He sighed and said finally, "It's a shame you didn't devote your time to becoming a writer, instead of an . . . an inventor? An adventurer?" He put his hands on the Time Traveler's shoulder.

"You don't believe me then?" asked the Time Traveler.

"Well . . ." began the editor.

"I didn't think so," said the Time Traveler, without anger. He looked about the room. "I'll tell you the truth. I almost don't believe it myself. But still . . . but still I recall everything that happened in such great detail. And there is this . . ." The Time Traveler gestured toward a flowering plant, which he'd claimed he'd brought back from the distant future. "Where could this have come from?"

The three men inspected an exotic flowering plant, which the Time Traveler had hastily replanted into a teacup filled with garden soil. A single large bloom of vibrant scarlet flamed with gold dropped from an impossibly thin stem. As each man passed his hand near the flower it retracted, moving independently.

"I'll admit," said the doctor, "The plant is like nothing I've seen before. May I take it home to study it?"

"Certainly not," said the Time Traveler. "No."

The men were silent for several minutes.

"Look at the time," said the editor, finally. "It is after midnight." He turned to the doctor. "We should go. We should find a cab."

The doctor nodded and the guests gathered their coats and moved toward the door. The doctor hesitated, "Where did you really get that plant?" he asked.

"A friend," said the Time Traveler. "She put it in my pocket when I was in her time. A gift. It was a gift."

The doctor sighed once again, tipped his hat, and headed down the walk. He turned back and said, "That's it then? That's all you'll say?"

The Time Traveler closed and latched the door. He looked around the empty foyer, then walked back to his laboratory. He pulled back a curtain to reveal his time machine.

FACT

A dialogue is a conversation between two or more characters. A monologue is a long speech by one character. Other characters are present and listening, but they do not interact. A soliloquy occurs when a character speaks his or her thoughts out loud, but does not directly address any of the other characters who might be present in the scene.

The dialogue in this excerpt provides information about the plot and the characters in the story. First, the reader learns some details of the Time Traveler's adventure. When he describes his return and the experience of traveling backward through time, the reader learns that he has gone ahead in time and that his machine has brought him back.

Second, the dialogue reveals the internal conflict the Time Traveler experiences when he admits that he might doubt his own story. The dialogue also portrays the external conflict with his friends, who definitely doubt his story. The Time Traveler is a practical man, and he is not one to fantasize. It seems, almost, that he would prefer that it were not true, but he cannot deny the details of what happened.

Also notice the tone of the interactions. The men are respectful. The only hint of a temper is when the Time Traveler replies with an abrupt, "Certainly not . . . no," when the doctor asks for his exotic plant.

The only character who notes that the Time Traveler might be lying is the Time Traveler himself. His friends are too polite to say such a thing. This formal, polite tone tells us something about the time or setting of the story, which is the nineteenth century, and the social class of the men, which is an upper class.

Finally, at the end of the excerpt, the interaction between the doctor and Time Traveler reveals that the doctor believes the Time Traveler is choosing to withhold the truth, and that he believes there is more to the story. When the Time Traveler, ultimately, unveils his time machine, only to himself, the reader knows that he has been telling the truth. The other characters, however, do not.

Reread the excerpt with this information in mind. Consider how the dialogue adds realism to what is not a very realistic episode. Consider, also, how the conversation creates a setting that a reader can picture: a group of men, talking late into the night, wrestling with an impossible story.

Understanding Connotation and Denotation

In the 8th grade your child will explore language by considering not only the dictionary definition of words, but also the feeling or tone of words:

- **Denotation** is the static definition of a word. It is the definition one might find in a dictionary.
- **Connotation** is the feeling a word invokes.

Often, connotation is independent of the denotation. For example, the definitions of boat and yacht, according to the Merriam-Webster dictionary, are somewhat similar:

- Boat: a small craft used for traveling on water

- Yacht: a large boat that is used for racing or pleasure

The denotation, then, notes only a difference in the size of the watercrafts. However, the connotation of the word *yacht* suggests wealth and luxury.

Connotation and denotation can also affect the tone of writing. Consider the following sentences:

Miriam was thrifty; she thought carefully before making any purchases.

Miriam was cheap; she thought carefully before making any purchases.

In the first sentence, Miriam is thoughtful and careful with her money. In the second sentence, however, the word *cheap* suggests that Miriam is miserly, and that she may be unreasonably cautious with her money.

To practice identifying the connotations of words, review the following word pairs with your child. Consider which have negative connotations, like cheap, and which have positive connotations, like yacht. Some words may also have a neutral connotation, or simply communicate an idea, without any underlying tone.

1. slim/skinny
2. assertive/pushy
3. cackle/chuckle
4. demonstration/riot
5. exotic/strange
6. sound/noise

You can practice applying and analyzing connotation with your child by editing sample sentences to change the connotation. For example, this sentence:

My brother gave me a cheap toy for my birthday.

How could this sentence be revised to remove the negative connotation, which suggests the speaker is unhappy with the gift?

My brother gave me an inexpensive toy for my birthday.

In the first sentence, the word *cheap* has a negative connotation. It suggests not only the cost of the gift but the quality of the gift. In the revision, the word *inexpensive* focuses only on the cost, and has a neutral connotation. Consider the following sentence:

My dad nagged me to take out the trash.

The word *nagged* has a negative connotation and suggests that the speaker is irritated by his father's request. In the following sentence, the word *nagged* has been replaced with a word with a neutral connotation:

My dad reminded me to take out the trash.

This sentence focuses on the purpose of the father's communication, rather than the speaker's feelings.

To help your child recognize how the connotations of words can change the tone of a text, focus on authentic texts, such as news reports. Find opportunities to compare different reporting of the same events. For example, consider the following sentences, both of which describe events related to demonstrations in Baltimore in 2015:

Demonstrations turned violent this evening in Baltimore.

Riots erupted in the city of Baltimore tonight.

Which suggests a more violent event? Which sentence highlights how quickly the problem emerged? Is there a difference in connotation between the words *evening* and *night*? Is there a difference between *turned* and *erupted*? These word choices determine the tone of the text.

Understanding Irony

Irony is a literary device that draws attention to dialogue or actions in a text. Your child may learn that irony occurs when the author says the opposite of what she means in order to create a specific effect, such as humor or suspense. This definition most applies to verbal irony. There are three main types of irony:

Verbal Irony

Verbal irony is sometimes called sarcasm, though this is not a completely accurate description. Sarcasm tends to be mean spirited, while verbal irony can be self-deprecating, kind, or humorous. Verbal irony occurs when the intended meaning is the opposite of what the words in the text say. Review these examples:

Adam's mom noticed his wrinkled clothes and uncombed hair. She said, "Thank you for taking the time to look your best for our trip to Grandma's."

In the example, it is clear from Adam's appearance that he did not take the time to look his best. The mother's dialogue reveals that she is displeased with his appearance even though she says the opposite of what she really means.

QUESTION

What is the difference between irony and coincidence?
A coincidence is something, perhaps unfortunate, that happens when another event or situation is happening. If, for example, someone built a brand new mansion and it was struck by lightning and burned down the next day, that would not be ironic. It would be an unfortunate coincidence. If that same person built a brand new mansion with money he earned from writing about the benefits of living in a very small living space, that would be ironic. One would not expect someone who extolls the benefits of "tiny living" to build himself a mansion.

Consider another example of verbal irony:

Jordan turned quickly and pushed his plate from the table; it shattered to the floor. "Just my typical, coordinated self," he said with a laugh.

In this example Jordan does not demonstrate that he is coordinated. When he pushes the plate to the floor, he comments on his own clumsiness by saying the opposite of what he means.

Verbal irony can be humorous, but it can be mean-spirited when it is used to point out another person's flaws.

Dramatic Irony

Dramatic irony is common in movies as well as in literature. It occurs when the reader or the audience is aware of something that the characters do not know. This can create suspense, as the reader waits to see how and when the characters will discover the information. Review the following example:

Jane and Marlie could not get over how much they had in common. Not only did they look alike, with the same color hair and eyes, they liked the same things: dolphins, blue nail polish, and dill pickles. Finally, they were both adopted! Little did they know that there was a reason for their connection. Although they didn't know it yet, Jane and Marlie were twins who had been adopted by different families.

This example is dramatic irony because the reader knows why Jane and Marlie are so alike, even though the characters themselves don't know. In addition, the author has included information that they don't "know it yet," which suggests that they will eventually learn that they are related. In this case, dramatic irony creates suspense as the reader looks for clues for how the characters learn the truth.

Situational Irony

In situational irony, what happens in a situation is the opposite of what the reader would expect. Often situational irony leads to humor. Review the following examples:

Acme Pest Control Company will be closed all week due to a termite infestation.

This is an example of situational irony because a pest control company is in the business of preventing insect infestations. It is ironic that the company is closed due to a pest infestation because they should be able to control insects in their own building.

The pilot gripped the wheel tightly. Beads of sweat formed on his brow. He took deep breaths, looked down the runway, and gritted his teeth. "I can do this," he thought to himself. "People fly every day. It's perfectly safe."

This is an example of situational irony because a pilot who is afraid to fly is the opposite of what one might expect. This situation can build suspense, as the reader wonders if the pilot will be okay during the flight.

Irony is a complex concept. Your child will benefit from opportunities to identify and discuss irony in what he reads, as well as what he sees on television or in movies. Irony is almost always deliberate in literature and is intended to call attention to an important plot point.

Noting and Analyzing Common Themes from Myths and Religious Stories

In the 7th grade, your child worked with mythical and religious allusions in texts. In the 8th grade, he will continue to analyze these allusions and will, in addition, independently consider themes from these stories and how they are applied to other works of literature.

Some common themes in mythology and religious texts include:

- **The danger of hubris:** Hubris is pride, arrogance, or exaggerated self-confidence. In Greek mythology hubris is demonstrated when humans try to make themselves equal to the gods. In Greek mythology, Icarus dons wings and attempts to fly close to the sun, as a god might. The sun melts the wax in his mechanical wings and he plunges into the sea. In contemporary literature a character that is overconfident or fails to realize her own weakness may suffer the effects of hubris.
- **The inevitability of fate:** Fate is the notion that one's future is preordained and that people are powerless to control what will happen to them. One example of the power of fate is the myth of the King of Thebes. The king learns that his son will kill him, so he takes steps that he believes will result in the death of his son. His actions, however, result in his son being separated from him so that many years later the two do not recognize each other, and the son kills his father.

- **Goodness is rewarded and evil is punished:** This universal theme is so prominent that in almost every story a reader can expect that a villain will suffer consequences for his behavior. It is also typical that an inherently good character will, despite setbacks and obstacles, eventually get what he most desires. The biblical story of Job is an example of a good character who is eventually rewarded. Despite many trials, Job maintained his faith and maintained a pious outlook. Eventually he is rewarded.
- **The possibility of redemption:** This theme promises that people can change and that those who act inappropriately can be shown how to be better people. A representation of this theme occurs in many films. For example, a grumpy older neighbor who doesn't seem to like people makes a connection with a child, and through that relationship the grump realizes that there is kindness in the world, and, in turn, is kind to others.

Help your child identify these classic themes in contemporary literature by working with him to review characters, plot, and literary elements that contribute to a central idea or message. When possible make connections to older, traditional stories that share similar themes.

Reading Informational Texts

In the 8th grade, your child will read many different kinds of informational texts, including nonfiction narratives, arguments, journalism, textbooks, encyclopedias, historical documents, and others. An important focus in the 8th grade is the writer's craft, that is, how a writer's choices help to develop meaning. When developing meaningful ideas, skilled authors of informational texts will build connections between individuals, ideas, and events so the reader can understand how actions have consequences, how events are related, and how ideas are developed over time. The topics covered in the Reading Informational Text (RI) strand that differ from those covered in Reading Literature (RL) include:

- Cite textual evidence that most strongly supports analysis.
- Determine the central idea of a text.
- Determine an author's purpose or point of view.

Cite Textual Evidence

In the 6th and 7th grade your child learned to identify evidence to support a point. In the 8th grade, your child will be required to identify the best or strongest evidence in a text that supports a conclusion. Learning to distinguish between relevant evidence and the strongest relevant evidence requires analytical skills and the ability to understand how to support a main idea.

Review the following passage and questions:

On Thursday, January 15, 2009, at 3:25 P.M., US Airways flight 1549 took off from LaGuardia Airport in New York City. It was a clear day, with hardly a cloud in the sky, but the temperature was bitterly cold, dipping as low as 18–20°F. In fact, the flight was delayed almost forty minutes, as airport personnel needed to spray the plane with a de-icing solution to prevent ice from forming and interfering with its operation. The pilot of the plane was Captain Chesley Sullenberger III, who was known to his friends as "Sully." Just a few days shy of his fifty-eighth birthday, on January 23, Sully had been a pilot with US Airways for nearly thirty years. Assisting Sully in the cockpit of the Airbus A320 jet was first officer, Jeffrey B. Skiles, who had recently completed training to fly the Airbus A320. In addition to these two men, there were three additional crew members and 150 passengers on board the plane.

Jeffrey Skiles spotted a flock of birds in the sky just before takeoff. About three minutes after flight 1549 had left LaGuardia's runway #4, when the plane had reached 2,700 feet, the flock of Canada geese and the plane collided. The result was catastrophic, or completely devastating, to the plane. Both engines shut down. Since the plane was climbing, or ascending in altitude, very rapidly, the timing was particularly dangerous. Both Sully and Skiles heard several thuds. Their window was obscured, which made it impossible to see what was in front of them. Finally, just as the plane passed about 2,800 feet in altitude, both engines completely stopped. Captain Sullenberger radioed the tower at LaGuardia, "Hit birds. We've lost thrust in both engines. We're turning back toward LaGuardia." The situation was dire, but initially both Sullenberger and Skiles were confident they could simply turn back and land at the airport they'd left just a few minutes earlier.

Captain Sullenberg was granted clearance to return to LaGuardia, but soon realized the plane did not have the power necessary to turn and land safely. He asked the tower if he could land in New Jersey, which was just minutes away by air. Granted clearance to land at Teterboro, a regional airport in New Jersey, Sullenberg again realized the plane would not make it. He radioed back to the control tower, "We can't do it. We're going to be in the Hudson." Sully was referring to the Hudson River, a deep river separating New York City and the state of New Jersey. That day, the water temperature of the Hudson River was just over freezing at 36°F. People who plunged into the frigid water could survive for, at most, 30–90 minutes, before perishing from hypothermia, or an extreme decrease in body temperature. If any passengers were completely submerged, they would most likely lose consciousness within fifteen minutes, and possibly drown. Sully's decision had potentially fatal consequences. He turned on the microphone to his stunned passengers and said, "Prepare for impact."

Just 208 seconds after striking the flock of birds, Flight 1549 touched down onto the river. By all accounts, Captain Sullenberger demonstrated exceptional skill in choosing the location and controlling the descent of the plane. One eyewitness reported, "If someone's going to land a plane in the water, this seemed the best possible way to do it. The way they hit was very gradual. A very slow contact with the water." Since the plane was travelling at about 150 miles per hour, and had no engine power to control its descent, the skill with which Sully landed the plane is impressive. Also remarkable was the location he managed to select for the emergency landing. The section of the river on which the plane touched down was close to several commuter ferry terminals as well as the terminals for tourist ferries that travel to the Statue of Liberty and Ellis Island.

Within minutes of the plane touching down and coming to a stop, ferryboats began to pull up alongside. The plane, however, was not stopped for long. The strong currents of the river began to move the plane as the crew scrambled to evacuate the passengers. Inside, Sullenberger spoke over the address system one last time, saying, "Evacuate." The flight attendants led passengers through the two emergency window exits over the wings as well as onto the front exit's emergency inflatable exit slide, which also served as a life raft. Unfortunately, in the rear of the plane, a frantic passenger opened a fourth door, which was partially submerged, and allowed icy water to course into the plane's cabin. In addition, when the plane touched down, a hole had been ripped into the bottom, the cargo doors had been breached, and water was slowly entering the cabin from below. Despite these challenges, and the fact that the plane was sinking and drifting down the river, the flight crew was able to get every passenger, including one person in a wheelchair and an infant, safely out of the cabin and onto the wings or the life raft. Captain Sullenberger inspected the inside of the plane, not once, but twice, walking up and down the aisle and checking under every seat before he stepped out of one of the emergency exits.

Outside of the plane, passengers waited just four minutes for the first commercial boat to begin rescuing them. Although the conditions were brutal, and some people stood up to their knees in cold water until they were pulled to safety, by all accounts, the rescue was swift and efficient. Back on shore, more than fifty ambulances and hundreds of firefighters waited to provide immediate first aid and to transport victims to local hospitals.

All 155 people on board flight 1549 survived. Seventy-eight people were injured, but only five had serious injuries, and only two people had to be hospitalized overnight. Almost immediately the media referred to the landing of flight 1549 as "The Miracle on the Hudson," and it was, in fact, the most successful emergency water landing in the history of commercial aviation. Today, visitors can see the salvaged wreckage of Flight 1549 on display at the Carolinas Aviation Museum in Charlotte, North Carolina.

Now review the following question:

Which quote from the passage best supports the claim that Captain Sullenberger prioritized the safety of his passengers?

1. "He turned on the microphone to his stunned passengers and said, 'Prepare for impact.'"

2. "Despite these challenges, and the fact that the plane was sinking, the flight crew was able to get every passenger, including one person in a wheelchair and an infant, safely out of the cabin and onto the wings or the life raft."

3. "Captain Sullenberger inspected the inside of the plane, not once, but twice, walking up and down the aisle and checking under every seat before he stepped out of one of the emergency exits."

4. "All 155 people on board flight 1549 survived."

All four of the answer choices show, in some way, that Captain Sullenberger cared about the safety of his passengers. To answer this question accurately, the reader must first thoroughly understand what is being asked. The question asks for evidence that Sullenberger *prioritized* the safety of his passengers, or put it ahead of other concerns. Some readers might even infer that the question asks for evidence that Sullenberger put the safety of his passengers before his own safety. Since the evidence should best support the idea that passenger safety was a priority, the best answer is number three.

The reader knows from the passage that the plane was sinking and drifting down the river. The crew worked to get all of the passengers out of the cabin and onto the wings to be rescued quickly, before they were exposed to the freezing-cold water. Despite these dangers, Sullenberger made two passes of the plane to make sure no passengers were left behind. The analytical reader can combine what she knows from the rest of the passage with this information to determine that this quote is the *best* evidence that Sullenberger prioritized passenger safety.

Note the following steps that went into determining the *best* evidence to support a point:

- Confirm a complete and clear understanding of the point to be supported. In the case of this question, the point hinged on the word *prioritized*.

- Develop a preliminary summary or understanding of what kind of evidence would support that point, based on the text in its entirety. In this example, the reader understood that the water was very cold and the plane was filling with water.

- Find or identify evidence that fits based on an overall understanding of the text.

With the time constraints of testing, some students are tempted to make an educated guess. In the case of questions that ask for the "best" or "strongest" evidence, it is difficult to do so without a full understanding of the text. Good annotation and active reading strategies, which are skills that students develop in the 7th grade, can help. (Please see Chapter 8 for a detailed examination of 7th grade reading strategies.)

Review the following question:

Which detail best supports the claim that all passengers survived because of the location of the water landing on the Hudson River?

1. Fifty ambulances and hundreds of firefighters waited on the shore for victims to ensure they were quickly transported to local hospitals.
2. Sullenberger landed the plane near several commuter ferry terminals.
3. Ferryboats pulled up alongside the plane within minutes of it touching down.
4. The passengers were quickly led out of the emergency exits and onto the wings.

This question, like the first one, requires an overall understanding of the text. Yes, it was beneficial that there were ambulances and firefighters onshore. And it was definitely helpful that the ferryboat captains acted quickly. The question, however, asks for the best evidence to support the claim that the *location of the water landing* led to the survival of the passengers. One answer choice, number two, best supports the claim that the location of landing was responsible for all passengers surviving.

As you help your child evaluate evidence in a text, keep in mind the following characteristics of strong support:

- Strong evidence is concrete information. It is something that can be proven or has been observed by many people.
- Strong evidence often has a cause/effect relationship to the main idea. Without the strong evidence, the main idea would not be possible.

- The strongest evidence is not contradicted elsewhere in the text. If, for example, this text mentioned that some witnesses saw Captain Sully on the wings, awaiting rescue before all the passengers had escaped, the evidence that he walked the length of the plane would not be strong.

Determine the Central Idea of a Text

Your child may already be familiar with the "main idea" of a text. The central idea is like the main idea: It is the most important idea the author of an informational text wants to communicate. In more complex texts, there may be more than one related central idea. The central idea is supported by strong evidence. The central idea could be a thesis statement that appears in the first paragraph, or it could be a main idea that the reader infers after reading the text.

Read this text and refer to the steps that follow to determine the central idea:

> Although fewer teens than ever are smokers, every year thousands of teenagers light their first cigarette and become smokers. Smoking has no benefits, but can lead to a host of diseases, including diseases of the lungs, heart, and skin. More attention must be paid to making smoking less attractive to young people. One solution is to ban all tobacco use shown on television and in the movies. While cigarette commercials have been banned for decades, it is still common to see television or movie characters light up. If a teenager finds a character interesting, he or she might try to emulate the character by trying smoking. Some magazines still carry cigarette ads. All advertising for cigarettes, in any form, should be banned, even in magazines intended for adults. All states have a minimum age for cigarette purchase, but it remains relatively easy for an underage smoker to buy cigarettes. Fines should be increased for stores that do not consistently check customers' identification and confirm that customers are legally allowed to purchase cigarettes.

When determining the central idea, your child should start by reading for the "big picture" and ignore the supporting details.

Begin by establishing the topic of this passage: Teenage smoking.

Then determine what the author has to say about the topic. What does the author want the reader to know about teenage smoking? The author wants the reader to know that teenagers are encouraged to try smoking by watching portrayals of smoking in movies, on TV shows, and in magazine articles. Further, the author says that advertising should be banned and fines should be increased for stores that sell cigarettes to underage smokers.

Finally, determine which supporting details provide the best evidence for the central idea:

- Teenagers might emulate attractive movie and TV characters.
- It is relatively easy for teenagers to buy cigarettes.

This three-step process (establishing topic, determining the author's purpose, and gathering supporting details), can be used to discover the central idea for most informational passages.

Review this process while reading the following text:

Even the best athletes can't win every game or match. Losing can be discouraging, and some athletes even quit a favorite sport if they lose too frequently. Rather than give up, there are other ways to prepare for and deal with a loss. The first solution is to be realistic. No one wins all the time. Whenever you play a sport, visualize winning, but understand that the other team is doing the same, and prepare for the possibility that you may not win. Think about what your reaction will be, and be prepared to lose gracefully and move on. Second, try to find a positive moment in every game. Even if you've lost, focus on one thing you did well in the game. Consider how to extend that success in future games. Finally, think of every loss as a learning experience. Think about what the other team or player did better. Did they use a strategy you have not thought of? Do they have stronger skills in some aspect of the game? Learn from the losses to improve in the future.

The topic of this text is: Losing.
The main point of this text is: Losing is no reason to give up.
The supporting details are:

- No one wins every game.
- It is possible to find something positive in a losing experience.
- Losing can be a learning experience.

Finding the supporting details is an important step in the process of identifying a central idea. Often, a reader will adjust his or her central idea when called upon to support it with evidence from the text. If a central idea can't be supported by text details, then the central idea should be revised.

Finding the central idea is a skill you can practice frequently with your child. Textbook readings, news reports, and even fun readings on Internet websites like mental floss (*mentalfloss.com*) can be used for practice and further discussion.

Determine an Author's Purpose or Point of View

Your eighth grader has had several years of experience in determining the author's purpose. Authors write with three main purposes:

- To persuade or argue a point
- To inform or explain
- To entertain

Understanding the specific features of each purpose help a reader determine the author's intent.

To Persuade or Argue a Point

In the 8th grade your child will likely begin working with the components of a formal argument. A formal argument is an essay that proves a disputable point using credible evidence. The parts of a formal academic argument are:

- The claim: the point of view or opinion of the writer
- The reason(s): why the writer holds the point of view (a "because" statement)

- The evidence: facts, data, and examples that support the writer's point of view
- The argument: how the evidence leads to the claim

The following is an argumentative essay. Follow along to identify the different components:

Fifteen years ago, if someone wanted to be able to make a phone call, take a photo, or look up something on the Internet, she would have to have had a backpack full of equipment with her, including a bulky cell phone, a digital or film camera, and a laptop computer. Today, anyone with an iPhone can do all of these things, and more, with a device that fits in her back pocket. I can't imagine getting through a single day without using my iPhone. Without a doubt, the iPhone is the most significant invention of my lifetime because it combines all three functions (phone, camera, and computer) into a single compact device.

First, of course, the iPhone is a phone. It offers all of the expected functions of a phone, plus some additional features. For example, an iPhone user can set up a voicemail account so that callers can leave a message. Also, the iPhone allows three-way calling, which means three people, on three different phones, can participate in a single conversation. Finally, the iPhone offers features to manage calls, such as Mute, and Hold, which makes it easier to talk to someone in the room without the person on the phone hearing the conversation. These features, combined with the fact that a user can talk by holding the phone to her ear, by using the Speaker-Phone feature, or by using headphones with a built-in microphone, makes the iPhone much more flexible and easy to use than earlier cell phones and traditional land lines.

In addition to a phone, the iPhone also functions as a camera. The iPhone's digital camera is not, of course, the first digital camera, but it is probably the most convenient. With the iPhone camera users can take either photos or video. The high-quality photos are sharp enough to be used online, or printed into hard-copy photos. Short videos make it easy and fun to make a record of special events and share them with friends and family. Because the iPhone has Internet access, photos and videos can be easily sent to others.

Finally, the iPhone is basically a minicomputer. The basic applications, or apps, include e-mail and an Internet browser. Users can download thousands of other apps to personalize their phones to their own lives. For example, for students there are dictionary apps, apps that provide practice in math and vocabulary, and apps that review major concepts from almost every subject a person might study in school. Users can type and send documents, reply to online posts, and even play games using the iPhone. Because it can be personalized with each user's favorite apps, the iPhone is like having a personal computer in your pocket.

Although the iPhone is an amazing technological development, there are those who might argue that it is not the most important of our lifetime. Some might argue that the hybrid car, which uses a special engine that captures electrical energy and uses less gas, is a much more important invention. While it is true that hybrid cars, like the Prius and Volt, are helping drivers preserve natural resources, hybrid cars are not as widely used as the iPhone. The most significant invention has to be the one that has reached the greatest number of people and affected the greatest number of lives. Most people know about hybrid cars, but millions of people drive other kinds of cars or don't drive at all. There are not enough hybrid cars on the road today to make a big difference in the use of natural resources. However, iPhones are widely available and many more people can benefit from them.

All in all, the iPhone has been the most important technological development of my lifetime. While there are other developments that are important, and could eventually be available to many people, nothing is as accessible and important as the iPhone. Because it combines the functions of a phone, camera, and computer into one pocket-sized device, the iPhone is the most important development.

After reading this essay, have your child determine the claim, the reasons, the evidence, and the argument:

- The claim: The iPhone offers tremendous functionality; that is, it can be used in many different ways.
- The reasons: The iPhone can be used as a phone, a camera, and a computer.

- The evidence: The iPhone has many different features and functions, which are detailed in the essay.
- The argument: The iPhone is the most important invention in the writer's lifetime.

Notice that the argument is separate from the claim. The claim is based in fact, which in this case is that the iPhone has three different types of functions. The argument is where the writer includes his or her personal point of view. It is based on an opinion, which in this case is that the iPhone is the most significant invention of his or her lifetime.

When reading and analyzing an argumentative text, your child should practice identifying a claim that is separate from the argument, keeping in mind that the claim is based in fact or evidence and the argument is based on the author's point of view or opinion.

To Inform or Explain

When an author writes to inform, his goal is to teach a lesson, explain a concept, or provide instructions. Some examples of writing to inform include:

- Newspapers
- Textbooks
- Maps and atlases
- Travel guides
- Scholarly journals

Information in a text that is intended to inform is organized in a logical order. The main points might be explained in order of time, in order of importance, or in a spatial order. Spatial order is useful when giving instructions because it explains things as they relate to others. An example would be, "Press the red button that is to the left of the steering wheel."

To effectively study an informational text, your child must have an understanding of key vocabulary words and possess related analytical skills:

Summary: The summary of an informational text is, at most, a paragraph that expresses the main point of the text and the most important details. It is objective; that is, a summary does not include the writer's opinion on the text that was read.

Critique: Unlike a summary, which is objective or unbiased, a critique is an evaluation. When your child is called upon to critique an informational text, she should be able to identify the most important information and consider how the information in the text is presented.

Review this short informational text and the summary and critique that follow:

It would seem logical to believe that having more choices in any situation would make people happier. The more choices one has, the more likely she is to get the thing that will most satisfy her. Ironically, according to Barry Schwartz, an American psychologist, that is not the case. In his book *The Paradox of Choice*, Schwartz explains that having too many choices actually has negative consequences.

First, according to Schwartz, people have difficulty determining the best option when they are presented with more than two or three choices. When asked to choose from a collection of ten or more items, people begin to focus on what they will lose by not picking one option, rather than on what they gain by choosing one. In addition, an abundance of choices can lead to feelings of depression, as it can seem like one is being denied several options, instead of being given a single option. This feeling of loss can lead to feelings of sadness. Finally, choosing one of many options can lead to regret and self-doubt, as one focuses on what he believes he did not get in the option he selected.

The summary of this text pulls together the main idea and most important supporting details. It might read as follows: "According to researcher Barry Schwartz, having too many choices can lead to difficulty when making selections, as well as feelings of sadness and self-doubt."

Notice that the summary is focused exclusively on the content, but not on *how* the text was written.

A critique, on the other hand, considers how the text is constructed, as well as the content. It might read as follows: "The writer uses the work of psychologist Barry Schwartz to establish the point that too many choices can lead to negative consequences. While the author has not included specific examples, he makes several well-supported claims about the consequences of too many choices, including sadness and self-doubt. The text would be stronger with more concrete data, including specific anecdotes and results from specific studies."

Notice that the critique provides an overview of the main point as well as information on how the author makes the point. The writer of the critique also identifies ways the text could be stronger.

Your child will be asked to critique the work of other writers and provide information on how the work could be improved. One great way to practice is to get into the habit of asking questions about reading. Such questions could be like, "What do you wish the author had told us?" or "How did the author provide examples of this idea?"

Much of what your child reads in the 8th grade and beyond will be informational texts. Learning to interact and read information actively will help to improve her comprehension skills.

To Entertain

Writing that is created to entertain is often fictional, meaning it is based on invented stories or events. Such types of writing can include stories, novels, jokes, and poetry. Informational texts can also be intended to entertain, such as the retelling of a funny situation.

In the 8th grade your child will likely encounter a genre of writing called creative nonfiction. Creative nonfiction is, obviously, a retelling of actual events. However, events and situations in creative nonfiction are told like stories. Examples include historical biographies that retell important events in the life of a well-known figure as a plot. The text is dramatic, and some minor details might be omitted or compressed. However, all of the information is factual. Creative nonfiction does not include any invented or fictional information.

Memoirs are another example of creative nonfiction. Your child will most likely read at least one memoir during her middle school career. Some of the most popular recent memoirs include *Soul Surfer* by Bethany Hamilton, which is about a teenage surfer who lost her arm to a shark attack; and *I Am Malala*, by Malala Yousafzai, which is about a young girl who fought for her right to attend school in Taliban-controlled Pakistan and nearly lost her life doing so. Both of these memoirs are creative and tell compelling stories but are completely factual. When reading nonfiction texts that are intended to explain information, your child should focus on the author's purpose. That is, encourage your child to consider why the author shared his or her experience or ideas. Often the author hopes to share a lesson or insight that can be applied to the lives and experiences of others. You can help your child identify and respond to that lesson or insight through discussion and reflection.

Practice Exercises

These exercises are intended to help your child practice applying her newly learned skills. The questions are similar to those he may encounter on a standardized test.

Kinds of Irony

Read each excerpt and determine the kind of irony described.

1. A pest control company has to close because it is infested with termites.
   a. Verbal irony
   b. Dramatic irony
   c. Situational irony
2. A boy comes to the table in a wrinkled shirt. "Oh," says his mother, "I see you took the time to iron your clothes this morning."
   a. Verbal irony
   b. Dramatic irony
   c. Situational irony
3. In a movie, a girl is waiting for her friend to call. The audience knows that the friend has lost her phone and won't be calling.
   a. Verbal irony
   b. Dramatic irony
   c. Situational irony
4. A student begins doing an impersonation of the teacher. The other students see the teacher standing in the doorway, but say nothing.
   a. Verbal irony
   b. Dramatic irony
   c. Situational irony
5. A police car is towed for parking illegally.
   a. Verbal irony

b. Dramatic irony

c. Situational irony

Author's Purpose

Read each of the following and determine the author's purpose.

1. Sparky snapped awake at 4:00 A.M. on the dot. He knew his human would be waking up soon, and he knew how upset his human was when she over-slept. Sparky nudged his human with his nose several times. She stumbled out of bed, walked to the back door, and let him into the backyard. Now Sparky's real job had to be done. He ran to her bedroom window and began to yelp. "Get up Human!" he thought, as he barked louder and louder.
   a. To inform
   b. To persuade
   c. To entertain

2. Anyone can play tennis. All it takes is a few lessons and a willingness to learn. Don't miss your chance to be a part of this exciting sport. Visit the Colby Tennis Center and find out about our affordable lesson packages.
   a. To inform
   b. To persuade
   c. To entertain

3. At least 93 percent of all residents of Hawaii voted in favor of joining the United States in 1959.
   a. To inform
   b. To persuade
   c. To entertain

4. Do you want to lose weight, gain muscles, and be more attractive than you've ever been? Join John's Gym and get on the path to physical fitness!
   a. To inform
   b. To persuade
   c. To entertain

5. Alaska became a state in 1958, when the Alaska statehood act was signed by President Eisenhower.
   a. To inform
   b. To persuade
   c. To entertain

CHAPTER 12

Grade 8—Writing, Speaking, and Listening

In the 8th grade students will be asked to manage opposing points of view (counterclaims) and will work on developing an authoritative voice in writing and communication. Students will be asked to provide more thorough descriptions and explanations than in past grades. As well, students will likely engage in cross-curricular writing projects, through which they will apply their more developed writing skills to argue or explain topics studied in classes other than ELA, such as social studies and science. The narrative writing task will likely focus on analysis of personal experiences, and lessons learned from those experiences. During collaborative discussions, students are expected to listen and respond clearly and respectfully, as in earlier grades, but will now learn to build on the ideas of others, as collaborative skills are further developed.

What Your Eighth Grader Will Learn

In the 8th grade your child will develop her questioning skills and ask pointed questions of others in an effort to uncover new information through discussion. In addition, your eighth grader will begin to synthesize information from multiple sources in a discussion, including other students and resource texts, to develop new, independent ideas.

There are four main focus areas in the Writing standard:

- Writing arguments to support claims
- Writing informative/explanatory texts
- Writing narratives to develop real or imagined experiences
- Conducting research to build and present knowledge

In addition, your child will focus on the following topics in the Speaking and Listening standard:

- Being a collaborative participant in a range of discussions
- Presenting claims and information to others

Writing Arguments to Support Claims

Argumentative writing in the 8th grade adds new focus areas to instruction and assessment. In addition to introducing a claim and acknowledging the counterclaim, which is an opposing point of view, your child will logically address the counterclaim and explain the difference between his own ideas and those who disagree. Eighth grade writers know that it is reasonable to expect disagreement with a claim, and they develop the research and writing skills necessary to respond to an opposing viewpoint. There are several assessed components to argumentative writing in the 8th grade.

Introduce a Claim

The claim is also called the thesis. It is the main point the writer intends to prove. The thesis often offers the writer's point of view and the opposing viewpoint, using a clause that begins with "although." Review the following writing prompt, claim, and counterclaim:

In 2000, the Federal government passed the Children's Internet Protection Act (CIPA) to protect school students from inappropriate content that may be harmful. As a result, all schools have Internet filtering software installed that prevents students from accessing many websites. In recent years, student groups have argued that Internet filters prohibit students from accessing many websites that pose no threat to their safety.

Here is an example of a writing prompt your eighth grader may see associated with this text: Should the CIPA legislation be repealed to grant students greater Internet access in school?

The claim for this essay can also introduce the counterclaim:

While the goal of protecting students from inappropriate online content is a good idea and maintaining a safe learning environment in schools is important, CIPA legislation should be repealed because search engines like Google offer safe searching options, security software often keeps students from accessing valuable websites, and most students have access to the unfiltered Internet on their phones and home computers.

This example provides two points of view on the same question. Both can be logically supported. The writer has formed a claim that will lead to the development of an essay to prove that while protecting students from inappropriate content is a good idea, the CIPA legislation isn't necessary and may be ineffective.

This claim or thesis "promises" the reader that the following points will be covered:

- The goal of protecting students from inappropriate content is a good one.
- It is important that students have a safe learning environment.
- CIPA isn't required because Google already has safe searching options.
- Security software often blocks valuable content.
- Students can easily access inappropriate content anyway.

It will help your child to think of an argumentative essay with a counter-claim as a friendly argument or debate. Her goal is not to be more enthusiastic about her side of the issue but to be methodical in the use of credible information that directly supports her point of view.

In the 8th grade your child will directly respond to counterclaims, rather than only acknowledge them. The two counterclaims in this argument are:

- The goal of protecting students from inappropriate content is a good one.
- It is important that students have a safe learning environment.

The response to a counterclaim does not necessarily have to prove that it is wrong. In the case of this topic, the writer could support the counterclaims, but respond by providing information that supports his own point of view.

The goal of protecting students from inappropriate content is definitely important. In the years since this legislation was passed, many safeguards have been put in place on the Internet, making blocking software obsolete. Since the legislation specifically requires Internet blocking software, it is no longer the most effective way to protect students, and actually does more harm than good, as it denies them access to valuable resources.

In this response, the writer agreed with the basic premise of the counterclaim, but explained that while the purpose of the legislation was a good idea, the implementation no longer makes sense. Notice, specifically, that the writer did not simply dismiss the counterclaim as "wrong," but provided a nuanced explanation.

It will take practice for your child to learn to respond to opposition logically and calmly. Encourage your eighth grader in conversation to acknowledge what is "right" about opposing points of view. For example, imagine you decided that your child had to stay home all weekend to finish a school project. His first response might be to be angry at being denied his free time. Encourage a constructive, analytical response, such as, "It makes sense that I should have to stay home this weekend to make sure I finish my project by

Monday. However, it is not likely that the project will take me two full days to complete, so I will probably have to stay home even after the project is finished. It makes more sense for me to stay home *until* the project is finished."

Supporting a Claim

Throughout middle school your child has researched evidence to support her claims. She will continue to call on these skills in the 8th grade to support a point of view, and will demonstrate more independence in locating credible, appropriate sources. In addition, in the 8th grade your child will continue to learn about the importance of writing logical arguments and avoiding logical fallacies. A logical fallacy is a flaw in reasoning. Writers can use them inadvertently in an effort to support a point of view. In addition to the logical fallacies covered in the 7th grade, your eighth grader should review her work, as well as potential sources, for the following types of logical errors:

Hasty Generalization

A hasty generalization is a broad claim based on limited evidence. For example: "The first time I visited that mall it took an hour to find a parking space; therefore, the mall has inadequate parking and it is always nearly impossible to find a spot." This is a hasty generalization because the writer makes a broad statement about what the parking situation is at the mall all the time based on a single experience. The day the writer visited the mall might have been Black Friday, the busiest shopping day of the year, so all the spaces were taken. This anecdote is not evidence to support a claim that the mall needs more parking.

The Circular Argument

In a circular argument the claim and the reason are the same. For example, "Internet blocking software is a bad idea because it blocks parts of the Internet." In this sentence the reason simply restates the claim. An improved claim that is not a fallacy might read, "Internet blocking software is a bad idea because it blocks valuable educational websites." In the revision, the writer has clearly indicated the problem with the software.

Here is another example of a circular argument, "The president is a good communicator because he effectively shares information." A communicator does indeed share information, but this claim basically says that the president is a good communicator because he is a good communicator. An improved claim that does not include an error of logic might be, "The president is a good communicator because he responds directly to questions from reporters, provides specific details to support his statements, and frequently checks for understanding when explaining complex concepts." In the revision the writer has listed three specific characteristics of the president's communication that support the claim.

Slippery Slope

The name of this fallacy, which may conjure an image of a hill coated with ice, is meant to express the idea that one idea can quickly lead to a conclusion that is not logically supported. A slippery slope fallacy may begin with a sound premise, "We must preserve CIPA legislation to protect students from inappropriate Internet content." The slippery slope conclusion, however, equates the premise with an unrelated consequence: "If we do not preserve CIPA legislation, students may be exposed to inappropriate Internet content, which could lead to them being abducted or kidnapped by Internet predators." Obviously there are dangers to viewing inappropriate content, but it is not logical to propose that viewing an Internet website that might include inappropriate language or R-rated content, for instance, will lead to abduction by a predator.

When writing an argument it is important that the evidence your eighth grader uses is concrete and specific. The best way to provide a logical argument is to use specifics. Help your child find specific information and avoid using fallacies to counter opposing viewpoints.

Make Connections Between Claims

An argumentative essay has three components: the claim, the reason, and the evidence. The following sentence is a claim. It is the main point of an argumentative paper:

CIPA legislation should be repealed.

The claim states the main point that the paper intends to prove. It is a claim because it is an arguable point that someone could reasonably disagree with.

The reasons for the claim provide the logical support. Reasons are valid statements that support the claim. The following are the reasons for the CIPA legislation claim:

- It requires Internet blocking software that is ineffective.
- There are other ways to block inappropriate content, such as Google SafeSearch.
- Students have access to content on their phones and home computers, and such devices are not protected by CIPA-mandated Internet blocking.

The evidence of a claim is proof. Evidence is found through research and by reading and reviewing credible sources. Evidence is necessary to support the reasons for a claim. The first claim regarding the CIPA is that Internet blocking software is ineffective. Evidence for this claim could include:

The most common type of Internet blocking software used by schools automatically blocks any website that allows reader comments. Many credible and appropriate websites, such as the *New York Times* (*www .nytimes.com*) and CNN (*cnn.com*) allow user comments, and are therefore blocked. The software is imprecise.

In a fully developed essay, the writer might go on to explain other common features of Internet blocking software and how those features interfere with research. The evidence would then provide examples that support each reason.

To connect the claim, reasons, and evidence, your child will use transitional words and phrases.

Transitions that link claims and reasons include:

TRANSITIONS THAT LINK CLAIMS AND REASONS	
Transition	**Example sentence**
Because	Smart phones are the most important recent invention *because* they provide access to information.
Due to	*Due to* the fact that they offer users security, smartphones are the most important recent invention.
Since	Smart phones are the most important recent invention **since** they allow users to communicate with others anytime and anywhere.
In view of	*In view of* the fact that smartphones offer access to information, communication, and security, they are the most important recent invention.

Your child should also use transitions to connect evidence to reasons. Evidence usually provides a specific example of information in a reason, and so the most effective transitions are those that link examples to general statements. These transition words and terms include:

- Such as
- For example
- Like
- In particular
- Including
- To illustrate

Here is an example of a paragraph that uses transitions to create cohesion between a claim, reason, and evidence:

> CIPA legislation should be repealed *because* it requires schools to use Internet blocking software that is inefficient. *In particular*, the software blocks websites based on very broad criteria. *For example*, the most common type of Internet blocking software used by schools blocks any website that allows reader comments on articles.

In this example, the writer uses transitions to link the claim, the reason, and the evidence so that the reader understands the logical connections between ideas.

In the 8th grade your child will also write to distinguish a counterclaim from his own claim. Using transitional words and phrases that show contrast will help organize his writing so that counterclaims are distinguished from his own claim. Effective transition words to show contrast include:

- Although
- But
- However
- Instead
- Nevertheless
- Rather than
- Yet

A reasonable counterclaim for this essay might be:

It is important that schools take steps to protect students from inappropriate content on the Internet.

This is a reasonable counterclaim, and a writer would not immediately dismiss it, but it is not well-developed. Notice how the expanded counterclaim that follows is contrasted with the writer's claim.

Of course it is important that schools take steps to protect students from inappropriate content. *However,* the most common types of Internet blocking software are not the most effective ways to do so. *Rather,* schools should investigate different approaches to Internet safety, such as Google SafeSearch.

This writer of the counterclaim does not dismiss the writer's claim; rather, he offers an alternative that is more logical and feasible.

Maintain a Formal Style

Your eighth grader has been working on maintaining a formal style in academic writing all through middle school. By the 8th grade he should be consistently using third person pronouns in academic writing, avoiding contractions, and replacing informal words with more precise and formal diction. *Diction* is a domain-specific term for word choice and sentence structure. In the 8th grade, formal writing also considers other ways of maintaining an objective point of view. It also explores ways of revising first person pronouns and other words that suggest bias. Review the following sentence:

CIPA legislation was obviously not well thought out because it requires schools to use poorly designed Internet blocking software.

In the preceding sentence there is an obvious bias. The sentence is not objective. It doesn't make its point based only on evidence. Instead, it uses judgmental language such as "not well thought out" and "poorly designed." Review the following revision:

The goal of CIPA legislation was to protect students from inappropriate content. Schools quickly implemented Internet blocking software that used broad criteria to determine which websites should be blocked.

Notice that the revision acknowledges the value of the legislation and is very specific about the problem with the most commonly used software. The writer could then go on to explain that the broad selection criteria leads to appropriate websites being blocked along with those that are inappropriate.

Using Concluding Statements

The end of an essay is just as important as the beginning. The conclusion is the writer's last word on a topic and should make the point of the essay, once and for all. Some strategies for writing a successful conclusion include:

1. Return to the theme or main point of the introduction. In the first paragraph, your child set out what he was going to write about. In the conclusion, he can tell the reader why he was successful.
2. Answer the big question, "So what?" A successful conclusion very specifically asserts why the argument matters in the first place, and why anyone should care.
3. Provide suggestions for next steps, especially if something needs to be done about the issue.

Here is an example of a conclusion that uses all three strategies:

In conclusion, it remains important to find ways to protect students from inappropriate content while they use the Internet at school. While the CIPA legislation was a good first step, the Internet blocking software it requires is not effective, and can actually get in the way of student learning. If students are to become effective users of digital information, they must have greater access to that information; otherwise, they will not develop the skills they need to succeed as high school and college researchers. Contact your legislators today and ask them to consider repealing CIPA legislation so that students can take advantage of all appropriate resources the Internet has to offer.

Notice that the conclusion also offers a final rebuttal or explanation for why the counterargument isn't valid before restating the thesis and summarizing the reasons. The reader is left with a clear overview of the argument, the most compelling reason why the counterargument isn't valid, and an idea for what he can do to change this law.

Informative/Explanatory Texts

Informative writing is also called expository writing. Its purpose is to inform or explain. Your child has been writing expository texts for several years in school. In the 6th grade she learned how to organize and write papers to compare/contrast, show cause and effect, define a subject, and to write about events in history using chronological order. In the 7th grade she explored the definition essay for what was likely the first time. In the 8th grade your child will learn about several different types of informational essays, all of which she has been exposed to in the past. In the 8th grade greater focus is placed on analysis of information, rather than simply recounting information.

In the 8th grade your student will investigate an idea or a concept, analyze information, and use that information to explain a concept clearly and concisely. This type of essay is most often used as an assessment tool, or a way for your child to demonstrate his understanding of class topics.

A writing prompt for an expository essay used as an assessment might be very simple, such as:

- What is climate change?
- Explain the most important events leading up to the Vietnam War.
- Explain how poets and artists responded to WWI.

For each of these prompts, the writer would need to conduct research, call on information he has learned in class, and synthesize information into a single, well-organized paper.

There are several assessed components to an informative/explanatory text:

The Introduction

The introduction includes the controlling idea, or thesis of the paper. Even though this isn't an argument, and your child will not be proving a point, there still must be a thesis statement that establishes the focus of the paper. An example might be:

> Climate change is a measurable and observable change in worldwide weather patterns that began in the twentieth century and is caused by an increase of carbon dioxide in earth's atmosphere.

The controlling idea such as this one does two things:

- It responds directly to the prompt.
- It provides a very specific explanation of the term that will be expanded on in the essay with examples and evidence.

Once the controlling idea is in place, your child can write the rest of the introduction. The purpose of the introduction is to hook the reader, provide necessary background information, and present the controlling idea, usually in that order. Here is a sample of an introduction for the preceding climate change essay writing prompt:

> According to the World Wildlife Fund, nearly every glacier in Alaska is currently melting more than twice as fast as they did just one hundred years ago. If glaciers continue to melt at this pace, there will be a catastrophic rise in sea levels, leading to flooding of coastal cities worldwide. Many scientists believe this accelerated melting is caused by climate change. Climate change is a measurable and observable change in worldwide weather patterns that began in the twentieth century and is caused by an increase of carbon dioxide in earth's atmosphere.

This example used a startling fact as a hook. A startling fact is an actual statistic or researched fact that a reader may not be familiar with. In this introduction the fact that glaciers are melting and sea levels will rise creates a sense of urgency and stresses that the topic is important.

Other strategies for beginning an essay include:

- A quotation from a famous person
- An anecdote
- A humorous comment
- A description
- A figure of speech

As in earlier grades, your child should avoid introductions that begin with a sound effect or question. Instead, the essay should begin with concrete and specific information. Some essay topics lend themselves well to using an anecdote or short story that is related to the topic. Be sure to stress to your child that the anecdote must be based in fact. It is not acceptable to invent evidence, even as a way to start an essay.

The introduction should provide a very clear idea of what the essay will be about, but should never include phrases such as "in this essay . . ." or "this essay will . . ." The thesis will provide the information about the topic.

Graphics

Another component of an expository essay is graphics, which can include images, illustrations, charts, and tables. Writers may choose to use tables or charts created by others and available in resources, or they can create their own. If materials from outside sources are used, the original author must be properly cited.

FACT

More often than not your child will be asked to write an expository essay to show that he understands a concept. Clearly communicating information is just as important, if not more important, than using clever word choice. When you help your child with an expository essay, focus on using direct quotes, paraphrases, and summaries from sources. Also, encourage your child to find and analyze statistics—real numbers that are evidence of his main point.

Charts, tables, illustrations, and other graphics can be valuable, but they must be explained in the body of the essay. For example, the topic of climate change could be very well supported by charts or graphics showing measurements of glaciers, average temperatures, or other specific data. It is very important that your child explain this data in the body of his paper. Charts and graphs don't speak for themselves. The writer has to explain what is relevant.

Body Paragraphs

Once the introduction and the formatting are in place, your child will develop her essay with information from research. This information is organized by categories into separate paragraphs, each with a topic sentence.

The controlling idea used in regard to climate change had three main points:

- Climate change is a measurable and observable change in weather patterns
- Climate change began in the twentieth century
- Climate change is caused by an increase of carbon dioxide in the earth's atmosphere

Introducing the categories of information in the introduction or controlling idea will strengthen your child's paper and give him the opportunity to demonstrate his ability to address different categories of evidence, which is a grading criterion.

Each paragraph in the body of the essay should include a topic sentence, which identifies the category of information, and concrete examples, definitions, or details that elaborate on the information in the topic sentence. Here is an example of a topic sentence for the first category of information in this essay:

Climate change is a measurable and observable change in worldwide weather patterns.

The supporting details for this paragraph should be specific. It is not enough, for example, to simply say that weather events are becoming more severe. The student writer might include details such as:

- Evidence that shows an increase in powerful storms in certain parts of the world.
- Evidence of higher than average annual temperatures.
- Evidence that ocean currents are changing.

The strongest essay will include at least three body paragraphs, each covering a different category that has already been introduced in the thesis. A good way to plan an essay is to outline it first, based on the controlling idea.

In the 8th grade your child will likely be asked to integrate information from sources into sentences and paragraphs he has written independently. As in past grades, your child will be asked to cite his sources and give credit to the researchers who initially published the information. Review the following example, which combines the writer's own words with a researched statistic:

There is no doubt that burning fossil fuels has added carbon dioxide to the atmosphere. In fact, since the start of the Industrial Revolution, the amount of carbon dioxide in the atmosphere has increased more than 30 percent (*NASA.gov*).

Notice that the student writer did not quote directly from the source. Instead, he used information from the source to support a specific point, and strengthened that point with the use of a statistic.

Notice also that the writer has cited the source, but that this time the source is not an individual but an organization. When there is no named author, which is sometimes the case for scientific information, the organization that published the information should be cited. This citation will coordinate with another citation at the end of the essay. Again, your child's teacher will likely have a very specific requirement for citing sources. The Common Core standards do not require a specific style, only that sources are cited.

Using Transitions to Clarify Relationships Between Ideas

Like the argumentative essay, the informative essay is strengthened with transitional words and phrases between paragraphs. In the 8th grade, your child should begin to think of creating cohesion in an essay by doing more than just using the transitional words she learned in grades 6 and 7.

Cohesion: This is the connection between sentences. Each paragraph should be cohesive so that one sentence is related to the next. If there is data from research, it should be clear to the reader why it is there. If the student quotes from a text, he should write one or two sentences explaining how the quote is related to the rest of the paragraph. You can help your child develop more cohesive writing by encouraging him to try some of the following strategies:

Amplification: One sentence provides more information about an idea that is first introduced in a sentence that precedes it.

Almost all of the Alaskan glaciers are shrinking. While 95 percent of Alaska's more than 10,000 glaciers have shrunk by as much as 35 percent in the past few decades, a few, such as the Hubbard Glacier, are gaining ice each year.

In this example, the specific evidence in the second sentence amplifies the claim in the first sentence.

Repetition: Cohesion can be created by repeating key terms or ideas in more than one sentence. Review the following example:

When a glacier loses ice, scientists refer to it as glacial retreat. Glacial retreat results in large areas of land being uncovered for the first time in centuries, and can actually benefit wildlife by providing more grazing area.

In those two sentences, the key term *glacial retreat* is repeated. First the term is defined, and then further elaboration explains the effect.

Accumulation: The same idea is explained with two different examples.

Rising sea levels caused by glacial melting will result in more frequent flooding of coastal areas. For example, mangrove forests in southern Florida could be completely destroyed by floodwaters. Likewise, coastal cities like New York and Boston may lose land to the ocean. It will become more expensive and less practical to rebuild in flood zones.

In this example, the writer provides two illustrations of the problems caused by the flooding that will result from rising sea levels. These two examples explain the consequences to natural phenomenon and manmade structures. This accumulation of evidence creates cohesion, or connections between ideas, and strengthens the reader's understanding of the point.

Amplification, repetition, and accumulation are three ways your child can connect ideas as he becomes a more skilled writer. While you will likely continue to see basic transitions in his writing, try to encourage him to create the more advanced connections described here.

Use Precise Language

Precise language is clear and specific. As your child works more frequently with research sources, it will become more important for him to use the language of the expert research in his writing. Domain-specific words are terms that are used in a specific field of study or when writing about a specific subject. Your child may have to look up unfamiliar words when researching a topic. You can help your child by reviewing his use of unfamiliar domain-specific vocabulary in his writing. Consider the following sentence:

> NASA relies on data from the atmospheric infrared sounder flying on the Aqua satellite to measure climate change.

This example uses domain-specific vocabulary including "atmospheric infrared sounder" and "Aqua satellite." Are these terms meaningful in this context? Probably not. Another important part of using domain-specific vocabulary is that it will provide your eighth grader with context or information. This, in turn, will demonstrate his own understanding of the material and help the reader understand highly technical concepts and language. Review the following revision:

> NASA's Aqua satellite carries six different measurement instruments and is in place in orbit around the planet to study precipitation, evaporation, and water cycles all over the earth. One of its instruments, the atmospheric infrared sounder, measures the infrared brightness of the earth's surface. This information provides data on the temperature and amount of water vapor in the atmosphere. As the climate changes, scientists expect to see increases in both temperature and water vapor.

The revision of the sentence still uses domain specific vocabulary and, in fact, adds even more vocabulary words such as *data*, *atmosphere*, and *water vapor.* The additional elaboration clarifies the terms from the first sentence and makes the passage more informative.

Getting into the habit of using domain-specific language is something you can practice with your child. Think about how often you hear a term and simply ignore it or skim over it, assuming the meaning will eventually become clear. When you use a term your child might not be familiar with, ask him if he knows the definition, and then provide him with more information until it makes sense to him. Do the same in return. There are many school-related terms that might be unfamiliar to parents and other adults. Ask your child to explain concepts such as rubrics or benchmarks. Doing so will be good practice for him as it will illustrate the kind of elaboration that is important when using specific vocabulary.

Maintain a Formal Style

As in argumentative writing, informative writing uses a formal style. There are specific characteristics of formal writing. The obvious characteristic is that it avoids slang, text-speak, or writing shortcuts. There are several specific characteristics of formal writing that your child should be aware of when he writes academic essays:

- **Formal writing avoids colloquialisms.** A colloquialism is a phrase that is used in everyday speech, but is not appropriate in academic writing. Some examples include *buzz off* instead of go away, *wanna* instead of *want to*, or *feeling blue* instead of *feeling sad.* Some colloquialisms are so familiar that your child will need support removing them from his formal writing.
- **No abbreviations.** Some abbreviations are so common that your child may forget to use the complete word. Words like automobile, television, and photograph are often abbreviated to auto, TV, or photo. Help your child catch these sorts of abbreviations to ensure his writing is formal.
- **Remain objective.** Objectivity can be challenging. Keep in mind that as soon as a writer says that something is "good" or "beautiful," the text is no longer objective. Any word, especially an adjective, that makes a judgment about the appearance or quality of an object is, by definition, subjective and should be revised.

- **Avoid commands or the imperative voice in writing.** Even when the second person pronoun isn't used, an imperative sentence directly addresses the reader. Sentences such as, "Please contact local officials to find out more . . ." are imperative and are not appropriate for formal writing.

Review the following sentences with your child and consider how to revise them so that the writing is more formal.

Dr. Johnson, a brilliant scientist, has appeared on TV many times to warn the public about climate change.

Take a look at the article about his work in *Time*; it includes several shocking photos. He proves that climate change isn't a fairy tale.

Here the same sentences have been rewritten using formal language:

Dr. Johnson, a scientist with the University of Pleasantville, has appeared on television many times to explain climate change.

In a recent issue of *Time* magazine, there is an article about Dr. Johnson's work, which includes several photographs. Johnson proves that climate change is a reality.

Notice that the colloquialisms have been replaced with more formal terms, and that potentially subjective language, such as referring to Johnson as "brilliant," or the photos as "shocking," has been removed. The information remains identical, but the delivery is formal.

Provide a Concluding Statement

Every strong essay ends with a conclusion. In shorter essays that conclusion might be a single sentence that wraps up the main points. For a longer essay, the conclusion could be a full paragraph. The goal of a conclusion is to answer the question, "So what?" or stress why a topic is meaningful or important. It should also provide closure, and let the reader know that the essay is ending with a specific point. For the past few years your child has learned the nuts and bolts of an effective conclusion. In the 8th grade he might want to experiment with different approaches, such as:

- Conclude with a quote from an authority used as a resource in the essay. Be sure the quote is specific and expresses a clear concept, rather than a general opinion.
- Link a global concept to a local issue. For example, in the case of this essay on climate change, your child might link the information he used to develop his idea to recent weather patterns in your part of the country, such as increased rainfall, frequent flooding, and so forth.
- Offer a new, more precise definition of a key term. In the sample essay the writer worked hard to provide a clear explanation of global warming. He can then end the essay by defining the term again, but this time calling upon the evidence he used in the paper.

It is important that the conclusion is definite, and that it end with a clear idea of the importance of the topic. Remember that the conclusion should not bring in any new information. If there is additional information needed to support the topic, it should be in its own paragraph, before the conclusion.

Writing Narratives

In the 8th grade the purpose of narrative writing is usually to assess a student's understanding of narrative plot structure, or how a story is constructed. Your child will complete narrative writing assignments less frequently than argument or informative writing. As students move toward high school, more and more emphasis is placed on nonfiction texts and students' ability to understand and analyze texts.

Engaging the Reader

In the 8th grade students are expected to engage in a lot less "throat clearing" or general information leading up to the main point of a narrative. Your child should work on establishing a connection with the reader, before he begins writing what the purpose of the narrative will be. He should also include only the information needed to achieve that purpose. Consider the following narrative writing prompt:

Think of a time when you broke a school rule and were given a consequence as a result. Write about that experience and what you learned from it.

A weak introduction might begin with a very broad background:

Rules are in place to protect students and make sure everyone can learn without distractions. While people don't always agree with school rules, it is important to follow them. To help people remember to follow rules, school administrators have set up consequences for breaking the rules. Some of the consequences are very unpleasant and can even be embarrassing. I try very hard to follow school rules, but sometimes I break a rule . . .

In this excerpt, the student has written several "throat clearing" sentences, but hasn't gotten to the point of the paper, which is to write about her own experience. Consider the following revision:

In my school, students must go directly to the cafeteria at lunchtime, even if they have a pass to be somewhere else in the building, like the library or a teacher's classroom. I have a pass to the library almost every day, so after a while, I just stopped checking in at the cafeteria and used the check-in time to organize my locker or visit with friends before I went to the library. I knew I was breaking a rule, but I didn't think it mattered, until I was reported missing from a fire drill, and ended up getting three days of detention for not being with my group during an emergency drill.

Notice in the preceding revision that the writer starts by explaining the rule. Then, she describes how she broke the rule and the consequences for doing so.

Using Dialogue, Pacing, and Description

One of the best ways to make a narrative seem realistic is to use dialogue, which are the words spoken by the characters. Dialogue should reveal what characters are thinking or feeling; it is a window into the "real" person behind a character. Your child should avoid dialogue that simply fills space, such as *"Wow," I said*, because it doesn't really tell us anything about the character. Dialogue should also be realistic, but not too convenient. Review the following example:

> "No," I said to my friend. "I don't care about school rules like this one, and I'm not worried that there will be consequences for not going to the cafeteria. I'll be in the library in a minute, and that's all that matters."

The previous example is too convenient and not realistic. It isn't representative of a real conversation between two students.

Dialogue doesn't have to be hyper-realistic. When people talk, they use filler words like *um* or *yeah*. That isn't necessary in dialogue. Compress language to leave out the fillers and unnecessary words.

Dialogue doesn't explain unfamiliar terms. Save explanations for the narrator. Review the following examples:

> "I'll be in ISS, the in-school suspension classroom, for the rest of the week," I explained to my friend. "I can't meet you in the library."

This is a conversation between two students in the same school. It isn't likely that the narrator would have to explain what ISS means to a peer. Through the narrative, the story can provide that additional information, but it should not be part of the dialogue.

Pacing is another important aspect of narrative writing. The pace of a story is the rate at which the narrator takes the reader through the events. A slower pace builds suspense. A fast pace creates excitement. Consider the following examples:

> I leaned against the locker bank. The fire alarm was loud, and I felt like it was pulsing through my heart. I couldn't hear anything but the steady beep, beep, beep and began to wonder if it would damage my hearing. I didn't know where I should go. I began running in the direction of the cafeteria, but I wondered if I would get in trouble for being late, so I stopped, turned around, and headed back to the library. The door to the library was locked, and nobody was there.

All I could hear was the pulsing beep of the fire alarm. My first thought was to get to the cafeteria, so I dashed down the hall in that direction. I skidded to a stop just before the doorway though. Would I be in trouble for being late? Should I be at the library? I ran back in the opposite direction, finally reaching the door to the library. I tugged on the handle, but it was locked. I peered in the window . . . empty . . . all gone. Now what?

The first example is much more pensive. The narrator spends a lot of time *thinking* about what to do. The second example, which is faster paced, has more action; the narrator dashes, skids, runs, and tugs. The pace is quicker and the story is more exciting. The faster pace has built narrative tension.

Using Transitional Words and Phrases

Just as in argumentative and explanatory writing, transitions are crucial in narrative writing to move the story from one point to the next. Two types of transitions especially helpful for narrative writing are those used to show the passing of time and those used to show spatial relationships.

COMMON TRANSITION WORDS AND PHRASES	
Type of transition	**Word or phrase**
To show time	soon
	later
	then
	by the time
	eventually
	before/after
	until/since
To show spatial relationships	near, far
	farther, closer
	up, down, right, left
	in front of, behind
	nearby, beside

Whenever a character moves within a setting, writers can help orient the reader by using spatial transitions. Remember that the reader doesn't know the setting of a story, so it is important to spatially orient the reader so he has a sense of distances between locations and features of a specific setting.

Use Precise Language and Descriptive Details

Narrative writing also relies on precise language. Precision is developed using very clear and vivid details. It takes practice for a writer to determine what kinds of details are most important to a narrative. It can be easy to focus on details that are interesting, but unnecessary to the narrative. Part of the revision process your child undertakes should be to edit out description that does not improve a narrative.

Provide a Conclusion

Every good narrative has an ending. The ending will share a lesson learned or draw a conclusion, as in the case in the following example, which will draw a conclusion about the importance of rules. There are some other techniques that can add an interesting ending to a narrative, such as ending with an image or describing a final scene with vivid detail.

I stared at the dull green walls of the detention room. Old wooden desks lined the sides and a bored teaching assistant sat at the front of the room, trying not to nod off as she flipped idly through a newspaper. This would be my lunchtime home for the next few days . . .

The vivid description of the detention room here stresses the conclusion of the essay, which is that the narrator faced a consequence for her actions, and that it was not a pleasant consequence.

Another interesting technique is to end with dialogue: Strong dialogue leaves a memorable impact on the reader. The dialogue should be interesting and share a key point about the story.

A 7th grade boy, seated on the other side of the detention room noticed that the teaching assistant had nodded off. He whispered loudly, "What did you do?" I thought for a moment, and glanced at the teacher before I replied, "I thought school rules didn't matter, until yesterday, that is."

The previous dialogue exchange is realistic and gives the narrator a chance to leave a parting idea proving that she has learned that school rules do matter.

Another good way to end a story is to end with a reflection. A reflection is a chance for the narrator to review everything that happened in the story and to share her final thoughts or realizations.

Until a few days ago, I didn't think school rules were that important. But, after I realized the trouble I had caused, and the number of people who were worried about me when they thought I was lost during the fire drill, I know that most rules are in place to keep everyone safe. I'm not saying I'll never break a rule again; but I'll definitely think about why some rules exist before I decide they don't matter.

The reflection reviews some key plot points and resolves the lesson-learned aspect of the writing prompt.

Conducting Research

In the 8th grade your child will complete short research projects to answer a research question. He will learn to access multiple sources to find information that develops a response and to consider topics for further study. There are several important skills required for effective research:

- Developing a research question and other questions related to a topic.
- Choosing relevant sources and combining information from multiple sources to answer research questions.
- Avoiding plagiarism and using sources appropriately.

By the 8th grade your child's teacher will have several expectations for research projects. For example, your child will be expected to have the ability to develop a focused research question and identify and eliminate questions that are related to the research topic but are outside the scope of a specific project. Your eighth grader will also be expected to know how and where to find credible sources. Finally, your child's teacher will expect that all 8th grade students will understand how to use sources appropriately.

Teachers will, of course, support students as they work on research, but they will likely give less direct instruction on how to complete the different steps in the project. To complete a research project with greater independence, your child should try to follow these steps:

1. Develop a research question. The research question provides the focus for the project and puts limits on what your child will investigate. A strong research question might be, "What are the health risks of using performance-enhancing steroids?" This question provides a topic (steroids), and a very specific focus (the health risks of using steroids).

2. Conduct research. Find preliminary sources that help develop the thesis for the topic. Sources can be found on the Internet. However, your child must continue to apply what he knows about judging the credibility of sources. The school library may subscribe to academic databases that provide articles and other resources that are definitely credible.

3. Develop a thesis statement. After spending some time reviewing resources, skimming websites, and reading short summaries of longer articles (abstracts), your child should develop a preliminary thesis statement. In the example of steroid use, such a statement could be, "Using performance-enhancing steroids can result in unattractive body changes, high blood pressure, heart disease, and increased risk of some kinds of cancer."

4. Create an outline. Once the preliminary research is complete and the thesis is in place, your child can plan his essay. Creating an outline is the best way to begin. He can use the details from the thesis to create topics for each body paragraph. In this case, the body paragraphs would include unattractive body changes, high blood pressure, heart disease, and cancer.

5. Research and record sources. For each section of the essay, your child should research the topic and collect notes. He should record the name of the source for each fact he gathers.

6. Write a rough draft. Once he has gathered the information he needs, your child can write a draft of his essay. Encourage your child to write a draft without a lot of concern about grammar, sentence structure, or spelling and other mechanics. The goal is to get ideas on paper in a longer form. He should make an effort to use some sort of citation for ideas

that are not his own. At this point, it isn't necessary to quote directly from any sources.

7. Seek feedback. Your child's teacher may want to review rough drafts or may offer a peer review opportunity where students share their drafts with each other. If neither of these opportunities is offered, help your child by providing feedback on the strength of his ideas. Avoid focusing on mechanics. Instead, ask questions to help him fill in blanks and make his paper more thorough.

8. Make revisions. In the first revision your child will include any direct quotes from sources he wants to use, rearrange ideas to ensure his paper is developed logically, and answer any questions that came up by providing more information.

9. Conduct a final edit. Editing, or reworking and addressing the mechanics of an essay, should be the last step. Help your child identify sentence errors, word choice errors, and other mechanical issues that can interfere with clarity and meaning.

10. Publish. Print the final paper, including a title page and reference page, and prepare it to be submitted.

ESSENTIAL

Encourage your child to work on a timeline that leaves time for the paper to "rest" between drafting and revision. Most writers find that they can more effectively find errors in logic and mechanical errors when they've stepped away from a paper for a few days. In addition, encourage your child to read his paper out loud, or read it out loud to him. Hearing a paper read is an excellent way to identify sections that just don't "sound right."

As always, it is important that your child's paper is his own work, and that he does not use the work of others as his own. Most eighth graders understand what plagiarism is, and work hard to avoid it. However, there are several reasons why a student might unintentionally plagiarize, and they are worth noting:

- Unintentional plagiarism can occur when a student writes about a concept in her own words and forgets a citation. Remind your child that any idea that is not her own must be cited, even if she has written about it in her own words.

- Using parts of a paper he has written in a different class for another paper is considered plagiarism. Students sometimes don't realize that their own work can be plagiarized. Most schools have a rule that students cannot receive credit for the same work in different classes. If your child has a great interest in a single subject, be sure he conducts new research each time he writes about it, and that he doesn't mistake his learning from other projects for common knowledge. To help him avoid this type of plagiarism, encourage your child to address a familiar topic with a completely different research question or to look at another side of an issue.

- Students might inadvertently plagiarize by punctuating direct quotations incorrectly. Encourage your child to use quotation marks around all words copied directly from a source. If part of a quote is within quotation marks, but another part is not, the unquoted and uncited portion could be considered plagiarism.

- Students might not realize that they are plagiarizing when they take quotes from television shows or movies without citing a source. Television programs and movies are citable sources, just as texts are. Encourage your child to cite the original source of any information he has learned from watching movies or TV.

Outside sources can be of great value, but they must be used responsibly. Encourage your child to use research as a tool to make his own ideas more detailed, but guide him so that he does not use the work of others as a substitute for his own ideas.

Engage in Collaborative Discussions

In the 8th grade your child will be asked to discuss topics with others. He may have an assigned discussion group, or he might need to participate in a whole-class discussion. As well, he may be asked to discuss a topic with a small group and report findings to the class.

Proper preparation is essential for participating in a class discussion. Your child should prepare by carefully studying any related readings and annotating them to address the assigned purpose. By the 8th grade, your child's teacher will expect students to have had many classroom discussion experiences, and there will likely be less direct instruction for how to contribute. Consider reviewing the following tips with your child so that he can be reminded of the expectations of a collegial discussion:

1. Arrive to class prepared with a strong understanding of the assigned reading or topic. It can help to prepare some "talking points" or questions in advance. To create these talking points, your child should review his annotations on a reading and consider what he wants to know more about, and what he considers to be a unique or new insight.
2. When others speak, pay close attention. Your child should make notes on his own paper when a speaker addresses an idea or answers a question.
3. Begin speaking by summarizing what the last speaker said in a sentence or two. This shows the other participants that the speaker is paying attention. This practice also gives the previous speakers a chance to correct any misunderstanding about a given point.
4. Each speaker should make it clear when he has stopped summarizing the last person's point, and is going on to add his own insight. Your child can do this by simply saying something like, "My opinion is . . ." or "My interpretation of the story is . . ."
5. When a speaker has finished, ask for feedback. The speaker might ask if anyone agrees with him or has anything to add. Reaching out in this way encourages further discussion.
6. Participants should not focus on who is right or wrong. Your child should think of a discussion as a way to bring up many different points of view. It is possible that there are several right answers to a question that requires interpretation.

Remember that class discussion is intended to be collegial. That means that no one person should dominate the conversation and every opinion or idea should be given equal attention and respect. Encourage your child to be respectful, even when he strongly disagrees with another person's point of view. Learning to engage in a shared discussion is a crucial life and career skill.

Presenting Claims and Information to Others

In the 8th grade your child will be asked to present information to the class. This will be an individual activity. By the 8th grade your child will have presented individually and as part of a group many times. He will have experience researching a topic, and should have a working understanding of standard presentation tools, including PowerPoint, Prezi, and other options. His teacher will be looking for evidence of development from prior years.

FACT

A fear of public speaking is not uncommon. However, research has shown that reluctance to speak in front of groups can lead to lack of success in one's career. More than three-quarters of all Americans claim a fear of public speaking. Most are able to overcome it to the degree necessary to participate in collegial and professional discussions. If your child shares that he is afraid of speaking in front of the group, encourage him to prepare as thoroughly as possible. Being thoroughly prepared can reduce speaking anxiety tremendously.

There are several criteria your child's teacher may use to assess the presentation skills of 8th grade students. These can include, but are not limited to:

- **Purpose and organization.** Your child will be assessed on the focus and organization of his presentation. Purpose is determined by a clear thesis statement. Just as in his argumentative and informative writing, your child should have a clearly established point to his presentation information. In addition, key details about the topic should be revealed logically and in a way that allows the audience to follow along.
- **Awareness of audience.** By the 8th grade your child will be expected to consider the audience of his work, and to think outside of himself to a greater degree than before. Encourage your child to think about to whom he'll be presenting. Will it be other students? Just a teacher? Students from several grades? What can he reasonably expect his audience to know about his topic? Encourage him to include explanations, definitions, and other information that will help the audience understand what he's talking about.

- **Effectiveness of presentation.** This criterion includes everything from body language to volume. Help your child thoroughly prepare for his presentation so that he appears confident and knowledgeable. Encourage him to make eye contact with members of his audience and to look for signs of agreement or confusion among those watching him.
- **Content.** This is hardly the least important aspect of a successful presentation, but it is likely the area your child will feel most confident about. Be sure that he has used credible sources and that he supports his points with evidence.

Your child may be required to use visuals in his presentation. Some teachers may ask students to prepare handouts or notes. If your child is asked to create a notes page or handout to accompany his presentation, keep the following tips in mind so that you can ensure his notes are useful and easy to understand:

- **Keep it brief.** Remember that a handout is for reference. Your child's presentation will deliver most of the information. The handout should define key terms, provide important dates, or include other specific information. The handout should not be something students will use to follow along with the presentation.
- **Include references.** One purpose of a handout might be for students in the audience to identify what they'd like to learn more about. A handout should include a list of references your child used to create the presentation.
- **Make sure the handouts don't include information that is not introduced in the slides.** In some cases, it might be worthwhile to offer more details in a handout, but this is not the place to introduce an entirely new topic.
- **Make sure there is white space on the handout, or room for readers to annotate and add notes.** Leave wide margins and space between main points.
- **During your child's presentation, he might want to let the audience know what information is covered in the handout.** Doing so will help audience members focus their notes, questions, and requests for elaboration.

Encourage your child to practice her presentation thoroughly, and to prepare additional notes on her topic. If a teacher has assigned presentations as a way to disseminate content in the classroom, it is likely there will be a question and answer period. Your child will feel more confident if she has considered potential questions about her topic, and how she might respond. Remind your child that it is okay to tell an audience if she doesn't know the answer to a question. In fact, it is much better for a speaker to offer to find the information and get back to someone at a later time than it is to provide information that might not be accurate.

Practice Exercises

The following exercises will help your child practice her newly acquired skills. These are similar to questions she would find on a standardized test.

Identifying Arguments

Read each of the following. Highlight the sentences that would be strong argumentative claims.

1. The chow is the only dog that doesn't have a pink tongue.
2. The chow is an ideal family dog because it has a pleasant temperament.
3. The only mammal that can fly is the bat.
4. The world population of honeybees is diminishing, and issues such as global warming must be addressed if they are to be saved.
5. People should not kill spiders.

Types of Fallacies

Read each statement and determine the type of fallacy.

1. Starting school an hour earlier is a bad idea because students will be required to get up an hour earlier.
   a. Hasty Generalization
   b. Circular Argument
   c. Slippery Slope

2. I don't enjoy books by Mark Twain. I read *The Adventures of Huckleberry Finn* and didn't like it at all, so I know I won't like any of the other novels he wrote.
   a. Hasty Generalization
   b. Circular Argument
   c. Slippery Slope

3. If we don't require students to complete homework every night, they won't study, will likely do poorly on exams, will be less likely to finish high school, and may never earn a college degree.
   a. Hasty Generalization
   b. Circular Argument
   c. Slippery Slope

4. I never eat seafood. I had lobster one time and hated it. All types of seafood are disgusting.
   a. Hasty Generalization
   b. Circular Argument
   c. Slippery Slope

5. Parking on this side of the street is illegal because it is against the law.
   a. Hasty Generalization
   b. Circular Argument
   c. Slippery Slope

CHAPTER 13

Grade 8—Language

In the 8th grade your child will continue to delve into the more complex aspects of grammar and language. These new skills are introduced on the foundation of prior years' instruction. For example, students should come to the 8th grade with an understanding of the parts of speech, which is crucial for learning new grammar concepts such as gerunds, participles, and infinitives, and how they work in sentences. As with language studies in all of the preceding grades, the purpose of learning these different aspects of language is so that students can become competent and confident communicators.

What Your Eighth Grader Will Learn

As in grades 6 and 7, in grade 8, students are expected to have mastered the Language standards from prior grades. Each of these categories of study builds upon what was taught the year before.

There are four categories of study in the language standard:

- Conventions of grammar
- Knowledge of language or style (verb moods)
- Punctuation: commas, ellipses, and dashes
- Vocabulary
- Figurative language

The grammar section focuses on verbals, or words and groups of words that are formed from verbs but function as different parts of speech. Your child will also learn to use verbs to create sentences that are either active or passive. Continuing the study of verbs, your child will learn to form and identify the different moods of verbs: indicative, imperative, interrogative, conditional, and subjunctive. Finally, your child will be able to identify and correct errors in verb usage, including voice (active or passive) and mood.

Punctuation study in the 8th grade covers commas, ellipses, and dashes as ways to indicate pauses in speech. In addition, since students will be working with sources throughout their academic experience in the 8th grade and on, they will learn to use the ellipses to indicate an omission in a quoted passage, which is a crucial skill for maintaining academic integrity.

Your eighth grader will learn to use the active and passive voices in the conditional subjunctive moods in order to achieve a specific effect in their writing. For example, using the subjective mood of a verb, students can write about wishes or desires, or write about situations that are not true, such as sentences like, "If I were president . . ." (In this example sentence the verb indicates that the statement is contrary to fact.)

In the 8th grade, students will continue to develop the skills necessary to understand unfamiliar words and add those words to their own vocabularies. As in prior grades, your child will learn to use context to determine a word's meaning, particularly the overall meaning of a sentence or paragraph. Additional Latin and Greek affixes are introduced, bringing new ways for students to understand unfamiliar words. As in prior grades, your eighth grader will learn to make use of reference materials to understand definitions and pronunciations of unfamiliar words.

In the 8th grade, readers begin to work with language in new ways. Your eighth grader will understand the definition of a pun, be able to identify a pun in a text, and write puns independently. Your child will also identify and discuss different types of irony and how authors use irony to stress concepts and ideas in a literary text. In addition, students pursue precision in their vocabulary understanding by considering the nuances and connotations of words, and how the meaning of a word can be determined by the context of a sentence and be affected by that text as well.

Conventions of Grammar

Your eighth grader's grammar study will focus on the use of verbs and verbals. Verbs are words that show action or state of being. A verbal is a word or group of words that is formed from a verb but does not function as a verb. The three types of verbals are gerunds, participles, and infinitives.

Gerunds

A gerund is a verb with the ending -*ing* that functions as a noun in a sentence. Nouns are people, places, or things. Gerunds are used in the following sentences:

Swimming is my favorite sport.
My father enjoys *cooking*.
The teacher warned us about *talking*.

In the first sentence, *swimming* functions as the subject of the sentence. In the second sentence, *cooking* is a direct object, and, in the last sentence, *talking* is the object of the preposition *about*.

Writers can use adjectives to modify gerunds, just as they would with nouns.

Her *quiet singing* soothed the children to sleep.
Sam's *thoughtless complaining* offended his mother.

In the first sentence, *quiet* modifies or provides more information about the gerund, *singing*. In the second sentence, *thoughtless* modifies the gerund, *complaining*.

Any action can be made into a gerund and used as a noun. Gerunds are useful in describing activities rather than the action of the activity. For example, the verb *swim* describes the action, but *swimming* describes the activity. *To cook* describes the action, but *cooking* describes the activity. Gerunds should not be confused with participles.

Participles

The verbals formed with participles function as adjectives in a sentence. Participles are formed by adding *-ed, -d, -t, -en, -n,* or *-ing* to a verb. When *-ing* is added, the adjective adds information about something happening in the present. When any other affixes are added, the information is about something that occurred in the past.

The *fried* chicken smelled delicious.
The *frying* chicken smelled delicious.

FACT

When combined with a helping verb or forms of *to be* or *to have*, participles form several verb tenses, including present perfect, past perfect, present perfect progressive, and past perfect progressive. These tenses are used to more precisely indicate when events in the past occurred.

In the first sentence, the chicken has already been fried when the smell is noted. In the second sentence, the chicken is in the process of frying. Both *fried* and *frying* modify the noun, *chicken*. Here are two more examples:

The *fallen* branches littered the driveway.
The *falling* branches crashed onto the cars.

In the first sentence, the branches have already fallen, while in the second, they are falling. Both *fallen* and *falling* modify the noun, *branches*.

Infinitives

An infinitive is a verbal formed by adding "to" to the base form of a verb.

to run
to read
to swim

Generally, an infinitive functions as a noun in a sentence, although sometimes it can modify another word and function as an adjective or adverb. It can be confusing to determine what part of speech the infinitive is working as, but identifying its placement in a sentence can help.

In the following sentence, the infinitive *to leave* is the subject of the sentence and functions as a noun in the sentence.

To leave now would be foolish.

In the following sentence, the infinitive also functions as a noun. This time, though, it is the object of a verb, *want*.

Marti complained that she didn't want *to leave*.

In the following sentence, the infinitive functions as an adjective, modifying the noun, *nerve*.

She didn't have the nerve *to leave*.

Finally, in the next sentence, the infinitive functions as an adverb, modifying the verb, *prepared*.

We prepared *to leave*.

In all of the example sentences the same infinitive functioned as three different parts of speech in four different forms. Help your child identify these distinctions by discussing what is being modified in a sentence. It can be easy to identify an infinitive, but challenging to note the part of speech.

ALERT

The split infinitive is a common grammar error. The infinitive, *to +* verb, should never be interrupted with a modifier. *I like to frequently swim* is incorrect. The correct sentence is, *I like to swim frequently.*

Active and Passive Voice

When the subject of a sentence performs the action of the sentence, that sentence is in the *active voice.* When the action of the sentence is performed *on* the subject, the sentence is in the *passive voice.*

Active voice: Seth moved the couch to the other side of the room.
Passive voice: The couch was moved to the other side of the room by Seth.

Sentences written in the active voice are more concise, meaning they require fewer words to communicate an idea. They are also more precise, as the subject is the noun that completes the action. In the case of the examples, in the first sentence Seth is the subject and he completes the action, *moved.* In the second example, Seth still completes the action, but the focus is on the object receiving that action. In most situations sentences written in the active voice are stronger and more direct.

QUESTION

When are sentences in the passive voice better?
In scientific writing, or descriptions of experiments or studies, scientists often use the passive voice as a means of focusing the reader on a process or results, such as, "The seeds were planted in two inches of enriched soil." In this sentence, the writer wants the reader to focus on the seeds not on the researcher doing the planting, who isn't even mentioned.

Sometimes students confuse passive voice with more formal writing, as in this sentence:

The issues managed by the founding fathers included taxation and property and voting rights.

This sentence is actually no more formal than the following sentence, which is stronger because it is more concise:

The founding fathers managed taxation and property and voting rights.

Encourage your child to review her writing and identify where she is using the passive voice. Changing a sentence to the active voice usually requires a revision, rather than simply rearranging the order of a few words. Here are some examples of sentences that need revisions:

Dinner was served at 8:00 P.M.

In this sentence, the reader doesn't know who served dinner, so information has to be added to the sentence to make it active.

Janet served dinner at 8:00 P.M.

Sometimes the subject is included in a passive voice construction, usually preceded with *by*.

Dinner was served at 8:00 P.M. *by* Janet.

The use of *by* makes it easy to identify the passive voice, and it is easy to revise.

Janet served dinner at 8:00 P.M.

Verb Moods

The mood of a verb indicates the attitude of the sentence or attitude of the speaker. Moods are classifications of verbs. Verbs have several moods:

- Indicative
- Imperative
- Interrogative

- Conditional
- Subjunctive

The mood indicates the reality or the state of being. (By contrast, verb tenses indicate *when* something happens in the past, present, or future.) The mood is the way something is expressed, and makes the distinction between a statement or question, a wish, or a command.

Indicative Mood

The indicative mood makes a statement of fact. It is the most common mood in writing. The main verbs in these sentences are in the indicative mood.

We will leave in an hour.
She plays tennis.
He spent his allowance on video games.

In each of these sentences, the speaker considers that what she is saying is a fact. The indicative mood is used when the statement is a fact or what is believed to be a fact.

Imperative Mood

The imperative mood is used when a sentence is a command or a request. The imperative includes an understood subject, which is "you."

Please be seated.
Finish your homework.
Hand me that pen.

In each of these sentences, the subject is unstated. The command is addressed to the unstated subject.

Interrogative Mood

The interrogative mood is used to ask a question.

Who is that?
What time does the bus leave?

Mom is picking us up, isn't she?
Is that your dog?

Notice that some questions ask who, where, what, when, or why. Often in the interrogative mood the subject and verb are reversed, as in "Will you go?" rather than "You will go." Other forms have a question tagged to the end of a statement, such as, "You won't leave without me, will you?"

Conditional Mood

The conditional is used when the action of a verb can only happen if a certain condition is met. The helping verb *would* is used with the conditional, and the sentence usually includes either the words *if* or *but*.

I would come over, but I'm studying for my math test.
Marty would be a good pitcher if he could relax.

Students sometimes confuse the conditional with the imperfect past tense, as in this sentence:

When I was younger I would watch cartoons every day.
When I was a third grader, I used to walk to school with my brother.

If you can substitute *used to* for *would*, and the sentence has the same meaning, it is not the conditional, but the imperfect.

Subjunctive Mood

The subjunctive is used to indicate wishes, dreams, and other conditions that are not facts. The subjunctive is formed with the verbs *were* and *had*, and the prepositions *if* and *as though*.

In the example that follows, the subjunctive indicates that the speaker has not studied. It is followed by the clause that includes a conditional, *would have passed*.

If I had studied, I would have passed the test.

In the following example, Jon is not a cheater, thus, he did not do well on the test. The statement is not true and the subjunctive is used to express that.

If Jon were a cheater, he would have done well on that test.

The subjunctive can also be used to express wishes or desires, as in this example:

If I were a billionaire, I would fund space travel.

The speaker is not a billionaire, and will not be funding space travel, but may wish that she were, as indicated in this sentence.

Usually the word *if* is a clue that the mood is subjunctive, but not always. Readers should also review the verb tense.

If I practice every day, I will become a better pitcher.
If I were to practice every day, I would become a better pitcher.

In the first example, the daily practice is likely to occur and lead to improved pitching skill. In the second example, the daily practice is much less likely, and the possibility of becoming a better pitcher is slim.

The subjunctive is often used with the conditional mood. In the following example the dependent clause, beginning with *if*, is in the subjunctive mood; while the independent clause, following the comma, is in the conditional mood.

If I were an astronaut, I would go camping on an asteroid.

Going camping on an asteroid is conditioned upon the speaker being an astronaut. Since the subjunctive is used in the dependent clause, it is unlikely that the speaker is an astronaut, so the asteroid camping trip is not going to happen.

Commas, Ellipses, and Dashes

Ellipses, commas, and dashes are used to indicate pauses in speaking or writing. Writers use these punctuation marks to add interest, build suspense, or show shock or surprise. Your student will learn the difference between these three punctuation marks and how to use them correctly.

Commas

Commas are used to indicate a very brief pause that does not suggest emotion or content. The main purpose of a comma is to help the reader better understand what is being read. The separation of ideas and the pause is intended to clarify meaning. Use a comma in the following situations:

- Between items in a series of three or more.
- After a dependent clause, if it precedes an independent clause.
- After the introductory words *yes* or *no*, when they appear at the beginning of a sentence.
- To set off parenthetical phrases or nonessential phrases in a sentence.
- To separate a city and state.
- To separate a direct quote from the rest of a sentence.
- To separate the date from the year.
- To separate an appositive phrase.

All of these situations require a pause in speaking or reading in order to provide clarity. In the example that follows, the commas in the series cue the reader to pause in a way that helps make meaning of the items listed:

I had a salad that was made from goat cheese, lettuce, raisins, and pecans.

Now read the sentence without the commas:

I had a salad that was made from goat cheese lettuce raisins and pecans.

In the second example, is there any way for the reader to know that the first ingredient is a kind of cheese made from goat's milk? Or does the second example suggest that the salad includes the meat of a goat? The comma provides clarity so the reader knows for certain what is being described.

When clarity is the main goal, a comma is the correct punctuation to indicate a pause in reading or speaking.

Ellipses

Ellipses are used to indicate a longer pause than a comma. The ellipsis can add suspense in a story by slowing down the narrative. It can also show that a thought has trailed off. The most common uses for ellipses are:

- Signal an unfinished thought.
- Show hesitation, as though the speaker is searching for the right words.
- Show that part of a direct quote has been omitted.

ESSENTIAL

An ellipsis is always three dots, even when it appears at the end of a sentence. A writer should not add a fourth dot for the period at the end of the sentence.

In the following example, an ellipsis is used to show that words have been omitted from a direct quote:

"To be, or not to be. That . . . question."

The words "is the" are omitted from the quote from *Hamlet*. The full quote is, "To be, or not to be. That is the question." Writers of research papers will find it helpful to omit unnecessary introductory information before and after evidence from the sources they use.

FACT

The singular form is *ellipsis* and the plural is *ellipses*. It is correct to write "An ellipsis is . . ." or "Ellipses are . . ." It might be confusing to note that *ellipses* is also the plural of another word, ellipse, which is a type of mathematical curve.

In the sentence that follows, an ellipsis is used to show an unfinished thought. Notice how it builds suspense. This technique is most often used in narrative writing:

Tom had many questions. He began to wonder, "What if . . ."

The writer doesn't indicate what Tom is wondering about, so the reader becomes curious. Because of the building suspense, the reader is encouraged to continue on with the text.

In the example that follows, the ellipsis is used to indicate a hesitation:

"Excuse me," said Peter, "Could I see that . . . that . . . medallion in the case?"

In this example, the writer is showing that Peter needed a moment to gather his thoughts.

Dash

The dash shows a sudden and abrupt break in a sentence. If a comma suggests a short pause and an ellipsis suggests a longer, slower pause, then the dash suggests an emphasized stop within a sentence. A dash can be used for the following:

- To indicate something that has interrupted a sentence.
- To indicate a change in direction or off topic comment.
- To show surprise, anger, or another strong emotion within a sentence.

ALERT

Dashes should be used in pairs, unless the information set off continues to the end of the sentence: *I met my brother—my favorite person—at the airport,* is correct, as is *I met my brother at the airport—the new one that just opened.*

In the following example, the dash is used to show an interruption to the main point of the sentence:

296

I don't know where—or even when—I'll see my cousins again.

In the following sentence, the dash is used to set off an expression of strong emotion from the rest of the sentence:

My little brother—that jerk—broke my computer.

Dashes are the strongest type of pause in a sentence and, like exclamation points, should be used sparingly. If dashes are used too frequently they lose their impact and the pauses they convey will be no different than the standard pauses created with commas.

Vocabulary Acquisition

In the 8th grade, students use context clues to determine the meanings of unfamiliar words. As they did in the 6th and 7th grades, they use their knowledge of Greek and Latin affixes and root words to understand unfamiliar words. Finally, they use reference materials to confirm understanding of unfamiliar words.

Using Context Clues

In the 7th grade, your child began using the context of an entire paragraph or passage to determine the meaning of an unfamiliar word. Those skills are further developed in the 8th grade with longer texts and more subtle clues. For example:

Patrick snatched his phone out of the puddle almost instantly. He worried that it might be too late. He tapped fiercely on the screen, but it was *unresponsive*. He sullenly stashed it in his backpack and trudged home.

Using several different clues, the reader can conclude that the phone is not working. The reader can use her *schema*, or background knowledge, of what happens to a phone that falls in a puddle, along with the clues about Patrick's mood (the words *sullenly* and *trudged*) to determine that the phone did not work when Patrick tapped it. The reader can arrive at the contextual meaning of the word *unresponsive*, which in this case means inactive or no longer working.

Here is another example:

> Jonas was *appalled* by his friends' behavior when they had a substitute teacher. The teacher was obviously displeased as well, but she may have been more accustomed to that type of behavior than Jonas was, as she simply sighed and wrote the boys' names down to report to the principal.

In this sentence, the reader can tell that *appalled* is somewhat similar to *displeased*. With continued reading, the reader learns that being appalled is a stronger feeling than being displeased. The reader can then guess that appalled means disgusted or shocked.

Learning to use extended context to determine the meaning of an unfamiliar word can be challenging. You can help your child by encouraging him to keep reading if he doesn't find a clue in the same sentence as the unfamiliar word. It can also help to discuss the overall subject or tone of a passage.

Greek and Latin Affixes and Roots

As in the 6th and 7th grades, your child will learn the meanings of common Greek and Latin word parts and apply that knowledge to determining the meanings of unfamiliar words. There are hundreds of Greek and Latin word parts, and some of the most commonly studied in the 8th grade are detailed in the following table:

COMMON GREEK AND LATIN WORD PARTS		
Word Part	**Meaning**	**Example**
auto-	self	automatic
biblio-	book	bibliography
capitis	head	captain
dentis	teeth	dental
dormio-	sleep	dormitory
frater	brother	fraternity
homo-	same	homophone
mater	mother	maternity

mid	middle	midnight
neo-	new	neonatal
pater	father	patriarch
ped-	foot	pedicure
unus	one	unit
vivo	live	revive

In the sentence that follows, the unfamiliar word is underlined:

The choir members sang in <u>unison</u>.

Based on his study of root words, the reader knows that *uni* means one. He can reasonably infer that in this sentence, the choir members are singing as one, or together, following the same notes and lyrics.

In the next sentence, the unfamiliar word is underlined:

The class was divided into <u>homogeneous</u> groups, based on the students' reading ability.

The reader knows that the word part *homo* means *same*, so she can infer that the readers in each group had similar reading abilities. The groups are made up of students who are the same.

Consulting Reference Materials

Despite the many tools and strategies your child has to help him determine the meaning of unfamiliar words, there will be times when a dictionary or other reference is necessary. Using a glossary, an online dictionary, or a traditional dictionary are excellent strategies for confirming meaning, and can help your child add new words to her vocabulary. Students in the 8th grade will continue to practice identifying the correct meaning of a word through context. They will also use their knowledge of parts of speech to discover meaning.

In the example that follows, the unfamiliar word is underlined:

Filthy floodwaters <u>course</u> through the streets.

An astute reader identifies that *course* in this sentence is the verb. Reviewing the following dictionary definitions provides additional information:

1. (noun) the path or route along which anything moves
2. (noun) a class that is part of a unit of study
3. (verb) to move swiftly

Since the reader knows that *course* is being used as a verb, the only applicable definition is the third definition, *to move swiftly*.

In the following sentence, the unfamiliar word is underlined:

Nina was afraid she might <u>jam</u> her fingers in the car door.

The reader might believe that *jam* functions as a verb in this sentence, but she is uncertain. She consults the dictionary and finds the following definitions:

1. (verb) to crush or bruise
2. (verb) to block or bump a pass receiver in football
3. (noun) a food made by cooking fruit and sugar until the mixture thickens

The reader can eliminate the third definition, as the sentence has nothing to do with fruit. The remaining definitions are both verbs, so the reader can be sure that the word is a verb, and that the first definition is correct, *to crush or bruise*.

The key to successful vocabulary acquisition is persistence. Help your child try multiple strategies to determine the meaning of unfamiliar words. Encourage her not to simply skip words she doesn't understand. As texts become more complex, her rate of reading may become slower. That's fine, because it takes longer to understand more complex information. Ultimately, it is more important that she understands what she reads than it is to break speed-reading records.

Using and Understanding Figurative Language

In the 8th grade your child will continue to study figurative language learned in earlier grades. These include allusions, alliteration, and the like. Your eighth grader will also learn about puns and irony. Puns will likely be familiar to your child, as they are the basis of many childhood jokes. More than likely, your child will be able to use his schema or prior knowledge to make sense of puns and create them on his own. Irony can be trickier. The following sections explain and provide examples of the three common types of irony. Once you've read about them, it is likely you'll begin to recognize irony used in television programs and movies, which you can point out to your child.

Puns

A pun is a sort of joke that relies on the fact that words have multiple meanings or that words that sound alike can mean different things. The joke relies on the reader's understanding of the multiple meaning of the word or words used in the joke.

The example that follows relies on the reader to know that the words *patience* and *patients* sound alike. This pun could mean that the doctor was impatient, or that he was angry about losing business because his customers are called patients.

The doctor was angry because he had no patients.

In the following sentence, the pun relies on two different meanings of the word *beat*:

You can't beat a boiled egg for a quick breakfast.

One meaning of *beat* in this sentence is "to do better than"; so, the sentence says that nothing is better than a boiled egg for breakfast. However, the word *beat* can also mean to whisk or mix rapidly, which one cannot do to an egg that has been boiled, meaning one cannot have a beaten, boiled egg for breakfast.

While the puns your child will be most familiar with are those from jokes and children's books, puns are also used by well-known authors and in classical literature. The following example is a play written by Oscar Wilde:

The Importance of Being Earnest

Ernest is a man's name, and in the play, a female character wants to marry a man named Ernest. Earnest, as it is written in the title, means honest or sincere. So, the title is a pun.

William Shakespeare was a fan of puns as well, as evidenced in this line from *Richard III*:

Now is the winter of our discontent / made glorious summer by this sun of York;

In the example, the word *sun* is used as a pun. York is a family name, and the man about to be crowned king is a member of the York family, a *son* of York. Shakespeare also contrasts winter and summer, but saying the *son* is also the *sun* who will bring new life to the nation.

As you read, watch television, or even look at advertisements with your child, keep an eye out for puns that you can mention or ask him to explain.

Irony

Irony is a kind of figurative language that relies on contradiction or the difference between expectations and actual events. In some cases, it requires a reader to use his or her own background knowledge or experience to understand why a situation is ironic. There are three types of irony your child will study in the 8th grade:

- Verbal
- Situational
- Dramatic

Verbal Irony

Verbal irony occurs when the speaker says the opposite of what he or she means. Verbal irony can be in the form of an overstatement or understatement. The following is an example of verbal irony in the form of an overstatement:

Oh good! A flat tire! That's exactly what I need today.

The next statement is an example of verbal irony in the form of an understatement:

My computer crashed and I lost all of my files, but that's fine; it's no big deal.

People sometimes consider sarcasm the same as verbal irony, but sarcasm is usually used to make a cruel or insulting comment, while irony is not. Review the following examples:

You call that music?
Oh good, my iPod is broken.

The first statement can be considered sarcastic. The speaker is insulting the person he is talking to, suggesting that whatever is playing is not really music. In the second statement, verbal irony is used, as the speaker is not likely pleased that her iPod is broken.

Situational Irony

Situational irony is when the expected outcome isn't what happens. Situational irony is not necessarily an unfortunate coincidence. For example, rain on one's wedding day is not ironic; it's unfortunate. A meteorologist being caught in an unexpected rainstorm *is* ironic, as one would expect a meteorologist to know that it is going to rain. Other examples of situational irony might include:

- A ski area closes because of heavy snowfall.
- A tow truck needs to be towed.
- A hospital has to close because the entire staff is sick.
- A reading teacher hates books.
- Someone posts on Facebook about what a waste of time Facebook is.

It can be interesting to point out situations that would be or are ironic in everyday life. For example, you could mention that it would be ironic if the orthodontist's children had crooked teeth, or if the veterinarian were allergic to dogs and cats.

Dramatic Irony

Dramatic irony is almost exclusively a plot device. It is when the reader or viewer knows something the characters in the story do not know. A good example is a silly horror movie where the characters run to the basement for safety, but the viewer already knows that the monster is in the basement waiting for them.

What is a plot device?
A plot device moves the story in a narrative forward. It is used to show something important about a character or event that will help the reader better understand what will happen next.

Dramatic irony can be used to build suspense and tension in a plot. For example, in a romantic comedy, Jane is about to leave and is walking through the airport. She doesn't know that Tom is trying to find her because he has fallen in love with her. There is the possibility that Jane will get on an airplane and leave before Tom can tell her how he feels. The reader feels tension, knowing that Tom is searching for Jane. The reader is invested in the plot, hoping that Tom finds Jane before it is too late.

In another example of dramatic irony, two characters, Melissa and Sam, might be complaining about their teacher, Mrs. Jones. They refer to Mrs. Jones as being cruel, ugly, and unfair. The reader knows that just a few pages earlier Mrs. Jones accidentally locked herself in a closet in the classroom, so she is listening to everything Melissa and Sam are saying. The reader feels bad for Mrs. Jones, and for Melissa and Sam, who are likely to be embarrassed when they realize Mrs. Jones is in the room.

Many story plots rely on dramatic irony. As your child reads or watches television and movies, remind him to look for and identify the dramatic irony that results in suspense, comedy, or other effects.

Helping Your Child Succeed

Your eighth grader will be presented with a lot of new information in language study. It is likely that your child will find some aspects of the curriculum challenging, as it is unfamiliar. A great first step in helping your child succeed with the new material is to point out examples when you see them. That can be especially effective in your child's study of verbals. Find examples in newspapers, magazines, and books. When your child sees grammar in authentic situations, the uses and applications will make more sense. Notice out loud when someone uses the passive voice in speech and start a conversation about why that might be the case, and how you might change that statement into active voice.

When terms or labels are unfamiliar, it is always good practice to use them as much as possible. Think back to when your child was very young. How did you teach him the alphabet? Did you use body parts? Common words around the house? Or did you teach him through repetition and labeling? Whatever strategy you used then, more than likely it will continue to work with your eighth grader.

Be sure your child has access to different kinds of reference materials, including a traditional paper dictionary. Using online dictionaries is usually the first option these days, and that's fine. But it is also important that your child understand how a dictionary is organized, and what the abbreviations are for parts of speech and usage.

Revisit some of those childish jokes that rely on puns and ask your eighth grader to explain what the joke is. Why did he think it was funny when he was younger? For example, there's an Internet trend called "Dad Jokes," which are almost exclusively puns. For example: "What's a duck's favorite dip? Quakamole." The puns are silly and the jokes are marginally funny, but they provide great ways to review and talk about this kind of figurative language. Spend some time searching the Internet together for examples. Finally, point out irony when you see or hear it. Teenagers are masters of verbal irony. Let your child know that you notice when she uses it.

Practice Exercises

These exercises will help your child practice the skills covered in this chapter. They are similar to the types of questions she will encounter on standardized tests.

Identify Gerunds

In each of the following sentences, highlight or identify the gerund.

1. I always have breakfast before going to work.
2. Washing a cat can be dangerous.
3. Holding down the cat to be bathed is a great effort.
4. Cats don't like having soap in their faces.

5. In addition, cleaning behind their ears is tricky.
6. Luckily, bathing isn't necessary for all cats.
7. My favorite sport is running, and I run almost every day.
8. When I'm not watching television, I'm thinking about my next painting.
9. The performer worried that her singing was not as strong as it once had been.
10. My mother returned to school and pursued a career in accounting.

Identify Participles

In each of the following sentences, highlight or identify the participle.

1. My dad was angry when he saw the dented fender on his car.
2. The performer was worried her singing career was in decline.
3. Another word for a mirror is a looking glass.
4. The baked chicken is a healthy alternative to junk food.
5. I placed the cookies on a baking sheet.
6. The burning sun blazed in the window.
7. I dreaded walking to school in the freezing cold.
8. We laughed when the trained horses danced.
9. The pouting child sulked in the corner.
10. We gathered around a crackling fire to tell stories and make s'mores.

Identify Infinitives

In each of the following sentences, highlight or identify the infinitive.

1. Thomas looked back at his warm, comfortable bed. "I don't want to go to school," he thought.
2. In order to pass, you'll have to study.
3. Eighth graders usually are eager to go on to high school.
4. It can be challenging to be the youngest person in a class.
5. I reminded my mother to save empty water bottles for my science class.
6. I was eager to hike to the top of the mountain.
7. This summer I plan to learn French.
8. You'll need a combination to unlock that trunk.
9. I need to practice so I can audition for the advanced orchestra next year.
10. To give up now just doesn't make sense.

Appendix: Exercise Answers

Chapter 5 Practice Exercises

Making Inferences
1. A
2. C
3. B
4. C
5. B

Identifying the Author's Purpose
1. C
2. B
3. A
4. A
5. C

Chapter 6 Practice Exercises
Transitions
1. A
2. C
3. C
4. A
5. C

Using Precise Language (answers may vary)
1. The cashier gave us tickets to enter the movie.
2. We rode in my mom's Volvo to the Justin Bieber concert.
3. The ship traveled from the United States to England.
4. Tom didn't complete his math assignment because he was thinking about baseball.
5. She bought a skirt at Forever 21.
6. I need a hammer to get that nail into the wall.
7. We put on our swimsuits and went to the beach.
8. I have to read *The Adventures of Huckleberry Finn* for my English class, which is right after lunch.
9. The astronauts landed on Mars.
10. They have two dogs named Peanut Butter and Jelly.

Using Formal English (answers may vary)
1. That movie was funny; it made me laugh.
2. Mother told me to be quiet and not make any comments.
3. My father joked that my mother was getting older at her last birthday.
4. I enjoyed the party.
5. Are you all right?
6. I do not know when we will be there.
7. I do not know what the assignment is.
8. My project is not finished yet.
9. I am sorry. My throat is irritated, and I am coughing.
10. He is a good and honest person.

Chapter 7 Practice Exercises
Pronoun/Practice

1. **We** students wish we had less homework.
2. Everyone should turn in **his or her** homework before leaving class today.
3. Either Robert or **I** will play goalie in tomorrow's game.
4. My brother said, "You and **I** are going to shovel snow in the morning."
5. The students didn't seem to know where **they** should go when the fire alarm rang.
6. The governor **himself** attended our graduation ceremony.
7. That is Amy's backpack; it belongs to **her**.
8. Timothy said he lost **his** homework and would have to turn **it** in tomorrow.
9. One of the librarians parks **his or her** car in that parking spot.
10. The substitute teacher gave **us** a quiz.

Shifts in Pronoun Practice

1. B
2. A
3. C
4. C
5. B

Indefinite Pronoun Agreement Practice

1. Everybody on the boys' basketball team keeps **his** equipment in the locker room.
2. Anybody who is late for class must put **his or her** name on the list by the door.
3. Each of my aunts called me **herself** to wish me a happy birthday.
4. Someone left **his or her** phone on the bus, so I gave it to the bus driver.
5. Neither my brother nor his friend Rob will let me borrow **his** skateboard.

Vague Pronoun References (answers may vary)

1. Many students like either math or history, but math has always been my favorite subject.
2. Lisa complained to her mother that she didn't like the cake her mother made.
3. Both Faith and Kim are good at basketball, but Kim is a better volleyball player.
4. Jimmy told his brother, Tom, he should talk to Tom's teacher.
5. Bob found his dad's missing watch and told him.

Use Commas to Set Off Parenthetical and Nonrestrictive Information

1. That movie, in my opinion, is one of the best of the year.
2. Aiden, who is an excellent hockey player, volunteered to coach the youth league.
3. This dog, for example, has learned to open the door and dial the phone.
4. In other words, I am really looking forward to the game.
5. My favorite song, which is playing on the radio right now, came out last year.

Dashes to Set Off Nonrestrictive Expressions

1. The new *Hunger Games* movie—it is my favorite so far—is showing at the plaza cinema.
2. My aunt Mary—she's a wonderful lady—volunteers at the hospital three days a week.
3. My dog Duke—he's the greatest dog—was a gift from my grandparents.
4. Lake Wautaska—the jewel of the northeast—is a popular tourist spot.
5. My favorite TV show—it is so exciting—is on tonight.

Chapter 8 Practice Exercises Reading Literature

1. C
2. B
3. B
4. B
5. C

Symbolism

1. C
2. C
3. C
4. C
5. B

Chapter 9 Practice Exercises Transitions

1. A
2. C
3. C
4. C
5. C

Formal versus Informal Language (answers may vary)

1. I am writing because I am having difficulty with my homework and hope you can help me.
2. I am referring to the homework you said should take no more than thirty minutes to complete.
3. I think you were mistaken. I have been working on this homework for more than an hour and have found it very difficult.
4. I hope you will return my e-mail and offer me some advice.
5. Thank you for your help.

Chapter 10 Practice Exercises
Identifying Phrases
1. A
2. B
3. C
4. B

Independent and Dependent Clauses
1. Dependent
2. Dependent
3. Independent
4. Dependent
5. Independent
6. Independent
7. Dependent
8. Dependent
9. Independent
10. Dependent

Compound and Complex Sentences
1. B
2. A
3. B
4. A
5. B
6. A
7. B
8. A
9. B
10. B

Chapter 11 Practice Exercises
Kinds of Irony
1. C
2. A
3. B
4. B
5. C

Author's Purpose
1. C
2. B
3. A
4. B
5. A

Chapter 12 Practice Exercises
Identifying Arguments
1. The chow is the only dog that doesn't have a pink tongue.
2. **The chow is an ideal family dog because it has a pleasant temperament.**
3. The only mammal that can fly is the bat.
4. **The world population of honey-bees is diminishing and issues such as global warming must be addressed if they are to be saved.**
5. **People should not kill spiders.**

Types of Fallacies
1. B
2. A
3. C
4. A
5. B

Chapter 13 Practice Exercises
Identify Gerunds
1. I always have breakfast before **going** to work.
2. **Washing** a cat can be dangerous.
3. **Holding** down the cat to be bathed is a great effort.
4. Cats don't like **having** soap in their faces.
5. In addition, **cleaning** behind their ears is tricky.
6. Luckily, **bathing** isn't necessary for all cats.
7. My favorite sport is **running**, and I run almost every day.
8. When I'm not watching television, I'm thinking about my next **painting**.
9. The performer worried that her **singing** was not as strong as it once had been.
10. My mother returned to school and pursued a career in **accounting**.

Identify Participles
1. My dad was angry when he saw the **dented** fender on his car.
2. The performer was worried her **singing** career was in decline.
3. Another word for a mirror is a **looking** glass.
4. The **baked** chicken is a healthy alternative to junk food.
5. I placed the cookies on a **baking** sheet.
6. The **burning** sun blazed in the window.
7. I dreaded walking to school in the **freezing** cold.
8. We laughed when the **trained** horses danced.
9. The **pouting** child sulked in the corner.

10. We gathered around a **crackling** fire to tell stories and make s'mores.

Identify Infinitives

1. Thomas looked back at his warm, comfortable bed. "I don't want **to go** to school," he thought.

2. In order **to pass**, you'll have **to study**.

3. Eighth graders usually are eager **to go** on to high school.

4. It can be challenging **to be** the youngest person in a class.

5. I reminded my mother **to save** empty water bottles for my science class.

6. I was eager **to hike** to the top of the mountain.

7. This summer I plan **to learn** French.

8. You'll need a combination **to unlock** that trunk.

9. I need **to practice** so I can audition for the advanced orchestra next year.

10. **To give up** now just doesn't make sense.

Index